Transnational Management: Identity and *Nunchi* in Multinational Corporations

Steffen Kromer

Cover design by Julian Weber
Indexing by Clive Pyne, Book Indexing Services

Published by Berry Street Books, an imprint of Eifrig Publishing,
PO Box 66, Lemont, PA 16851, USA
Knobelsdorffstr. 44, 14059 Berlin, Germany.

For information regarding permission, write to:
Rights and Permissions Department,
Eifrig Publishing,
PO Box 66, Lemont, PA 16851, USA.
permissions@eifrigpublishing.com, +1-888-340-6543

Library of Congress Cataloging-in-Publication Data

Steffen Kromer
Transnational Management: Identity and *Nunchi* in Multinational Corporations
  p. cm.

Paperback: ISBN **978-1-63233-173-1**
Hard cover: ISBN **978-1-63233-184-7**
Ebook: ISBN **978-1-63233-185-4**

[1. Business anthropology 2. Management - Transnational studies 3. National Identity - Germany - South Korea 4. Emotional intelligence - *nunchi*]

22 21 20 19 2018
5 4 3 2 1

Printed in the USA on acid-free paper with recycled content. ∞

Transnational Management: Identity and *Nunchi* in Multinational Corporations

Steffen Kromer

Berry St BOOKS
an imprint of eifrig publishing

Lemont   Berlin

Acknowledgements

Firstly, I would like to express my sincere gratitude to Professor Fiona Moore and Professor Alice Lam for the continuous support of this study and related research, for their patience, motivation, and immense knowledge. Their guidance helped me in all the time of research and writing of this work. My sincere thanks also goes to the Aulbach and Lee families and all HanaEins members who provided me an opportunity to join their team as a researcher, and who granted access to their "lived realities" and the research setting. Without their precious support it would not have been possible to conduct this research. Also I thank my friends who always supported and believed in me.

Lastly, I would like to thank my family: my parents and my sister for supporting me spiritually throughout writing this volume and my life in general.

All translations from German and Korean to English, of written accounts and transcribed interviews or field notes, are my own.

Abstract

This book takes a case study of a particular population, German businesspeople working in German multinational corporations (MNCs) in Seoul, and examines *nunchi* (emotional intelligence), an important non –Western organizational phenomenon, and the role of symbols of identity in the recontextualisation process of adopting *nunchi* into strategic self-presentations. Firstly, I will briefly give the background of my study, first defining and exploring concepts relating to identity and *nunchi*, working across borders and identities and the way in which identity is expressed, to set the stage for later examination. In particular, I will examine the function of performative identity and presentation of self in everyday life (Goffman 1956) models for analysing identity in transnational settings.

This study concentrates on the connections between *nunchi* and identity of German transnational businesspeople, which is eventually enriched by Hochschild's (1983) depiction of emotion work and Brannen's (2004) theory of recontextualisation. One of the key contributions is the introduction and vitalisation of the non-Western concept of *nunchi*, which loosely translates to emotional intelligence in international business studies.

This study is based on approximately 145 hours of interviews of 27 formal and 31 informal interviews, which were undertaken between February 2014 and March 2015. Follow up interviews were conducted between July 2015 and November 2015.

This book will consequently be a unique source for both scholars and practitioners, as its ethnographic approach provides enlightening new insights contributing towards an improved understanding of *nunchi* and identities in MNCs. In contributing a challenge to peculiar perspectives by taking a non-Western concept and exploring its relevance, this study is unique in its findings. The findings imply that *nunchi* is not a fixed object but a strategic tool, which allows transnational businesspeople to promote their individual, drives, which leads on to new forms of self-presentation tailored to transnational business. This volume is therefore based on an ethnographic study, which stresses the complexion and complexity of *nunchi* and identity in transnational business settings.

Contents

List of Figures and Tables

Chapter 1

Introduction

This book explores *nunchi* (emotional intelligence) and its significance in strategic self-presentations as a symbol of national identity across borders and identities in German multinational corporations (MNCs) and the private sphere, which are located in Seoul and its surrounding metropolitan area. Specifically, this ethnographic study will look at the concept of *nunchi*. *Nunchi* is a Korean concept, which literally refers to 'eye measurement' and, in a broader context, means the emotional intelligence of individuals. Various aspects of *nunchi* in MNCs in terms of interpersonal and transnational relations—in which harmony often depends on symbols of identity, including non-verbal contact and understanding strategic self-presentation—will be explored, with close links to symbols of national identity, managing across borders and other contexts, in private and public life.

This ethnographic study will focus on the strategic self-presentation of transnational businesspeople in German MNCs in South Korea and their management and corporate performances, in which *nunchi* is a prerequisite for managerial success. The importance of international business and increasing mobility of Korean and German transnational businesspeople makes the recontextualisation of symbols of identity at different levels a daily necessity in management studies. Thus this ethnographic study makes use of Erving Goffman's (1956) theories of strategic self-presentation, which suggests actors to strategically present themselves trying to influence the perception of their image. Additionally, in order to explore *nunchi* in strategic self-presentations as a symbol of identity, Mary Yoko Brannen's (2004) theory of recontextualisation enhances this study, as recontextualisation allows us to introduce symbols of national identity such as *nunchi* from their original identity context to another, therefore recontextualisation implies a shift in meaning. It is hypothesized that *nunchi* is vital for the long-term endurance of corporate success, conflict resolution and managerial excellence between Koreans and their German partners, since the concept exists in both national identity contexts following different interpretations.

This is a study of the expression of symbols of identity and performances of Korean *nunchi* in strategic self-presentations of German and Korean transnational businesspeople working in German MNCs in South Korea. This is an interesting group for scholars of international management studies because transnational mobility has been identified as a significant force that is reconfiguring expressions and notions of the power of understanding symbols of identity, in this particular case emotional intelligence as a major management practice across identities, within and outside of South Korea (Butcher, 2009).

Therefore, this study introduces and inspects a principal organizational phenomenon; *nunchi* and the part core competencies play in the strategic expression of symbols of national identity in the recontextualisation process of adopting *nunchi* into strategic self-presentations. Ultimately, this study provides a way of viewing and comprehending *nunchi* as part of the presentation of self, hence identity, implying that *nunchi* is not merely an emotional response that is privately encountered by single actors; it however develops in the situation of the encounter, and consequently *nunchi* uncovers something about strategic self-presentations of the actors and produces righteously imputed expectations.

In this introductory chapter, I will present the study's background as well as concisely outline the issues that affect my research. This will contain a critical overview of the way in which emotional intelligence and the discourse of strategic identity is reflected in the literature on business management, particularly with a focus on MNCs and how this study relates to pre-existing studies. In the second chapter I will consider the literature on the role of national identity and its correlations to the interpretations of emotional intelligence, incorporating national symbols in the sphere of MNCs. I will then recapitulate the approach of this study, which originated from Erving Goffman's theories on strategic self-presentation. In the third chapter, I will elaborate the methodology of the study and provide an outline of its structure, a summary of previous research conducted in this field and the composition of a hypothesis based on this work. I will then present an ethnographic case study, concluding by reassessing the previous research in the perspective of the latest findings. I end here with a succinct restatement of my hypothesis: that *nunchi* and identity in transnational business are more complex and multi-faceted concepts than most of the literature of the subject suggests and that the changes within are driven to some degree in part of self-presentation of the single character groups and *HanaEins* as an entity.

1.   Known Gaps in the Research

The expression of symbols of identity and performances of *nunchi* as a specific form of emotional intelligence in MNCs' management practices between transnational businesspeople, in this instance most notably Koreans and Germans, are not well understood. This is particularly the case regarding the significance of transnational mobility on identities as well as the under-researched facets of identities and their related symbols of identity such as *nunchi* and its associated strategic self-presentations. Fundamentally, the identity formations of trans-nationally mobile managers and employees can be comprehended as a negotiation between global and various local elements brought about by the transnational mobility of people and products (e.g. Korean and German transnational businesspeople, and symbols of national identity). However, this type of ethnographic approach has not been well utilized in the research on temporary and long-term trans-nationally mobile managers and employees and their learning process of the local interpretation of emotional intelligence, especially *nunchi* as a specific form of it in management.

Emotional intelligence is a branch of social intelligence, which concerns the ability to supervise one's own and others' emotions, to differentiate among them and to use the information to guide one's thinking and actions (Salovey & Mayer, 1990). The emotional intelligence context categorizes the existing literature on individual differences regarding the capacity to process and adapt to affective information. Many managerial challenges contain emotional information that must be processed; this processing may proceed differently than the processing of non-emotional information (Salovey & Mayer, 1993:p.433). According to Salovey & Mayer, 1993, 'the scope of emotional intelligence includes the verbal and non-verbal appraisal and expression of emotion, the regulation of emotion in self and others, and the utilization of emotional content in problem solving' (p.433). With regard to refining organizational effectiveness, management scholars and practitioners highlight the significance of a manager's emotional intelligence (Cooper, 1997; Harrison, 1997; Hesselbein, Goldsmith & Beckhard, 1996; Morris & Feldman, 1996).

Emotional intelligence represents a set of attributes such as self-awareness, emotional management, self-motivation, empathy, and relationship management (Goleman, 1995; Salovey & Mayer, 1990). Earlier work (e.g. Cooper, 1997; Goleman, 1995; Megerian & Sosik, 1996) proposed that features of emotional intelligence might motivate a manager's display of transformational leadership (see Bass, 1985; Burns, 1978), which involves a strong emotional bond between the manager and the employee. Corporate interest seems to be intensely linked to the on-going pursuit of a way to acquire sustainable competitive advantage, which can be achieved through attention to 'people issues' (Kay, 1993; Senge, 1990; Sparrow, Schuler & Jackson, 1994; Ulrich & Lake, 1990).

An emotionally intelligent person is able to identify and use his or her own and others' emotional circumstances to resolve complications and control conduct (Nguyen Huy, 1999:p.325). Whereas managers were once expected to regulate, plan and review the overall management of an organization, currently, it is also a manager's role to motivate and inspire others, to foster positive attitudes at work and to generate a sense of contribution and importance with and among employees (Hogan et al., 1994). As a result, researchers have been exploring the underlying attributes and behaviours of managers who successfully perform emotional intelligence (Church & Waclawski, 1998; Pratch & Jacobowitz, 1998; Ross & Offermann, 1997; Sternberg, 1997).

To be an effective manager, it is argued that one needs to possess emotional intelligence or, as Boyatzis (1982) terms it, 'the underlying characteristics of a person that lead to or cause effective and outstanding performance' (p.21). In reviewing both direct empirical research (e.g. Boyatzis, 1982; Bray, Campbell & Grant, 1974; Howard & Bray, 1988; Kotter, 1982; Luthans, Hodgetts & Rosenkrantz, 1988; Thornton & Byham, 1982) and meta-analytic syntheses (e.g. Campbell et al, 1970; Goleman, 1998; Spencer & Spencer, 1993), it becomes apparent that there is a set of characteristics that determine a manager's success. Regardless of the author or study, all appear to include some sort of definition of emotional intelligence as identified by Salovey and Mayer (1990), that emotional intelligence includes attributes such as, self-awareness, emotion management, self-motivation, empathy and relationship management. The concept of emotional intelligence appears to be based on extensive scientific literature and research evidence (Cooper, 1997; Cooper & Sawaf, 1997; Goleman, 1996). However, little field-work-data based research has been carried out in organizational contexts, and most of the existing studies have been drawn mainly from psychological research and education-based research (Damasio, 1994; Goleman, 1996; Higgs, 2000). However, transnational work and managing across borders and identities has become the standard for most multinational organisations (Adler, 1997; Dowling, Welch, & Schuler 1999; Schneider & Barsoux, 1997).

This is also the case in this study, which focuses on *HanaEins*, a group of German MNCs consisting of some of the largest German MNCs that operate in Korea and furthermore engage in the process of working across borders and identities due to *HanaEins* members' national and transnational commitments. *HanaEins* virtually contains close to all actors related to symbols of Germanness specifically, international German managers, settled Germans and German speaking Koreans, who work with and participate in the cross-border expression of symbols of identity and management of identities within *HanaEins*.

Furthermore, intercultural distinctions have long been a challenge facing multinational organisations, a challenge that has been intensified by the growing popularity of teams made up of entities from many different nations (Earley & Gibson, 2002; Snow, Snell, Canney-Daviosn, & Hambrick, 1996). Because managers must often function across borders in teams of trans-nationally diverse people, many MNCs express the demand for managers, who rapidly adjust to various identity specific settings and work well in transnational teams (Early & Peterson, 2004). Central to all forms of comprehension is an actor's capability to obtain, maintain, and read various types of information and experiences. Generally defined, this capability for adjustment is reflected by a person's intelligence (Gardener, 1983; Sternberg, 1985). This idea was explored by Salovey and Mayer (1990) and by Gardner in his book *Frames of Mind and Multiple Intelligences* (1993), as well as numerous works of Robert Sternberg (e.g. 1985). These works state that, people having high emotional intelligence are thought to be comparatively more able to empathize, work with, direct, and interact with other people. High emotional intelligence mirrors a person's capacity to perform actions e.g. problem solving with and through others. It also suggests a person's capacity to comprehend and express human emotions, as 'emotional intelligence captures a variety of attributes related to a person's ability to read and respond to the affective states of culturally similar others and to self regulate', (Early & Peterson, 2004 p.105).

Therefore the recontextualisation of *nunchi* captures this capability for adaptation across borders and identities, as it reflects a person's capability to gather, interpret, and act upon these radically different cues to function effectively in transnational business settings.

2.   Research Question

This study commences with the proposition that the experience of living and working abroad affects the identity expressions, in terms of emotional intelligence, of Korean and German transnational managers and employees. This arises from the experiences and interpersonal encounters with others that are part of the working abroad and managing across identities assignment. In turn, these experiences and interpersonal encounters may influence how Korean and German transnational managers and employees perceive a long-established business management style (Germany) and a newly developed business management style (South Korea) in terms of MNCs, which has important implications for understanding the Korean and German strategic identity performances in terms of *nunchi* and transnational mobility. Responding to the pre-existing literature's tendency to identify *nunchi* as a unique Korean phenomenon, in this work, I seek to evaluate whether *nunchi* is indeed a unique Korean phenomenon or if it simply follows different interpretations in the German identity setting. To direct my research towards the themes I have identified as interesting and significant, the following research question,

- What is *nunchi* and how can *nunchi* be learnt?

I have formulated the following research objectives:

- To examine the concept of *nunchi* and consider its relevance to international business studies;
- To discuss the ways in which the concept of *nunchi* relates to the Western

concept of emotional intelligence;

- To examine the role that *nunchi* plays in MNCs in Korea;
- To review the position played by the personal strategies of self-presentation of entities in shaping the philosophies of MNCs and collective groups, with a particular focus on *nunchi*;
- To consider the implications of the concept of *nunchi* for our understanding of identities of strategic self-presentation in MNC.

These objectives are deliberately broad and open to allow an inductive approach to this research, which requires the incorporation of participant feedback into the direction of the research and the protocols. As part of the ethnographic process, I hypothesize that some of these research objectives will be enriched as the research progresses and as the themes and topics most significant to my interlocutors emerge through my fieldwork experience.

Significance and Contribution

The following study explores and visualises prominent essential Korean and German symbols of identity and will allow the recontextualisation of such, which refers to the examination of how meanings shift according to different identity settings (see Brannen, 2004) in communicating and managing effectively across borders in transnational business and international business studies with close ties to *nunchi* across identities, especially in MNCs. Moreover, it explores the role of *nunchi* in expressions of symbols of identity and the strategic self-presentation of all actors in MNCs in transnational business. In short, it demonstrates to Koreans and Germans as well as a broader audience, including international managers, who work for MNCs that symbols of identity, which most of the time are taken for granted might be new or interpreted differently by actors of dissimilar national identity contexts and thus may cause confusion and misunderstandings for them. This study is therefore an insightful and helpful source for both researchers and transnational businesspeople, as its methodology harvests novel insights into the roles national and transnational identity formations and symbols of identity in the operation of multinational corporations: not as solid objects describing a certain group, but as strategic recourses by which transnational businesspeople advance their distinct ambitions, and through this, develop new forms of interaction remarkably adapted to transnational business.

Therefore, the significant contribution with the vitalisation and adaptation of *nunchi* is that it identifies as a fundamental tool for all actors in Korea in work-related settings and the private sphere.

The study that follows is thus centered on an ethnography, which aims to tackle one of the main shortcomings in anthropology and business studies: that both fail to consider the complexion and complexity of *nunchi* in transnational business settings. Using Erving Goffman's theory of strategic self-presentation, this study will explore that expressions of identity are not so much a matter of restricted, self-contained actions belonging to groups both national and transnational, but of multifaceted, continuously changing connections between different groups of changing degrees of national and transnational attachment (Moore, 2005). Therefore, the study will build a bridge between two identity settings and will lead to a mutual understanding of identity constructs in terms of strategic self-presentation and the use of symbols of national identity in MNCs, and the private sphere between Koreans and non-Koreans—in particular, Germans.

The work that follows is thus an exploration of the ways in which emotional intelligence, and *nunchi* as a specific form of it, is used by German transnational businesspeople in South Korea, as they negotiate their relationships with others according to their individual strategies of self-presentation. It also considers the origins and implications of the complexity of identity in transnational business, and whether it permanently affects transnational identities. This investigation will not only address the correlation between *nunchi* and self-presentation in global businesses and the way in which transnational actors use symbols of identity as a tactical tool for success, but will also contribute to our understanding of the effect of identity on business, and the implications for both researchers and practitioners.

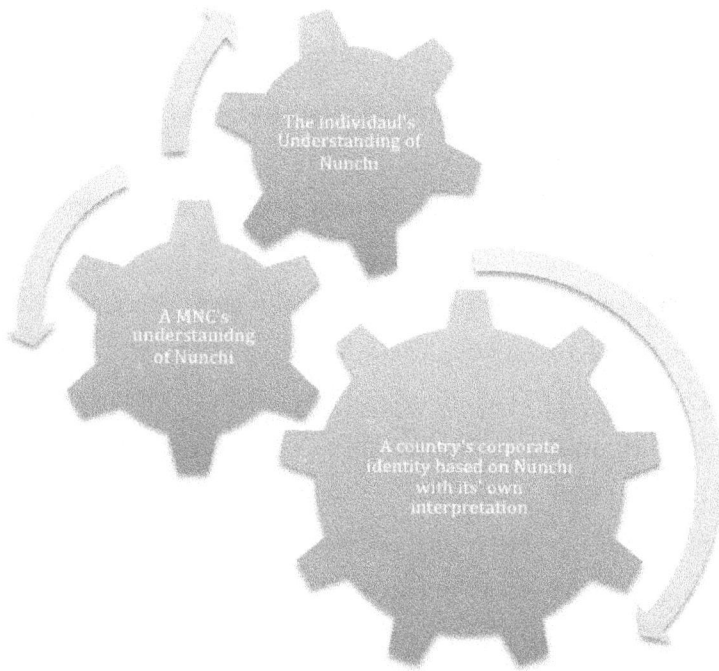

Figure I Illustration of Nunchi

3. Innovation and Advances in Knowledge

The innovation and advances in knowledge emphasise that "soft" symbols of identities, for instance *nunchi* are more susceptible to recontextualisation. This is a noteworthy contribution, because managing across borders and identities, leans towards transferring a somewhat transnational organizational system, which *nunchi* does not yet belong to, but shortly might will. I believe that *nunchi* is important for maintaining transnational business relationships and managing across identities between Koreans and their partners of non-Korean origin in MNCs. Therefore, this study contributes in outlining the process of how recontextualisation of symbols of national identity, in identity specific settings over time in order to be successful work instead of serving as a set formula of how to conduct business in Korea. Moreover, recontextualisation of *nunchi* provides an explanation for how and when symbols of identity might be seen as an asset, thus, are better utilised as a strategic way of self-presentation to secure organizational advantage. Korean management practices are based on informal—at times, social—mechanisms that are underpinned by embedded national traits. However, in transnational identity settings encompassing a diverse workforce, the expectations, regarding self-presentation of Koreans and their colleagues are commonly out of balance. Therefore, interpretations of *nunchi* and related concepts such as *jung* and *woori* need to be understood and contextualized (Yang & Kelly, 2009; Hong, 2008). Data will be used to illustrate how both partners in business relationships use *nunchi* interactively when tackling managerial processes to facilitate their partnership's long-term success.

I believe that the data will demonstrate the significance of *nunchi* for both the Korean and the non-Korean partner in their daily lives and interactions. Further, the interpretation of *nunchi* is a skill that has to be learnt by the non-Korean partner, and it will be interesting to examine how this occurs and the specific challenges of this learning procedure.

Additionally, this study provides the background for a more balanced evaluation of the impact of national and transnational identity on international business, and how individuals and groups use the concept of identity in strategic ways, ultimately developing transnational social connections through their strategic self-presentation actions. In addition, the data will shed light on how different individuals learn, make sense of and utilize *nunchi* in their interpersonal and business relationships, at different levels across borders and identities.

As will be outlined in the in the methodology chapter there have been moderately few ethnographies of business per se. Even studies, which have a high qualitative component, tend to be fixated on interviews and limited interaction with subjects rather than utter participation. The nature of methodologies used in this study thus provides a perspective on the actors working for German MNCs as a community, a group possessing similar symbols of identity and part of a broader society, which continuously sets it apart from many other studies conducted in a transnational German-Korean setting.

Finally, because the data was drawn from open-ended interviews (some formal and some informal), participation and observation, there were many opportunities to explore and expand upon the ideas introduced by the respondents themselves as they narrated their own stories and how they and their business partners in MNCs have experienced and embraced *nunchi*. In terms of the significance of this research, the findings and conclusions have the potential to assist in developing improved understanding of the way that international business affects transnational relationships and business relationships, transnational identity expressions and strategic self-presentation for Koreans and their partners of non-Korean origin.

In addition, the findings can be usefully generalized to international business studies, organizational studies and international human resource management more broadly because the field of recontextualising symbols of identity and strategic self-presentation can be applied to many other forms of relationships. By not purely looking at the findings as either being transnational or national, one can develop a different way of looking at transnational business, which takes into account the complete variety of ways of linking the national symbols of identity to the transnational setting. This study also underlines the significance of the roles, which self-presentation and individual strategy play in modelling and controlling businesses. As international business settings become progressively identity-focused, the strategic use of self-presentation, in terms of expressing symbols of identity becomes ever more meaningful and consequently more attention must be paid to its use in business.

The present study thus foregrounds the study of international business by proposing new ways of looking at symbols of identity of transnational businesspeople and how they present themselves in the organisations. In the long run, these may prove and supply more useful insights to studying international business settings and multinational corporations than theories based on more quantitative research. I argue that *nunchi* is important in the Korean identity context and that it is essential for outsiders to understand it; likewise, Koreans need to understand analogous concepts elsewhere. Therefore, the recontextualization of *nunchi* is needed to make use of it across borders and identities in MNCs.

Perceptions of Korean management practices and *nunchi*

The following paragraph is framed in the context of how Koreans and Korean management practices in relation to MNCs, transnational business and *nunchi* are perceived.

Korean managers are observed less positively by foreign subordinates abroad on a diverse spectrum of traits, including capability and trustworthiness (Ahn, 1998; Paik & Sohn, 1998; Waxin, 2004). Lee, Roehl and Choe (2000) argued that Korean managers are less open to considering employees' ideas in management operations. It appears that Korean companies overseas are unwilling to adjust their home practices to accommodate the national symbols of the host country's identity (Ahn, 1998; Paik & Sohn, 1998). These generate a notion that Korean managers do not trust non-Koreans, which in turn causes local staff to dislike them (Ahn, 1998; Paik & Sohn, 1998). As a result, Korean employers find it challenging to hire and retain talented non-Korean employees (Paik & Sohn, 1998). Thus, Korean MNCs' expansions abroad have faced many challenges, particularly in relation to human resource management (HRM) of local employees. Numerous endeavours have been made to elucidate these issues, such as hierarchical (Confucian) orientation of Korean MNCs (Chang & Chang, 1994), uncompromising HRM systems (Paik & Sohn, 1998), low levels of localization (Ahn, 1998) and Korean managers' lack of international experience (Waxin, 2004).

However, I point out that, even though these rationalizations stand as they are, they marginalize a fundamental aspect of the work background and the workplace interactions between Korean managers and their non-Korean co-workers, and the results of those interactions. In particular, I focus on the critical role of the resilient, informal concept of *nunchi* in the Korean identity context, which enables managers to uphold control in MNCs. The significance of the *nunchi* concept may be established as an explanation of Korean management challenges abroad. Koreans often point out their high levels of hard work and extensive working hours (Steers, Shin & Ungson, 1989) to the social pressure and the expectations of their manager and colleagues (Janelli, 1993). Confucianism stresses the importance of effort (Paik & Sohn, 1998), and this is displayed in the conduct and mindset of most Koreans in the form of *euiyok*, translated as 'will' (Paik & Sohn, 1998). In line with the Korean emphasis on group harmony or awareness (Mensik, Grainger & Chatterjee, 1999), those who fail to show *nunchi* are exposed and disciplined, commonly through precise, effective informal measures (Paik & Sohn, 1998), not just by management but also by equals. Although formal measures are seldom used (Paik & Sohn, 1998), informal social traits are used to report performance troubles and private concerns; co-workers apply *nunchi*—in other words, the capability to analyse someone else's mind and to be insightful and attentive (Lee, 1997; Robinson, 1985). A close connection between people permits them to practise *nunchi*, that is, read each other's mind and react to the other's requests without making overt inquiries (Choi, 1997), or without subsequently endangering each other's face (Yum, 1987).

Managers are expected to look after employees' professional and private desires, and, in return, employees are expected to show a high interest in their workplace; the fulfilment of these expectations is ensured through embedded, informal *nunchi*-grounded checks and balances (Yang & Kelly, 2009).

In sum perceptions of Korean management practices and *nunchi* indicate that Koreans are perceived less positively on the international stage as well as reluctant to consider inputs of those in lower ranks due to their uncompromising HRM practises that mirror higher inflexibility in (trans)national adjustment. As a result regular *nunchi* –grounded checks and balances are part of Korean management practices, which result in exposure of those, who fail to perform *nunchi* correctly through off-the-record measures not just by the top management but also by colleagues.

4.   Conceptual Framework

My research draws on two broad streams of literature. The first is the literature on national identity and management style construction, including transnational and performative identities, which I use to situate my study's focus on Korean and German transnational businesspeople and employees in MNCs and their identities and associated management working style. The second is the literature on emotional intelligence—or *nunchi*—its associated symbols of identity and how it is used in management studies. I argue that *nunchi* in management studies has rarely touched on (trans)national corporate identity and their (trans)formations. Specifically, I bridge these two streams of literature in my research using ethnography and narratives to understand how national identities (e.g. Germans) are transformed into transnational identities (e.g. embracing *nunchi*). This represents a novel perspective for studying the experiences and identities of Korean and German transnational managers and employees. Previous studies have focused either on national identity (e.g. Lee-Peuker, 2004), without understanding the role of *nunchi*, or on the immediate needs and concerns of Korean and German managers and employees, without understanding the implications these have for identities and their transformation. A further gap in the current literature is the correlation between emotional intelligence—or *nunchi*— and expression of symbols of identity.

The concept of recontextualisation

Brannen's (2004) notion of recontextualizing symbols in international management is vital to this study, in the understanding of *nunchi* and the process by which signs linked to *nunchi* evolve in social contexts: 'Semioticians term this phenomenon semiosis and define it as the processes and effects of the production and the reproduction, reception and circulation of meaning in all forms, used by all agents of communication' (p.603). Brannen's concept of 'recontextualization' derives from anthropology and tackles the semantic dimensions of internationalisation by examining how meanings shift according to different national identity contexts. The term recontextualization itself suggests that meaning is given to the contexts associated with systems, objects, language and, in this case, *nunchi*. According to Brannen, 'as semiotics teach us, people create meanings through systems of signification. The concept of recontextualization allows us to track such shifts in meaning attached to objects and processes as they move from one culture to another' (p.604). Brannen's established method for observing and applying recontextualization will help to establish and make sense of Korean *nunchi* in MNCs in and outside of Korea.

Strecker (1988 cited in Moore 2005, pp. 53-54) explored the ways in which narratives, jokes and expressions of one's identity may be used as means to trigger manipulation to fulfil one's aims without appearing to threaten the fulfilment of someone else's (p.74) or to establish hierarchic standings without causing conflict (p.172). This is achieved through the multiple powers of semiotic discourse. Such discourse is best described as the ability of symbols to carry various meanings, depending on the social context in which individuals find themselves (Brannen, 2004; Sperber, 1974 cited in Moore 2005, pp. 53-54). The study of symbols in the anthropology of (trans) national identities in relation to emotional intelligence thus implies that self-presentation may be a tactical instrument, which is used by individuals and groups to monitor, or even construct, identity discourses.

Anthony Cohen (1994, 1987, 1985 cited in Moore 2005 pp. 56-57) contributed to the above argument by confirming that membership in social groups is expressed through and defined by the use of shared commonalities, in particular, symbols, which carry group significant meanings and thus foster a sense of belonging, and hence identity. The importance of variances in semiotic meaning was pointed out by Cohen

(1986:p.9); however, he argued that some overlaps in meaning exist within all groups, which emerge through the experience of the individuals' civilizations. Korean *nunchi* can be considered a semiotic indicator because traditional as well as contemporary Korean national identity identifies it as the linchpin in all operations within Korean society, including business (Southerton, 2008). In understanding the prevalent symbols that construct identity, it is necessary to 'decontextualize knowledge', which then needs to be recontextualized according to the given circumstances (Brannen, 2004; Hannerz, 1990:p.246 cited in Moore 2005 p. 58). Given that symbols are a significant player in both self-presentation and the formation through which groups foster a sense of belonging, and hence identity, symbols are vital for understanding the way in which business is conducted in a specific identity context and how management styles are constructed.

The concept of Identity

The key theoretical position in this work derives from Erving Goffman's theory that the motivating force behind the dynamic method of *nunchi* (emotional intelligence), or the transitional identity of managers, is the self-presentation of characters and groups around them. Goffman's proposition, that the way in which people and organizations behave to present themselves in the most optimistic light possible, enabling the success of their own strategies, goes some way towards explaining the dynamic nature of emotional intelligence in transnational business settings, especially in MNCs. It is useful to consider the meaning of the English word *identity* and the implications it has for studies on identity. The English word stems from the Latin *identitas*, which derived from the Latin root word *idem*, meaning 'same' (Williams, 1989). According to his book *What is identity* (1989), there are two meanings of identity that are relevant for my study:

      a)   Identity propositions seem either to state trivially that something is the same as itself.

      b)   Or to state falsely that one thing is the same as another.

These two meanings are also very close to how the word identity is used in the vernacular and in popular texts, but the discourse on what identity constitutes is far more complex than these definitions. Nevertheless, these interpretations of the term identity provide a starting point for the on-going identity discourse.

Other definitions such as that of Goffman have to be taken into account in this study. Goffman shifted from his initial terminology of *the self* to *identity* for the first time in his 1963 work.

> Sociologists … tend to view identity as an artifact of interaction between the individual and society—it is essentially a matter of being designated by a certain name, accepting that designation, internalizing the role requirements accompanying it, and behaving according to those prescriptions. (Gleason, 1983 p.918).

Similar to Gleason, identity in this study is viewed as a set selection of symbols of identity through which the interactions of individual actors and society takes place.

Goffman's most important argument about the presentation of self—or, in other words, identity—consists of four major aspects. First, identity is a matter of performance (p.17). Second, a person's identity does not consist of one single identity; rather, it comprises a variety of facets or revelations of self, which depend on the societal circumstances. Third, the management of the difficult relationship between the anticipated performance of self and other, compensating aspects of one's profile and current condition, is of great significance. Lastly, validation of the performance by others, if not their embedded association, is vital to fruitful impression management (Goffman, 1969). Goffman emphasized studying the ways in which people express themselves and their commitments, most notably, in his monograph *The Presentation of Self in Everyday Life* (1956), but also in many of his other publications (e.g. 1979, 1970, 1963, 1961). Goffman (1963:p.243, 1961:p.101 cited in Moore, 2005) depicted individual and corporate actors as tactically merging and choosing between expressions of commitment to increase their advantages in particular situations. According to Goffman (1961:p.143 cited in Moore, 2005), actors may express themselves primarily according to an association with one group. However, within that process, there is a continuous interplay of commitments to many groups and institutions, each ranked differently in different circumstances, according to which the actor feels best fits his or her ambitions.

Identity by studying differences

From the meaning explored in *What is identity* (1989), the concept of sameness of identities refers to a relation comparison of 'a close similarity of affinity'. However, for an empirical study of identities, this concept can also be approached from the opposite angle by considering differences. By this, I mean that people may come to know who they are, or whom they identify as, through feeling dissimilar from others (rather than similar) and through a sense of *not* sharing an affinity with particular groups and others (Jenkins, 1996:p.4 cited in Moore, 2005 p. 63). In this study, both similarities and differences will be explored as a means for understanding identities, who use *nunchi* in MNCs.

The concept of Goffman and identity performance

Goffman's theory of 'the presentation of self in everyday life' grounds the study of identity in the dramaturgical performances of selves, as he conceives it, in either 'front' or 'back stages'. These dramaturgical performances of identity occur interactively within front- and back-stage audiences. This means that, for any individual, identities are dynamic and change with the context and structural conditions brought on by each unique stage and audience (Goffman, 1956; Burns, 1992).

The significance of identity performances

According to Goffman's (1956) *Presentation of Self in Everyday Life*, identities can never be understood unilaterally because, as performances, they must always be validated—or not validated—by those others with whom an individual interacts. Within a performance, individuals present information that 'helps to define the situation, enabling others to know in advance what he will expect of them and what they may expect of him' (p.13). In other words, the performance of identity is about expression on one side and impression on another side, providing two distinct vantage points for understanding an identity: using Goffman's language, that of the performer and that of the audience(s). It also concerns presenting identities to various others, including accomplices (i.e. 'team members' and those 'in on the act') and non-accomplices (Goffman, 1963, 1961, 1956). On the other hand however, Goffman's theory is not perfect and therefore subject to criticism. Jenkins (1996 cited in Moore 2005, p.67) points out that actors when presenting themselves strategically take into account strategic self-presentations of others (p.58), therefore the negotiations and interplays between actors, who all aim to achieve goals strategically contribute to the individuals' self-presentations. Ashforth (1998) points out that scholars of identity and organizations should pay more attention to identity processes, which contribute to a better understanding of the formation of identities.

The front stage

Goffman's concept of 'front-stage' performance of identity can be understood as an intentionally public projection of identity performance, which utilizes the conventions, knowledge and stereotypes that are meaningful for audiences—in a sense, the identity one purposefully constructs as public. This contrasts with the performances of identity in the back stage, which is spaces where performers are present, but not audiences. For front-stage performances of identities, 'clothing, sex, age, and racial characteristics; size and looks; posture; speech patterns; facial expressions; bodily gestures; and the like' (Goffman, 1956:pp.23–24) are all key parts of staging the performance. What this means for studying identity is that, according to Goffman, in the front stage, people consciously and purposefully present a particular performance of themselves to the audience, and this includes how they manipulate their dramaturgical performances as well as key 'props'. The key point is that front-stage performances are intentionally public and thus explicitly constructed with this in mind.

How and why *nunchi* is used and applied in Goffman's front-stage concept will be explored. Goffman's four major aspects contributing to the presentation of oneself—or, in other words, identity—mirror the applied interpretation of *nunchi* as performative identity. Primarily, he suggests that identity is a matter of performance. Suh (2002) found that all individuals have several views of themselves in Korean national identity. She argued that multiple selves are often co-occurring existences in East Asian cultures, especially Korean culture. Second, Goffman explained that one's identity does not consist of one single identity, but comprises a variety of facets or revelations of self, which depend on the societal circumstances. Consequently, actors' commitments are adjusted from setting to setting, and are informed by all the distinctive interpretations open to the actor communicating, and the actor obtaining, the symbols being used in group self-presentation (Jenkins, 1996 cited in Moore 2005, 65). Blackhall et al. (2001) examined the influences of truth telling and self-representation. Their findings were that truth telling varies from setting to setting depending on whether *nunchi* allows the actor to be direct or indirect. Thus, the actor's commitments adjust to the setting, thereby rendering fruitful impression management because of the effect of *nunchi* being part of someone's identity. Third, the management of the difficult relationship between the anticipated performance of self and other, compensating aspects of one's profile and current condition, is of great significance. Chung and Gale (2008:p.21) explored that typical Korean families encourage their members to withhold direct expression of personal opinions or feelings, and develop implicit and indirect modes of communication and sensitivity to others' needs. Lastly, the validation of the performance by others, if not their embedded association, is vital to fruitful impression management (Goffman, 1969). Yi and Jezewski (2000:p.725) found that *nunchi* is needed for the incorporation of non-verbal performance elements, such as when it is appropriate to smile and to make eye contact with other actors. Therefore, it appears that self-presentation or identity is subject to change and can be rectified to fit the social context in different circumstances (Hannerz, 1996, 1983). This suggests that actors are able to change their self-representations according to the commitments they have to a certain group.

The back stage

According to Goffman, back-stage performances are different from front-stage performances because the context and audience are different. Goffman believed that, on the back stage, there is no 'explicit' audience in the sense of the front-stage audience, and the audience that does appear in the back stage is comprised of 'accomplices'.

In regard to the back stage, Goffman, writing about 'team performances', asserted that in this environment 'the performer comes to be his own audience; he comes to be performer and observer of the same show'. This is to say that, within a team, defined by Goffman (1959) as 'a set of performers who cooperate in presenting a single performance' (pp.80–81), individuals are also performing an identity for their accomplices as observers. This has implications for my study because I observed German international managers and employees' interactions – perhaps imagined as 'accomplices' to some extent – and with Korean people, which may be understood as more of a front-stage-type performance.

An example can render Goffmanian front and back stages easier to comprehend empirically. Consider, for example, the case of an MNC and the staff who are employed there. How the staff conduct and present themselves in the front of house to customers (and other staff members in the front of house) will vary significantly from how staff conduct and present themselves in the back of house where co-workers are not able to view them (i.e. where their audience members are team members and accomplices) (Goffman, 1956).

In applying Goffman's front- and back-stage model to this research project, it is useful to consider how Korean and German transnational managers and employees present their identities to different audiences, which is indicative of either front- or back-stage performances. For instance, how do Korean and German transnational managers and employees present themselves in relation to various others—such as domestic managers and transnational businesspeople who have lived in Korea for a long time and might have not initially moved there purely for economic reasons? Korean and German transnational managers and employees can be usefully examined using the front- and back-stage model to recontextualize *nunchi* in MNCs and the private sphere in the twenty-first century.

Moreover, *nunchi* (emotional intelligence) and *kibun* (feeling of balance) are very much interlinked in Korean identity context, especially in business environments (Chaney & Martin, 2011). It is necessary to maintain an atmosphere of stable *kibun* at all times; therefore, one has to perform *nunchi* (Southerton, 2008) on both the front and back stages, in Goffman's terms. These performances take place through regulating another actor's *kibun* by using *nunchi* (Southerton, 2008). Conflict must be resolved by incorporating *nunchi* into the overall performance to achieve a harmonious stage setting for all actors involved (Kim, Sohn & Wall, 1999). Actors from different power levels directly help to uphold or reconstruct harmonious interactions at work through performative *nunchi* (Kim, Sohn & Wall, 1999; Lee, 2000). *Nunchi* is performed by actors in Korean management to avoid the highly sensitive possibility of losing social face on the front stage while others are watching; therefore, overt conflict is prevented through performative front-stage *nunchi* in Korean identity settings to ensure the maintenance of intentionally public projections of identity performance and harmony (Cocroft & Ting-Toomey, 1994). Organizational control in Korean management means monitoring the 'team performances', which assert that in the back-stage environment 'the performer comes to be his own audience; he comes to be performer and observer of the same show'. This is to say that, within a team, defined by Goffman (1956) as 'a set of performers who cooperate in presenting a single performance' (pp.80–81), individuals are also performing an identity for their accomplices as observers. When becoming the performer and observer, accomplices provide feedback to correct any misbehaviour (Jaeger, 1983:p.92). Organizational behaviour is regulated through actors' awareness of *nunchi*, which as pointed out by Jang & Chung does not follow an explicit procedure (Jang & Chung, 1995). Therefore, *nunchi* is the linchpin in performances of Korean management (Lee, 1998a, 1998b; Lee & Yoo, 1987).

In addition, Head (1992) examined the interlinking relationship between a company's advertising strategies and its country of origin's national self-image in domestic and international settings. In Head's monograph *Made in Germany*, this linkage becomes apparent and therefore may represents one interpretation of what identity constitutes. Kasmir (2001) supported this interpretation of identity by establishing the interlinkages between employees' self-presentations and the company's identity used in marketing agendas. Therefore, it appears that self-presentation or identity is subject to change and can be rectified to fit the social context in different circumstances. Hannerz (1996, 1983) defined this occurrence of alteration of self-presentation in transnational settings further in describing identity as a 'toolkit', from which actors select items to present themselves in the most positive way possible. "Ulf Hannerz … describes identity in such situations as a kind of "toolkit," from which actors select to present themselves in the most positive light possible" (Moore 2005, p.9). This suggests that actors are able to change their self-representations according to the commitments that they have to a certain group. As a result, actors may perform differently depending on the group. The best way of considering the construction of identity in transnational contexts may thus be to respect identity as an on-going process of 'our understanding of who we are and of who other people are and other people's understanding of themselves and others' (Jenkins, 1996:p.5 cited in Moore 2005, p. 63). Jenkins (1996:pp.5, 83–85 cited in Moore 2005, p.63) argued that a sense of group affiliation results from shared internal and external self-definition. Hannerz (1983:p.348, 355, 1992:p.65 cited in Moore 2005, 63) described the expression of group commitment not as a single identity but as a toolkit of symbols, from which people can select and combine elements in different ways and through which they view the world.

Hannerz (1992) also discussed the case of actors with various group commitments, or who are part of subgroups within a group, in which the same symbols can be said to define both or all the groups in question, but with different interpretations. Consequently, actors' commitments are readjusted from setting to setting, and are informed by all the distinctive interpretations open to the actor communicating, and the actor obtaining, the symbols being used in group self-presentation (Jenkins, 1996 cited in Moore 2005, p.64). Therefore, self-presentation in transnational situations is used not so much to create formulaic identities but to continuously define and redefine the connections between individuals or groups through alterations of its form and content.

The concept of emotion work in the wider literature

This section examines the wider literature on emotion work; the characteristics of expressed emotions are significant to my work. Developing a thorough theory of emotion is a task that has charmed writers from a range of disciplines, such theories are sometimes the subject of complete books (Darwin, 1965; DeRivera, 1977; Hillman, 1961); recognizing the full range of human emotion is however beyond this study. Emotions in organizations gained rising interest among scholars and practitioners in recent years (Ashforth and Humphery, 1995; Briner,1999; Fineman,1993). One of the topics is emotional work, in which the expression of organizationally anticipated emotions is part of one's job. Emotion work takes place principally when one has to work with people (Paoli, 1997).

The concept of emotional work was first introduced by Hochschild (1979, 1983) in her seminal book *The managed heart* (1983), in which she investigated flight attendants. Compellingly Hochschild established that their work could not be fully described by the physical aspects of their job, rather a considerable part of the job was dealing with passengers and their emotions. The concept of emotion work refers to the quality of interactions between sender and receiver (Zapf, 2002). Hochschild (1983) drew upon Goffman's (1956) work, arguing that in all social interactions, people tend to play roles and try to create certain impressions. Impressions include the display of normatively appropriate emotions following assigned display rules. Employees are not only required to work on tasks mentally and physically, they are also required to manage their emotions as part of their job. It is to note that this differs from considering emotions as a reaction to the conditions of organizational environments as investigated in the emotions at work literature (see Briner, 1999; Pekrun and Frese, 1992). Emotion work as part of the job, suggests that assigned emotions are a prerequisite. Morris and Feldman (1996) define emotion work as the 'effort, planning, and control needed to express organizationally desired emotions during interpersonal transactions' (p.987).

Authors differ somewhat in their conceptualization of emotion work. While Hochschild (1983) explored 'the management of feeling to create a publicly observable facial and bodily display' (p.7), other authors focused on the expressive behaviour (Ashforth and Humphery, 1993; Morris and Feldman, 1996).

Emotion work occurs in face-to-face or voice to voice interactions, emotions are displayed to influence other people's emotions, stances and actions and the display of emotions has to follow certain rules (Hochschild, 1983; Morris and Feldman, 1997). The core of emotion work is to influence others (Brucks, 1998; Strauss et al. 1980). Strauss et al. define what they call 'sentimental work', as a secondary task, which has to be carried out, while considering the receiver's response (Rice, 1963). Locke (1996) conducted an ethnographic study on paediatricians, who use 'comedic performance' to actively change the children's and parents' negative emotions into positive ones. In a 'mastery comedy', which is performed strategically, the physician examines a little girl. He starts joking, while touching her stomach, 'Is your breakfast there?' while playing around with her and trying to 'find her breakfast', he disguises his primary task of palpating the child's abdomen and internal organs (p.51). Goffman (1959) suggested that every social interaction follows some rules, which when strategically performed well, trigger the desirable emotions aimed for, much in the case of the 'mastery comedy'. Ekman (1973) defined rules on appropriate emotional expression display rules. Ekman classifies display rules as norms and standards of behaviour, which indicate the suitable emotions in a given situation and also how these emotions should be openly expressed. Hochschild (1983) speaks of feeling rules, because in her original concept, the management of inner feelings is fundamental, whereas Ashforth and Humphery (1993) emphasise the outer expression and choose the term display rules. Organizational socialization includes acquiring norms, or 'feeling rules' (Hochschild, 1979), about which emotions should be displayed and which should be hidden.

Many organizations provide in-house training about feeling rules. In the Walt Disney tradition, new employees study the sharp otherness between being "onstage" (where Disney patrons can go) and being "off-stage" (where only employees can go). When onstage, employees ought to follow succinct guidelines about which emotions can and cannot be conveyed (Peters & Waterman, 1982; Tyler & Nathan, 1985). New employees attend lectures and read in Disney handbooks (Walt Disney Productions, 1982, p.2): 'You were cast for a role, not hired for a job and "Our audience is composed of guests not customers … and we cast members are hosts and hostesses." *HanaEins* members when first arriving in Korea do not receive a handbook on how to fulfil their role expectations even though working and managing across borders and identities in MNCs in Korea is much like an "on stage" and "off stage" setting, as described by the Walt Disney tradition, this will be discussed in detail in the third part of this book.

Disney's tactic may seem extreme, but other companies place similar importance on the display of suitable feelings. For example Mrs Field's Cookies (Richman, 1984), Delta Airlines (Hochschild, 1983), and McDonald's (Boas & Chain, 1976). Emotional transactions can be viewed as "double interacts" (Weick, 1979). According to Weick (1979, p.115), the primary emotions sent by an employee (an "act") stimulate the target person to respond with implicit or explicit response about the continuation of the displayed emotion (an "interact"). The sender of emotions reacts to such feedback by readjustments incorporating, deserting, altering, or preserving the displayed emotion (completing a "double interact"). The sender and receiver of displayed emotion use one or more double interacts to achieve agreement, or reduce equivocality (Weick, 1979), about which feelings should be transferred and which should be hidden.

In summary, emotion work can be organized into emotional harmony, which is an indicator of good fit between person and setting (Caplan, 1983). Emotional dissonance, which according to Hochschild (1983) takes place when conveyed emotions fulfil feeling rules, but conflict with inner feelings. And emotional deviance, which occurs, when expressed emotions clash with local norms. Emotional deviance is the contrary of emotional dissonance because the organization member expresses inner feelings and neglects feeling rules. Hochschild's (1983) and fellow scholars' initial ideas on emotion work are mirrored in the *nunchi* discourse. Hochschild's (1983) concept of emotional dissonance may also be seen in Chung & Gale (2008) study which explores the fulfilment of feeling rules, which conflict with inner feelings, Chung & Gale (2008) describe such occurrence as good *nunchi*. The opposite, emotional deviance aligns with Mensik, Grainer & Chafferjee (1999) notion of group harmony and awareness. Those who fail to perform *nunchi* are classified as emotionally deviant and are subject to being exposed and disciplined in the *nunchi* literature, through precise effective informal measures (Paik & Sohn, 1998). Emotional harmony may be compared to the smooth practise of *nunchi*, where all actors are aware of their roles.

Conclusion

In sum, this study is an in –depth study of specific acts of strategic self-presentation, incorporating the recontextualisation of symbols of identity, events and processes related to the identity expressions of *HanaEins* members working for German MNCs in South Korea. Therefore I focus on the dynamic aspects and on-going challenges *HanaEins* members encounter when managing and working across borders and identities and aim at providing answers to the question what do *HanaEins* members see themselves doing.

Thus I attempt to establish a thick, descriptive and detailed understanding of the *nunchi* phenomenon, being close to experienced realities and everyday practices, focusing on specific examples of strategic identity performances and their meanings that *HanaEins* members attribute to them.

Therefore, based on Erving Goffman's theory, that actors constantly strive to present themselves in the best light possible and that meanings of symbols of identity shift depending on the identity context (Brannen, 2004), this study explores *nunchi* and its significance in strategic self-presentations as a symbol of identity across borders and identities in the case of *HanaEins* members in Seoul.

Chapter 2
Identity, Emotional Intelligence and *Nunchi*

Introduction

The following chapter is arranged in several sections to distinguish the various areas of the literature that are relevant for this study. The first part focuses on positioning this study amongst the literature. Secondly an overview of work on and linked to *nunchi* and how *nunchi* may either be seen as emotion work and/or as identity performance is presented. Thirdly, contemporary German and Korean identity are established and finally compared to each other. Fourthly, an illustration of Korean corporate identity and management is presented.

Positioning of this study

This opening section of the literature review severs to discuss and position this study amongst the realm of the quantitative studies on "cultural distance" (Kogut & Singh, 1988; Hofstede, 1980, 1991; Gomez-Mejia & Palich, 1997; Black & Mendenhall, 1991) in business management; and makes plain how this interdisciplinary, anthropologically infused study contributes to Shenkar et al. (2008) "cultural friction" focus when considering culture related subjects in management studies. Hickson and Pugh (1995) stress the importance of culture among the extensive literature, which according to them " shapes everything" (p.90).

The critical perspective taken here, exemplifies the shortcomings of the "cultural distance" literature to set the stage for the following selected literature relevant to this study. Therefore, the frequently citied study on "measuring the magnitude of differences in national culture" (Shenkar et al., 2008 p.905; Shenkar, 2001) by Geert Hofstede, *Culture's Consequences* published in (1980) is examined as a representative example for the "cultural distance" literature, because "the Kogut and Singh (1988) index is a rather simplistic aggregate of Hofstede's (1980) dimensions and is hence liable to the same criticism", (Shenkar, 2001 p.525). Culture is important for many aspects of business life especially when a business must interface with people, either as customers, employees, suppliers or stakeholders, however there is an ongoing debate as to the reliability and validity of the "cultural distance" discourse for studying culture and related subjects (McSweeney, 2002).

The following analysis of Hofstede's approach, as Morgan put it, cultural subjects were forced by management theorists to be " a phenomenon with clearly defined attributes ... often reduced to a set of discrete variables ... that can be documented and manipulated in an instrumental way" (1997, p. 151) is relevant to my study; because my research highlights the complex, fluid, and ambivalent nature of the phenomenon, hence also supports a paradigm shift from a positivist, functionalist thrust to an approach where the world is viewed as continuously enacted and re-enacted negotiation and renegotiation, thus drawing attention to the actual contact between actors, or what Shenkar (2008) terms "friction" allowing us to appreciate the complexity and dialectical nature of cross-border interaction.

Culture's Consequences (1980) by Geert Hofstede

Hofstede's study examines national cultural differences and their consequences. Although sociologists such as Immanuel Wallerstein (1990) are skeptical about operationalizing "the concept of culture" (p.34) and Benedict Anderson (1991) claims nations as "imagined communities", Hofstede asserts to have found four different criteria, termed "dimensions" through a combination of multivariate statistics (factor analysis) and theoretical reasoning. His primary data for *Cultural Consequences* (1980, 1984) were extracted from a pre-existing employee attitude survey undertaken with IBM approximately between 1967 and 1973. 117000 questionnaire responses were collected from 66 countries in which IBM was present at that time of which 40 countries were analysed. Hofstede found them to be validated to understand the informants "values" which in his terms are described as "broad tendencies to prefer certain states of affair over others" and hence built for him "the core element in culture" (1991, p. 35)

Relevance & Rigour

During the time of its delivery there was very little work on culture, and at this time many businesses were just entering the international arena. Scholarly attention was also turning toward culture during this period, and Hofstede was considered a pioneer (Sondergraad 1994, p.448-449; Shenkar et al., 2008, p. 907). The study raised awareness of cultural differences and lead on to the realisation that the recontextualisation of symbols of national identity is needed to foster greater understanding.

The research framework used by Hofstede was based on rigorous design with systematic data collection and coherent theory (Sondergraad 1994, p.448-449). The study may easily be replicated due to its rigorous design, which is a strength as it promotes transparency. The transparency of his research provides other scholars with the opportunity to clearly identify shortcomings, allowing a more vibrant scholarly discourse on the subject matter.

Moreover, my study contributes in redirecting management research away from the static "cultural distance" paradigm, stressing the dynamism occurring during interactions of real actors, working and managing across borders and identities in transnational business settings. Thus, taking Kirkman, Lowe and Gibson's (2006 in Shenkar, 2012) recommendation seriously, to "avoid further use of the overall cultural distance index" (p.303) to elude harvesting a "limited tunnel vision" (Shenkar, 2012, p.15) the weaknesses are outlined to set the stage for the wider literature considered in this study, because it is believed that only a truly interdisciplinary approach seeks to learn from and with other areas of study to achieve a perspective that embeds actual actors within their identity contexts, considering their contextual and political relationships in order to shed light on the essence of their self-presentations in transnational business.

Definition Problems

Definitions determine the research design, particularly when the relevance of the variables and factors are to be evaluated. Definitions provide the boundaries and limitations of the study, which enhance the reliability of the results. The first major problem with Hofstede (1980) is that there are definition problems. Hofstede describes culture as 'mental programming', as 'software of the mind', as 'subjective' (1980). Schein (1985) and Rossi (1989) share similar views and label culture as 'the unconscious infrastructure' and the 'basic assumptions of beliefs'. For all of them culture and social frameworks are treated analytically distinct but related, the second one being theorized as the dependent variable. This perception of culture and the attempt to analytically measure and statistically evaluate it differs from MacIntyre (1971) and Smelser's (1992) view to the degree that Hofstede's study could be completely rejected as an impetuous effort to measure the unmeasurable in using the "cultural distance" model, based on the criteria that "culture" does not have a clear-cut definition. Therefore the terminology used in research instruments; specifically the term "culture" itself is open to interpretation (Nasif et al., 1991 p. 82). There are more than 164 definitions for the term culture (Olie 1995 p. 128). Hofstede does not provide a clear-cut definition of culture in his study as discussed above. Without a clear definition of culture, doubts on the meaningfulness of research are enhanced, particularly when the definition of culture, while extraneous to the concern of the research, can "invalidate the findings" (Seliger and Shohamy 1989 p.5). When one considers other terminology used in the questionnaire these become subject to interpretation, undermining the objectivity of research, that is, whether the researcher is interpreting the results in a way that vindicates his or her hypotheses. It may become a case of: is the question defining the culture, or the culture defining the question? Problems of translating questions and responses add to these challenges (Henry 1990 p. 32).

Assumption of cultural homogeneity

The second problem is that Hofstede ignores that organisational cultures and identities vary from place to place as well as from time to time. Cultures and identities undergo a non-linear evolutionary process with actors constantly adapting to conditions. Hofstede's and subsequent models assume that only one IBM culture exists across all places in which the survey was distributed (Risberg, 1999 & Parker, 2000). Therefore, Hofstede fails to establish the matrix of identities within one identity, as he assumes organisational, national and occupational culture to be exclusively the same. Hofstede's concept assumes the domestic population is a homogeneous whole. However most nations are heterogeneous groups composed of various primordial units e.g. the UK, Malaysia, South Africa (Nasif et al.1991 p. 82 & Redpath 1997 p. 336). Analysis is therefore constrained by the character of the individual being assessed. Furthermore Hofstede's assumption of a uniform, singular and monopolistic organisational culture simply ignores the broad literature, debating for recognition of plural, cultures within organizations (Jelinek et al., 1983 & Smircich, 1983 & Spender, 1998). Assuming cultural homogeneity may have negatively affected the reliability, consistency or repeatability of his measures. Repetition of the results, which derive from the same survey in another cultural group may be distorted, due to measuring factors that cannot be completely compared with factors in the previous survey.

Factor analysis

Hofstede's assumption, which he used to justify the application of factor analysis, is subject to criticism. Factor analysis is a statistical technique, which replaces a large number of variables with a smaller number of factor, that reflect what sets of variables have in common with another (Dancey & Reidy 1999). Hofstede developed his model as a result of using factor analysis to examine the result of the IBM employee survey (Hofstede 1980). Hofstede's factor analysis had good intentions but was built on the assumption that organizational and occupational culture are the same, therefore his factor analysis can not support his empirical findings. The reliability of his research is further undermined by the assumption of equalizing organizational and occupational culture. He identified four bipolar dimensions (power distance; individualism/ collectivism; uncertainty avoidance; masculinity/femininity), which formed the foundation of his characterisation for each national character (d'Iribarne 1996 p.33 & Dorfman and Howell 1998 p. 129 & Hofstede 1980; Schneider and Barsoux 1997 p. 79).

Alasdair MacIntyre (1971) confirms the separation of occupational and organizational culture and therefore contributes towards rejecting the external validity of Hofstede's findings "No institution or practise is what it is, or does what it does, independently of what anyone whatsoever thinks or feels about it" (MacIntyre 1971, p. 263). Hofstede's study is most likely limited in its ability to generalise the findings to its target population. Furthermore Hofstede (1980) marginalises the occurrence of the coexistence of dimensions, since he defined all four as bipolar, e.g. a nation can either be masculine or feminine but not both at the same time. Slater (1970) supports the argument of coexistences of opposite dimensions, "An individual, like a group is a collection of ambivalent feelings, contradictory needs and values and antithetical ideas" (p.27).

Equivalency

Another contributing issue, rejecting Hofstede's approach is whether the specific wording and phrasing of the IBM questionnaire's terminology translates across cultures or as implied by Schwartz (1994) is meaningless if there is no equivalence of meaning. All quantitative research is subject to this potential criticism, but it is a case of acknowledging the issue of the difficulty of wording, and accepting that the research might never be perfect. Schwartz takes this further and argues that Hofstede did not address this issue, which therefore shows that it is unknown if the specific wording and phrasing of the IBM questionnaire's terminology used was conceptually equivalent across cultures and therefore Hofstede's model of national cultures. Hofstede's acceptance of the questionnaire design has been challenged by D'Iribarne (1991), Schwartz (1992) and Lytle et al. (1995), who claim that using different questions from his study to identify a nation's culture rendered dissimilar descriptions not matching Hofstede's findings. Salter and Niswander (1994) reassure the above counter argument. They found that Hofstede's methodology and accepted set of questions has not been entirely confirmatory when replicated, which adds to the suggestion that the "cultural distance" approach is not applicable in achieving accurate results in culture related studies and its' application in business studies.

Equivalency may be split into four dimensions: functional, conceptual, instrument and measurement equivalence (Cavusgil & Das 1997). Functional equivalence assumes that a functional part in one country is the identical in another (Hay, Anderson and Revicki 1993; Johnson 1998, p.4-6; Nasif et al. 1991, p. 83-84). For example considering the usage of pushbikes in Australia and Vietnam, the two countries would detect different uses. Australians would see the use as primarily recreational, while many Vietnamese would see it as a necessary type of transportation (Cavusgil and Das 1997). Conceptual equivalence regards the cultural value of behavioural or attitudinal constructs. For instance company devotion in Asia may be seen as loyalty to one's workplace and by following the rules, while in Australia it may be following instructions and not breaking the rules (Cavusgil and Das 1997). Instrument equivalence and measurement equivalence represent the cross-cultural consistency of the research instrument, whether is equally symbolised across the entire sample. This includes participant bias towards scaling. For example some cultures will tend not to provide extreme levels on a scaled question, while other cultures will tend to do so (Nasif et al. 1991, p. 85).

Conclusion and Applicability

Although a "friction" stance is taken in the study of "Korean *Nunchi* across borders and identities in Multi National Corporations and the private sphere in the 21st century" the above considered weaknesses of the "cultural distance" model influence my study's selection of literature and overall position in the international management literature as a supporter toward a "friction" focused shift in international business. Hofstede's limitations, one being definition problems encourage the present study to provide clear-cut definitions for the research design e.g. how are German and Korean identity defined. A rigorous approach in handling definitions through reviewing the extant literature on *nunchi* as well as on contemporary German and Korean identity enhances the validity of the study. Furthermore, Hofstede's assumed cultural homogeneity was avoided in my study. Breaching the streams of literature on *nunchi* and contemporary German and Korean identity as well as on Korean corporate identity grasps *nunchi's* significance in organisational as well as national identity. This will avoid the assumption that *nunchi* is used in the same way across organizational and national identity. In addition, close attention was devoted to the equivalency of terminology used in the literature while keeping the latter recontextualising of *nunchi* in mind.

Essentially cultures are still trying to be understood, which indicates that the "cultural distance" model, derived from filled in questionnaires has not detached this philosophical difficulty. Misleading assumptions essentially lead to wrong empirical descriptions irrespective of the mass of data and statistical analysis used. If the aim of a study is to understand national culture, national identity and symbols of identity the research approach, including the selection of literature considered should explore more about the fullness and variety of national practices. Therefore scholars need to participate with and focus on "cultural friction", which implies focusing on the interface between actors' transactions rather on the void between them. Thus applying a "friction" focus even when reviewing literature contributes to make sense of, understand and incorporate various influences and diversity to obtain valid results; and therefore offers a rich perspective alternatively to the "sterile views encapsulated in the concept and measure of "distance" (Shenkar et al. 2008, p. 15).

We shall now consider the first stream of literature relevant to this study, namely the various works addressing *nunchi*.

1.   *Nunchi* areas: An Overview

Few scholars whose work has been published in English or German have attempted to define and explain *nunchi*, which is a symbol of Korean identity that can loosely be translated as emotional intelligence in classic literature, however its nature and depictions suggest *nunchi* at times to be emotion work and at times as identity performance or a combination of the two. Due to the scarcity of the *nunchi* discourse, this section has been divided into several contexts in which *nunchi* has been discussed. Even though the single scholars, who concerned themselves with the *nunchi* phenomenon, seem not to engage with each others' works, which results in many one-sided depictions of *nunchi*, there seems to be a general trend, classifying *nunchi* as a regulating tool much like Salovey and Mayer's definition of emotional intelligence. The following examination of *nunchi* uses scholarly works, which directly or indirectly describe the nature of *nunchi* in different contexts and are therefore relevant to this study. It is worth mentioning that scholars whose identities have somehow been affected by Korean or German influences have conducted all of the works that are directly related to *nunchi*. Korean diaspora members and American scholars who have an interest in emotion work, identity performance and international business mainly represent the indirectly related literature.

An exploration of *nunchi* as emotion work and identity performance

Nunchi in the context of transnational nurses

This exploration of *nunchi* commences with Yi and Jezewski (2000), who closely observed and studied Korean nurses' emotional adjustment to hospitals in the United States, in evaluating their emotion work and identity performances in the formation of defining *nunchi* through self-presentation at work. Using a grounded theory method allowed them to gather their data from semi-structured formal interviews with a sample of 12 Korean nurses. Their study showed that Korean nurses had the most difficulty in non-face-to-face communication, for example, talking over the phone. The main reason to justify the Korean nurses' adjustment difficulties in non-face-to-face communication was that they could not include and read their counterparts' non-verbal codes. Yi and Jezewski indicated that the interviewees described the skills to obtain these non-verbal codes as *nunchi* in Korean. As explained by Yi and Jezewski, literally *nunchi* means, "eye sense". It is the skill in perceiving non-verbalized codes and understanding a situation. One nurse in this study defined *nunchi* as knowing what others need by just seeing their facial expressions' (p.725). Because the telephone does not provide the opportunity to experience the other's direct aura, many of the informants were scared, nervous and embarrassed. Further, they experienced difficulties in non-verbal behaviour such as when it is appropriate to smile and to make eye contact. According to Yi and Jezewski, 'Koreans rarely use these kinds of behaviour in Korea, because smiles are usually considered impolite and arrogant' (p.725). In cross-cultural communication, *nunchi* often conforms to high-context cultures, which communicate implicitly and strongly rely on context; as opposed to low-context cultures that rely on explicit verbal communication thus, as non-verbal codes; in other words, *nunchi* is generally part of a high-context culture.

American culture falls within the category of low-context culture, which explains the nurses' adjustment issues (Eliott et al., 1982; Hall, 1976; Kim, 1986). Depicting *nunchi* as "eye-sense" or non verbal codes as done by Yi and Jezewski, their characterisation of *nunchi* suggests it to be emotion work, which seems applicable to actors, who are familiar with symbols of a given identity setting e.g. when to smile or to make eye contact. However if such emotion work represents acquired knowledge of understanding symbols of identity such as in the case of the Korean nurses in the US, such processing of emotion work may turn into strategic identity performances.

Nunchi in the context of group affiliation

The significance of such context was investigated by Lee-Peuker (2004), who conducted a qualitative study, which included 20 interviews with international and local executive managers in South Korea's capital, Seoul, and its surrounding metropolitan area. Her hands-on approach to exploring the embeddedness of economic action in human relations in Korean MNCs investigated closely three elements: affiliation, indebtedness and mediation, which further allows the analysis of *nunchi* as emotion work and identity performance.

Lee-Peuker (2004) explained the importance of group affiliations in Korean MNCs and their origins. Group affiliation is not a result deliberately aimed for by people. Koreans have always belonged to some sort of group within the larger group of institutions, firms, society or the country as a whole, and 'people inadvertently grow into them during the course of life. Regional and familiar provenances as well as gender are determined by birth. From them all fundamental affiliations arise' (p.6).

Lee-Peuker (2004) explained that all Koreans spend their lives within several groups, which have a big effect on their lives:

> They form the inner circle of friendship and normally do not have more than seven to fifteen members per group. In such circles of friends, where all members are from the same generation, one ideally feels snug, at home, and such a group is just as natural as one's family.
> (p.6)

The feeling described in the above quotation, which can be defined as familiar security, does not just come from anywhere. It requires mutual intimacy, which can only be nourished through common shared experiences in everyday life. *Kibun*, which can be translated as sentiment, morale, affection or mood, and *nunchi* are closely intertwined. One cannot exist without the other. As Lee-Peuker (2004) explained, '*nunchi* denotes, tact, discretion, susceptibility, power of observation, courtesy, mind reading, and the ability to sum up the situation' (p.6). In short, *nunchi* defines the ability to empathize—to put oneself into someone else's shoes—particularly with their feelings and thoughts, and to behave, react and act accordingly for the sake of harmony and the other person's *kibun*. The level of *nunchi* given and expected varies among actors according to social class, status and age, which draws upon the strict social etiquette of keeping harmony in accordance with the aim of achieving persistent harmony. This can be observed within the Korean language, which comprises numerous different spoken forms of politeness according to age and authority level. For example, a younger person is always meant to use the politest version when talking to someone older. Further, it is considered rude to look older people in the eyes while drinking or serving food oneself. According to Lee-Peuker, many Koreans believe that any sort of relationship between Koreans and non-Koreans is risky because they assume that *nunchi* does not exist in other identity contexts:

> Intimacy is not a matter of chance or destiny, that suddenly binds two people together because of their congeniality, but the result of a long-term coexistence, through which—like in a family—all facets of one's character are learned. (p.6)

Personal relationships rely heavily on the possession of good *nunchi*, which provides guidance to understand another person's *kibun* and therefore helps in achieving harmony and respecting someone's 'face'. Lee-Peuker's hands-on approach is relevant for this study because I conducted formal interviews to supplement the ethnographic data collection. Lee-Peuker's approach differs from my approach because she is an 'insider' whereas I am an 'outsider'. Her prevailing Korean identity creates a limitation because she identifies herself with the subject matter completely and therefore views it from the inside rather than the outside, which might cause difficulties, especially in picking up small details.

Her own (Korean) upbringing in a group, life experiences, appearance and Korean-language proficiency (native) also impose limitations because she imports a great deal of pre-knowledge in behaviour and thought, which is rather natural opposed to being studied or observed. Therefore, her role as an insider is moderately negative for gathering data, which can be recontextualized in terms of the German identity context. Her judgement that many Koreans believe that any sort of relationship between Koreans and non-Koreans is risky because they assume that *nunchi* does not exist in other national identity contexts seems of great interest to this study as the recontextualisation of *nunchi* might not change her claims of Koreans not believing in the existence of *nunchi* in other identity contexts dissimilar to their own, however it will be interesting to see how they respond to recontextualised strategic self-presentations of German transnational businesspeople, which incorporates *nunchi*.

Taking into consideration Lee-Peuker's conclusions, *nunchi* represents emotion work, which is evoked through shared intimacy that needs to be emotionally triggered opposed to patently delivered in the form of an identity performance. An identity performance is the capacity of strategically presenting oneself in consummating an action, hence to construct and perform features of an identity.

However, when being in the same identity setting as indicated by Lee-Peuker e.g. any sort of group, *nunchi* may take on the form of an identity performance, because actors are regulated through symbolism e.g. overall harmony, to strategically create shared emotions through shared commonalities, experiences and memories in a performative manner. Thus in terms of symbolism and instilling symbols of identity such as harmony through the use of language (e.g. honorifics) or manners (e.g. eye contact, smiles, serving food), *nunchi* takes on the form of a clear identity performance; because symbols such as language do not follow the principles of emotion work, however necessitate logical reasoning to strategically deliver expected yet identity context appropriate identity performances.

Nunchi in the context of emotional interactions

Scherpinski-Lee (2011) compared German and Korean emotional interactions in various settings in her deep literature analysis. Her study examined more closely the importance of emotions in interpersonal relationships and associated networks in Korea. Her analytical approach systematically broke down the single components of Korea's emotional intelligence—or *nunchi*—and provided some background information on the formation of a national identity and how unique emotional interaction patterns have arisen as a result. Thus her comparison of German and Korean emotional interactions provides further motivations to explore *nunchi* and its facets as emotion work and identity performance.

Scherpinski-Lee (2011) also followed the cultural argument that philosophy and the thought of Confucianism built the essence of Korea's contemporary value system. Her definition of Korea's interpretation of Confucianism differs from that of other scholars. According to her analysis, *in* (인) 'be gentle', *eu* (의) 'righteous', *ye* (예) 'grace/manner/etiquette', *chi* (지) 'wise/sagacious' and *shin* (신) 'reliable/ trustworthy/dependable' are the main components that form Korea's interpretation of Confucianism and therefore its value system. Her study demonstrates that *nunchi* is the linchpin for all social interactions on all levels in Korea. Schrepinski-Lee described *nunchi* as the most important element in interactions, which either determines success or failure. According to her, it is the ability to interpret non-verbal signals that are often delivered while speaking, in other words, reading between the lines: 'Um non- und paraverbale Signale, die in kommunikativen Akten mittransportiert werden und Wünsche oder Absichten implizieren oder Shimjung-Eruptionen anzeigen, interpretieren zu können, ist es für ein angemessenes Verhalten unabdinglich, zwischen den Zeilen zu lesen' (p. 102). ['In order to be able to interpret non- and paraverbal signals, which are transported through acts of communication and imply wishes or intentions or indicate *shimjung* eruptions, it is paramount to read between the lines to demonstrate appropriate behaviour.'] Further, she noted that sense of tact (*Taktgefühl*), the importance to look ahead (*Weitsichtigkeit*) and empathy/intuition are also characteristics of *nunchi*.

Scherpinski-Lee (2011) explained that the emphasis on emotions and non-verbal communication in Korea categorizes the country as a high-context culture, just as Hall (1989) stressed that implicitness and indirectness in terms of communication and display of public emotions are prevalent in Korea. As mentioned earlier, *nunchi* is considered the most important element in managing human interactions because it offers a framework to incorporate and practise sub-elements such as protecting the other party's *chemyon* ('face') and to create and strengthen the other's *jung*. The *jung* element derives from *shimjung*. The first component is *shim*, which stands for 'disposition' and *jung* stands for 'affection'. *Shimjung* as a whole is mainly used to describe an immediate, spontaneously arising feeling that tends to be predominantly negative between two people who have been in a rather well-established relationship of any kind. 'Shimjung ist ein unmittelbares, spontanes, meist negativ besetztes Gefühl, das in einer bereits längeren bestehenden Beziehung zwischen zwei Menschen aufkommen kann' ('Shimjung is an immediate, spontaneous emotion that often entails negative connotations, which can arise in long pre-existing relationships between two individuals') (Scherpinski-Lee, 2011:p.97). When such a negative feeling arises, it is the other person's responsibility to take notice and, further, to take previous conversations and current circumstances into consideration to make sense of the other person's behaviour, mood and negative feelings to accommodate and provide emotional understanding. If misjudgement takes place, one changes the subject quite quickly, but at the same, tries to evaluate how one's misjudgement came into existence. Both parties involved need to possess *nunchi* in order to pick up non-verbal signals (read between the lines) to detect a prevalent negative feeling. As a response, *nunchi* facilitates the adjustment of one's behaviour to solve the problem by exchanging feelings of shared fortune and the relationship history as well as the importance of consolidating the relationship in the future. According to Scherpinski-Lee:

> Drittens müssen sie das Feingefühl besitzen, einen Shimjung-Diskurs
> zu initiieren, in dem der negative Gefühlsstatus gelöst, die Beziehung
> im Dialog extern validiert und neu austariert werden kann. In solch
> einem Dialog werden Gefühle offengelegt ... wobei die gemeinsamen
> Interaktionsgeschichte betont und die Notwendigkeit des weitern
> Zusammenhaltens aufgrund des gemeinsamen Schicksals, das beide
> verbindet, über die empfundene Differenz gestellt wird. (p.98)
> [Third, they must have the sensitivity to initiate a *shimjung* discourse,
> through which the negative emotional situation is relieved; thus, the
> relationship can be validated externally through dialogue and therefore
> a new balance can be established. Through this dialogue, emotions are
> being laid open ... whereby their shared history of interacting with
> each other is emphasized and the necessity of holding onto each other
> due to the shared fate, which connects both, is of higher importance
> than the perceived differences.]

Shimjung ultimately aims to provide a verbal exchange, which demonstrates the importance of the relationship and motivates all parties involved to engage in mutual understanding to restore overall harmony. The second component, *jung,* is described as the 'glue' that keeps relationships together. Scherpinski-Lee (2011) argued that the foundation for interpretation of non-verbal signals and conflict resolutions relies on *jung.* The intensity of *jung* is based on the amount of years and shared interactions in relationships. The framework for *jung* steadily increases with time and interaction. *Jung* is commonly used in the Korean language; hence, a person that possesses *jung* is portrayed as warm hearted and amiable opposed to people who lack *jung,* who are considered not capable of having a relationship, selfish and callous. Generally, people who possess *jung* avoid and do not share *jung* with people who lack *jung.* In close relationships, *shimjung* transfers automatically without using words—just trust and harmony—from one mind to another. *Chemyon* is the notion of maintaining harmony through the maintenance of face, which can only be implied if one possesses *nunchi* and uses it well in terms of *jung* and *shimjung.* Scherpinski-Lee provided an example to visualize *nunchi.* If a friend is currently experiencing money troubles, in most cases he will not address this problem to maintain his *chemyon.* As a result, the other person involved will use his or her *nunchi,* which heavily relies on *jung* and *shimjung* to manage the situation without violating the face of one's friends, and overall harmony is thus preserved.

This example shows that *nunchi* requires the decoding of non-verbal signals understanding of symbols of identity as well as the immediate implementation of expected actions. Schrepinski- Lee's (2011) deep literature analysis renders a platform for understanding the single components that form *nunchi.* Her analysis of *nunchi* points out that *nunchi* in the context of a *shimjung* process forms emotion work. Thus, such process entails several steps as indicated by Schrepinski-Lee, of which one of the most crucial steps is initiating emotion work to pick up on such process to then performatively act upon it through the required symbols present in the given setting. Such process might take place in any national identity context, however picking up on, expressing and executing it might follow dissimilar interpretations of *nunchi* as a symbol of an identity specific context. Amongst actors of dissimilar identity contexts, as in the case of this study, actors must implement *nunchi* as emotion work strategically, which may be seen as a form of performance, to then execute the context specific identity performance in order to manage a *shimjung* process and its annotated implications such as building *jung* and saving *chemyon*. Furthermore, Scherpinski-Lee's analysis raises awareness that the single components depend on each other. Her interpretations of the single components dismantle Lee-Peuker's (2004) secret behind *nunchi* and its associated elements and furthermore validate my critique of Lee-Peuker's personal identity to be a limitation, as she takes the *nunchi* phenomenon and its facets for granted and does not really interrogate. Her general trend does not deny that *nunchi* can be learnt in contrast to Lee-Peuker's argument that *nunchi* is strictly Korean. This shows Lee-Peuker's containment in thought and questions, whether her slightly subjective view derives from her insider perspective rather than Scherpinski-Lee's outsider perspective. The researcher's own identity matters in terms of reflexivity and reliability. Lee-Peuker's predominantly Korean identity versus Scherpinski-Lee's overweighing European identity show that researchers' own roots influence their work, whether it is based on literature analysis or interviews. The two examples show that the 'outsider', who is new to the topic and has not been brought up in "the Korean Way", interprets and views things differently compared with the 'insider'.

Nunchi in the context of intercultural communication

Meurant's critical review from an intercultural communication perspective on aspects of face and cultural dimensions in Chapter 6 of Kohls's (2001) popular guide to living and working in Korea contradicts itself. Meurant's major critique addresses Kohls's lack in explicitly addressing the key Korean-American cultural differentials of high- versus low-context culture and large versus small power distance, although it is clearly mentioned that the target audience are American businesspeople and not academics; hence, Kohls's publication is not academic to begin with.

Moreover, national identities are never transforming entities, and they cannot be categorized and labelled but have to be renegotiated at all times. In understanding symbols of identity such as *nunchi* and *kibun* and the associated elements such as *shimjung, jung* and *chemyon*, the outsider who is not familiar with a national identity context is much better equipped to understand the roots of an individual's behaviour in the Korean identity context. According to Meurant:

> *Kibun* is of great importance in understanding Korean relationships
> ... The persons interacting in one's life are responsible for assessing
> one's *kibun* through *nunchi*, so they can meet needs and communicate
> effectively. *Kibun* is easily disturbed, as when a young person is
> irreverent to an elder. (p.3)

Meurant's critique is imbalanced because he does point out the lack of high-culture-related facts but not the lacks that investigate and explain the roots of Korea's high-context culture, which is not standardized. To understand Korea's interpretation of its existing high-context culture, it is important to explain the significant triggers on which the existing identity context depends. Overall Meurant's *nunchi* representation classifies *nunchi* as an identity performance in relation to monitor and control *kibun*. The regulation of intertwined *kibun* elements such as *shimjung*, *jung* and *chemyon*, therefore rest upon the identity performances expressed through *nunchi*.

Moreover, Suh (2002) found that all entities have several views of themselves. She argued that the consistency between the different features of identity is highlighted in Western cultures; the multiple selves are often co-occurring existences in East Asian cultures, especially in Korean culture. Her argument contributes to the exploration of *nunchi* as emotion work and identity performance.

Nunchi in the context of self-identity

Suh (2002) argued that, between individuals, people with a more consistent self-view have clearer self-knowledge, are more confident and, most notably, have self-experiences that are less affected by the perception of others. Her comparison of Korean versus American citizens provides evidence that Koreans view themselves more adaptably across situations: 'Koreans, compared with American respondents, constructed themselves significantly more flexibly across situations, and the degree of consistency was less predictive of their subjective well-being' (p.1387). One of her outstanding findings is that consistent individuals received positive social appraisal from others in the United States but not in Korea. What is emotionally decent, vigorous, and worth rivalling is persistently redefined by the dynamisms of time and national identity. One idea that has been extremely persuasive in conventional psychology is that optimal emotional performance necessitates the person having a consistent self-identity across different scopes of experience.

Suh's findings suggest that this very individualistic recommendation might be less pertinent to the subjective well-being of members of a national identity who are motivated to think that the self is naturally collective, multiple and varying. Suh's argument in combination with Scherpinski-Lee's (2011) *shimjung* description in regard to *nunchi* shows that consistent self-identity has to be recontextualized. The practice of *nunchi* in Korea automatically implements the *shimjung* process, which in itself recreates a consistent self-identity. This interpretation of a consistent self-identity may differ from other perspectives and suggests that Koreans' optimal emotional performance necessitates *nunchi* and its associated elements. Shu's data revealed that consistent self-presentation without performative variations of self in adapting to a given identity context such as the Korean one was perceived negatively in Korea.

Shu's argument that some national cultures such as Korea are naturally more collective than what she terms Western cultures loses validity when considering *nunchi* as emotion work expressed through identity performances. Individuals do not just adopt naturally within identity contexts such as the Korean one, it is however through the expression of symbolism of *nunchi* as identity performances that actors function within such context. Furthermore Shu's data claims Korean identity to be naturally collective, when the literature on *nunchi* reflects a general tendency indicating *nunchi* to be a regulating tool, which highly impacts on the individual's position within groups that are part of larger groups, hence society. In that respect *nunchi* embodies identity performances in applying emotion work, through which actors adapt themselves to secure their own advantage in fulfilling the expectations of symbols of identity e.g. harmony. Furthermore, Shu's findings imply that symbols even if termed the same often carry different meanings and are subject to recontextualisation when working and living across borders and identities.

Nunchi in the context of filial piety

As a further matter, Blackhall et al. (2001) used an ethnographic study to examine more deeply attitudes and experiences of truth telling in regard to the diagnosis and prognosis of a terminal illness and the Korean-American point of view. The study is relevant because it outlines the relationship between the Korean concepts of *hyodo* and *nunchi*. *Hyodo* can be translated as 'filial piety'. It refers to the duties that family members owe each other, particularly the duties that grown children owe to their parents. Taking care of the relatives' emotional needs by protecting them from the cruel and harmful truth (Blackhall et al. 2001) is considered embracing *nunchi* because negative information is not conveyed directly (Alston, 1989). Korean-American participants were more likely to see truth telling as cruel and even harmful to the patients. Blackhall et al. indicated that 'only 47% of Korean-Americans … believed in telling the truth about the diagnosis' (p.61). Many Korean-Americans believe that the benefit of being prepared for death is insufficient to outweigh the pain caused by knowledge of the truth.

These justifications can be closely linked to Korean essential necessities such as *hyodo* and *nunchi*. According to Blackhall et al. (2001):

> *Hyodo* is usually translated as filial piety. It refers to the duties that family members owe each other, particularly the duties that grown children owe to their parents. One of these duties, as noted above, is the duty of the family to take care of sick relative, to take care of the relatives' physical need, and to take care of the relatives' emotional needs by protecting them from the cruel and harmful truth. (p.67)

Blackhall et al.'s (2001) study indicated that, because of *hyodo*, the family cannot tell their relatives about their medical condition if it is terminal; hence, most participants suggested that doctors should consult with the family first about whether or not and if so how the truth will be told. This is where *nunchi* enters the bigger picture. Blackhall et al. described *nunchi* as a guess or a hunch, which relates to non-verbal communication, and explained that: 'learning by *nunchi* is more acceptable … because it leaves room for hope and perhaps because it comforts you to know that your doctor and children love you enough to try to give you hope' (p.68). Many participants of Korean descent who stated that they would like to know the truth actually meant they would like to learn the truth by *nunchi*—in an indirect manner and through the right application of symbols of the Korean identity context. The preferred communication style is characteristic of high-context cultures such as Korea. Information is conveyed by non-verbal or indirect means. Communication style differs in low-context cultures.

According to Blackhall et al.:

> In low-context cultures, such as those of Germany and much of America, information is conveyed directly with detail and precision. Patients from low-context cultures who want to know the truth will expect to be told with this type of explicitness. (p.69)

Blackhall et al. (2001) found that patients from what they see as an identity context such as Korea strongly dislike frank and explicit answers about their prognosis. The authors described a scenario in which a returning patient complained about the blunt answer:

> 'How could you have said that to me? Don't you care about my feelings?' ... Instead of hearing you probably have 2 or 3 months to live, he was expecting to hear something like, we are doing everything we can, but you are very, very sick. (p.69).

This example demonstrates that people vary not only in whether they want to know the truth, but also in their understanding of what constitutes 'telling'.

Blackhall et al. (2001) confirmed that truth telling and its definition and interpretations are closely linked to *nunchi* and *kibun*, supporting Scherpinski-Lee's (2011) emphasis on emotions and non-verbal communication because Korea's national identity, as a high culture, stresses implicitness and indirectness. Love and trust are demonstrated differently; as Blackhall et al. identified, it is more important for the majority of Koreans to manifest a harmonious *kibun* through the knowledge of embracing *nunchi* than to use direct and hurtful answers. In learning through *nunchi*, love and care are expressed and conveyed better in the Korean context; this approach might be misinterpreted in low-context cultures, where integrity, trust and love are embedded in very honest and detailed answers. Truth presentations and representations are considered to be part of *nunchi*.

Blackhall et al. (2001) point out that *nunchi*, takes on the role of protecting someone's feelings, which defines *nunchi* in the form of both emotion work and identity performance. Blackhall et al.'s data shows that 'telling' as part of truth presentations and representations takes on different forms in different national identity contexts, thus understanding how 'telling' is constituted requires *nunchi* in the form of emotion work. Actors are meant to embrace *nunchi* in the form of empathy, in other words, trying to feel how someone from a Korean identity context would process truth presentations and representations based on symbols of identity in their national identity context such as *hyodo* and *kibun*. It is only after the establishment of what constitutes 'telling' through emotion work, that actors are able to apply *nunchi* as an identity performance.

Nunchi in the context of risk adversity

Kim and Park (2010) compared the cultural differentiations in attitude and choices regarding risk, at both individual and group levels, between Koreans and Australians. Their findings show that, when compared with Australians, Koreans do not demonstrate a higher preference for risk, regardless of gender. Further, Kim and Park provided evidence that Koreans, regardless of gender composition, are willing to take higher risk when making decisions in group situations as opposed to the individual decision-making process. Kim and Park reinforced the previous scholars' findings that Koreans feel more confident and comfortable within groups. Further, their findings underline Scherpinski-Lee's (2011) failure to identify a rising trend towards gender equality in the Korean contemporary value system. Scherpinski-Lee's as well as Stowell's (2003) analytical approaches commence with the proposition that Korea's contemporary value system is based purely on Confucian thought and philosophy, which, when considered logically, does not agree with Kim and Park's findings that Koreans, regardless of gender composition, are willing to take higher risks when making decisions in groups.

Nunchi in the context of family functioning

Chung and Gale (2008) examined the degree to which self-differentiation in relation to family functioning is valued differently by Korean and European-American university students. Pre-existing literature argues that, in low-context cultures such as individualistically driven societies, one of the main goals while growing up and at university or other tertiary education is independence and autonomy from one's family, especially one's parents. However, people of high-context cultures which are more collectively oriented, are encouraged to obey their parents' value system and to maintain connectedness between individuals (Ho, 1993; Hofstede, 1980a,b; Slote, 1992; Tang, 1992; Triandis, 1989, as cited in Chung & Gale, 2008). Therefore Chung and Gale's comparison provides insights on how *nunchi* may be seen as identity performance.

Koreans are encouraged to develop *nunchi* during adolescence. As explained by Chung and Gale (2008):

> The person who possesses *nunchi* is good at reading the feelings and state of mind of others by observing their non-verbal messages. Accordingly, typical Korean families encourage their members to withhold direct expression of personal opinions or feelings, and to develop implicit and indirect modes of communication and sensitivity to others' needs. (p. 21)

Chung and Gale (2008) indicated that self-differentiation relates to both intrapersonal and interpersonal processes: 'At the intrapersonal level, differentiation of self refers to the ability to distinguish emotional processes from intellectual processes and to choose goal-directed activities rather than feeling-directed activities' (p.22). Keeping the definition of self-differentiation in mind, Korean family dynamics differ from the ideal American family model; hence, Koreans need to focus on other aspects of healthy family functioning, such as harmony and cooperation based on *nunchi*, that reflect a high-context and therefore more collectivist value system.

Chung and Gale's (2008) findings support those of Suh (2002) that consistent self-identity and self-differentiation are closely linked to *nunchi*, *kibun* and their associated elements. Chung and Gale's data points out *nunchi* at the intrapersonal level to be emotion work, which allows actors to distinguish emotional processes from intellectual processes, which then guide their *nunchi* as an identity performance to achieve goal oriented activities instead of emotion driven ones. Such identity performances deriving from earlier emotion work are only possible in transnational settings, when the significance of symbols of identity e.g. harmony, are understood to strategically deliver identity performances guided by *nunchi* in context specific settings. Further, we can infer from what the say that *nunchi* and its practices need to be recontextualized in regard to other identity contexts and their values. It is also important to point out that, even though some scholars try to classify cultures as low context or high context, they always need to be examined separately and cannot be referred to as one entity.

Another aspect of *nunchi* has been explored by Choi, Park and Oh (2011), who investigated how cultural differences between Korea and North America in attitudinal and normative elements influenced informants' reasons behind their plans to tell the truth or lie. Their study shows that Koreans are generally less likely to perceive lying for a friend negatively, as opposed to Americans, who were more likely to perceive the behaviour of telling the truth positively. According to the researchers, 'Koreans were more tolerant of lying for a friend, while Americans were less tolerant. It seems that Koreans were more likely to focus on *for a friend* whereas Americans were more likely to focus on *lying*' (p.763). From this they conclude that Koreans foreground the relationship over the behaviour. For Koreans, a relationship-oriented excuse may be more acceptable in a high-context culture: 'In collectivist cultures, the relationship between the self and another is more intertwined than in individualistic cultures' (p.762). Saving another person's reputation could be as important as saving one's own reputation. As explained earlier, the *jung* element encourages Koreans to help their friend. In addition, Koreans might want to cover for their friend to preserve his or her *chemyon*. Further, the prominence of *nunchi* may lead Koreans to understand a friend's wish better and do what is necessary to maintain their friendship. Choi, Park and Oh's investigation on *nunchi* as a lying or truth telling practice, suggests *nunchi* to be an identity performance. The symbols underlying Korean identity such as *jung* and *chemyon* encourage, even force this variation of *nunchi* as an identity performance.

Nunchi in the context of non-verbal communication

Kang (2000) stressed that, in Korean culture, emotions and feelings are communicated more precisely and clearly without using words, ' … nonverbal messages are innate' (p.20). Kang explained that non-verbal behaviours are not easily controlled consciously; they are relatively free of distortion because they come out spontaneously:

> A blushing face, stammering speech, or clenching a jaw are all involuntary actions when a person feels nervous or embarrassed. The behaviour is automatic, an unconscious reflex. Likewise, when verbal and non-verbal communication conflict, the non-verbal message are characteristically the more accurate reflection of feelings. (p.20)

Kang (2000) argued that non-verbal communication is more effective than verbal communication to approach and convey messages in a less confrontational style, which therefore suits high-context cultures, in particular, Korea. Kang himself conforms to being an 'insider', as mentioned earlier, which suggests that his *nunchi* and *kibun* have been well developed throughout adolescence and therefore his argument has to be examined with caution because not everybody feels the same. A blushing face, stammering speech or clenching a jaw are all involuntary actions, which according to him express nervousness and shame, but could they not at the same time indicate that a person is cold or needs to go to the bathroom? Kang denotes *nunchi* in the form of non-verbal communication as an identity performance natural to Korean identity. Even though symbols of Korean identity suggest implicitness and indirectness in identity performances such as *nunchi*, the meaning underlying such identity performances needs to be recontextualised, in order for actors from different national identity contexts to work together across borders and identities. Even though Kang argues, that verbal messages need to be learnt and non-verbal messages are innate, he fails to address the importance of recontextualisation. From this we infer that verbal as well as non-verbal messages are linked to and based on symbols of identity, which as seen previously (see Yi and Jezewski 2000, Blackhall et al., 2001 and Suh, 2002) follow context specific interpretations that are subject to emotion work, in order to make sense of, thus being delivered in the form of identity performances.

Additionally, Stowell (2003) argued that among Korea, China and Japan, traditional Confucianism has the highest impact on communication, as observed in Korea's interpersonal communication style. Stowell suggested that the Korean communication style is more effective in implementing non-linguistic elements such as emotions and attitudes, whereas the Western style places higher emphasis on ideas expressed verbally, which incorporate individuals' thoughts. Stowell's perception of *nunchi* is tightly linked with the Korean communication style and the preservation of Korea's traditions. Stowell explained that:

> *Nunchi* is an interpretation of others' facial expression or what they say plus a mysterious 'alpha' hidden in their hearts. It is usually an interpretation by the lower social class of the feelings of the higher social class, necessary in an unreasonable society in which logic and inflexible rules have no place. (p.113)

Ideal Koreans strive at all times to uphold harmony through the communicational element of *nunchi* by attending to the relationship first, then the subject matter, using honorifics to indicate respect for others and modesty for themselves, according to Stowell (2003).

Moreover, Stowell (2003) classifies Korean culture as a culture giving much importance to hearing, in Korean culture hearing is used as a metaphor for understanding. Further, Koreans speak to grant each other *chemyon*, while encouraging group conformity, which is supported by the culture of the ear because it is passive, intuitive, sensitive and emotional and uses *nunchi* as a linchpin to make it work. Stowell (2003) classified Korean society as unreasonable and a society in which logic and inflexible rules have no place. Her description of Korean society completely contradicts Scherpinski-Lee's (2011) analysis of Korea's interpretation of traditional values, which differ from those of China and Japan. Scherpinski-Lee indicated that wisdom, grace, righteousness and gentleness are the main essences of Korean society. In contrast, Stowell characterized Korean society as unreasonable, lacking logic and a society in which inflexible rules have no place. Stowell's (2003) findings pointed out that the power of *nunchi* is effectively delivered through identity performances, which convey emotions and attitudes in a non-linguistic manner. The hearing component as indicated by Stowell gets exploited in tailoring identity performances around and on symbols of identity such as *chemyon* to achieve goal oriented activities instead of emotion driven activities much as Chung and Gale (2008) implied. Thus the strategic application of *nunchi* as an identity performance gives meaning to symbols of identity that follow at times unreasonable, logic lacking and inflexible rules to actors from a non Korean identity context. Stowell's definition of Korean society shows that her methodological approach explaining *nunchi*, lacks to identify *nunchi* as identity performance that is somewhat subject to emotion work and symbolism.

Conclusion

In summary, the complexities of *nunchi* call for complex approaches to understand and make sense of *nunchi*. The literature directly and indirectly related to *nunchi* has shown the significance of researchers' own identities in terms of being an 'insider' or 'outsider', whether they are using literature analysis or ethnography or other research methods. Scholars such as Scherpinski-Lee (2011) and Lee-Peuker (2004) have made a viable start attempting to define the complexities of *nunchi*, however the overall trend in the *nunchi* discourse indicates that scholars never quite connect the dots to identify *nunchi* as emotion work and/ or identity performance, which this study does. It is worth mentioning that these scholars' identities have both been internationalized through marriage (Korean–German) and it was not until after adolescence that they were exposed to being an outsider in the German or Korean context. Their conclusions support their findings and they present their results well, however their findings seem to be static and lack the dynamism, which symbolism and defining *nunchi* as emotion work and identity performance contributes to the overall *nunchi* discourse, particularly in transnational settings. The literature on *nunchi* agrees that the Korean management style, including managing conflict, must be handled with special consideration for overall harmony through the application of *nunchi* (Kim, Sohn & Wall, 1999). The concept of maintaining consistent overall harmony derives from Confucian ideas, which foreground calm and helpful interpersonal relationships (Paik & Sohn, 1998). *Nunchi* is described in Kim, Sohn and Wall's (1999) study. Both managers and employees directly help to uphold or reconstruct harmonious interactions at work in the case of an evolving difficulty. Neither party involved embraces a key set of rules to do so; however, *nunchi* is used to achieve overall harmony (Kim, Sohn & Wall, 1999; Lee, 2000). Thus the nature of *nunchi* may best be identified as an identity performance that most of the time necessitates some degree of emotion work to make sense of symbols present in a specific identity context, which may be seen as the set rules. The dynamism of symbolism underlying *nunchi* as identity performance thus allows actors to strategically present themselves in dissimilar identity contexts than their own. The emotion work component facilitates such identity performances of symbols of identity with means of sense making that give meaning to the formation of self-presentations of actors, who are not Korean 'insiders'. Therefore, *nunchi* is utilized in Korean management to avoid the highly sensitive possibility of losing social face in public; open conflict is therefore prevented through *nunchi* in Korean organizations to assure the maintenance of respect and harmony (Cocroft & Ting-Toomey, 1994).

Thus, *nunchi* in the form of emotion work and identity performance in an organisation may help to establish a cooperative context for strategic self-presentation. Organizational control in Korean management means monitoring the behaviour of company members and providing feedback to correct any misbehaviour (Jaeger, 1983:p.92). Korean management entails formal control (Weber, 1946) and informal as well as cultural controls such as *nunchi* (Jaeger, 1983). While most Korean organizations have a tall hierarchical structure (Gray & Marshall, 1998) with decision-making processes at the senior level (Chen, 1995), organizational behaviour is controlled through *nunchi*, which does not follow an explicit procedure (Jang & Chung, 1995). Such implicit procedure however may be visualised in defining *nunchi* as identity performance supplemented by emotion work. The emotion work aspect, which guides subsequent identity performances represents the descriptive nature of the *nunchi* discourse in a way that includes all existing facets of the phenomenon, but does not limit *nunchi* to being a static notion. Thus considering *nunchi* as emotion work and identity performance in all aspects including business opens new vistas for working and managing across borders and identities. Therefore, *nunchi* may be regarded the linchpin in personalized relationships in Korean management (Lee, 1998a, 1998b; Lee & Yoo, 1987).

Establishment of the German and Korean Identity Referred to as Germanness and Koreanness

Introduction

This section elaborates and attempts to establish the meaning of *Germanness* and *Koreanness* in relation to ethnicity—an arguably vague intellectual term—and the closely linked concept of identity, which may be renowned as the outcome of a social progression, a paradigm that is consistently in flux. Such concept is important and relates to this study, as symbols of national character along with German and Korean identity consistently change in times of globalisation, from this we may infer that the recontextualisation of symbols of Germanness and Koreanness are vital when working and managing across borders and identities. German transnational businesspeople have a long history of being present in many parts of the world. Before discussing German businesspeople in South Korea—in particular, Seoul—in line with the theoretical objectives of this study, it is important to examine briefly the ways in which Germans define and present themselves as a nation and how performative this self-representation is. In light of the theories of symbols and their correlation to identity discussed in the conceptual framework section, it is necessary to examine the most significant symbols that Germans use to explain themselves.

Germanness: An Overview

In this study Germanness and Koreanness are regarded as something collective rather than individual, to take Brubaker and Cooper's (2000) criticism into account that scholars use the term identity to discuss both individuals and collectives; which describes, "both something claimed for oneself and something externally attributed" (Maxwell and Davis, 2016 p. 1). This study suggests Germanness as a self-proclaimed and externally recognised notion, which is given meaning to through strategic self-presentation of symbolism. Ultimately, the following section is presented with the assumption that Germanness is viewed as neither absolute nor momentary, but permanently constructed within the current day and age's particular social and historical context. Such assumption implies that symbols making up the essence of Germanness carry meaning, which is presented differently by actors of symbols of identity over certain periods of time. The aim of the following section is to point out the meaning of such symbols and how they construct or maintain the understanding of Germanness. Thus this study will not discuss the shift in meaning over the last decades, which has been extensively studied by scholars (see Dumont, 1986,1994; Le Gloannec, 1994; Maxwell & Davis, 2016), however it will look at the symbols used in Germany's contemporary self-presentation and how such meanings are expressed and relate to earlier ones.

Germanness in the context of the "New Germany": German identity and symbolism

David Wetzel (2008) reminded contemporary identity and Germanic studies scholars that Germany once sent emigrants abroad. Currently, Germany is taking immigrants in, which has evoked ferocious political debate in the country over what it means to be German and how German identity is formed. The idea of a new immigration law was first introduced in the 1990s and "since 1 January 2005, Germany has a new immigration law... It was supposed to symbolise the beginning of a new era, in which Germany acquired a new identity as an immigration country" (Bauder, 2008 p. 95). An attempt to establish the history of Germanness and what forms Germany as a country has been on-going for over one and a half centuries. An extensive body of literature concerned itself with the notion of Germanness (Weidenfeld, 1983; Watson, 1995; Bruhn, 1994; Elias, 1996; Forsythe, 1989; Borneman, 1992; Haberman, 1994; White, 1997; Moore, 2005; Bauder, 2008; Bade, 1992). This study however marks the change of law in 2005 and the shortly following FIFA World Cup in 2006 as a fresh start, during which Germany drew the world's attention to look at the "new "Germany and how it strategically presents itself to the world through the use of symbolism.

Therefore, to be German is not to belong to a particular national group but to present oneself using significant symbols of identity. Additionally, to be German is not to belong to a single entity, but to take part in the collective identity search, which is expressed through symbols that underwent cycles of self-reflexivity and self-reinvention to allow Germans to collectively embrace their meanings especially during the time before and after the World Cup in 2006 (Sark, 2012).

This section examines the identity construction, through the use of symbolism of an audience of roughly eighty-two million people, who make up the "new" Germany consisting of, " former East Germans, former West Germans, immigrants in various stages of becoming new Germans or not interested in becoming Germans, and a new *Wendegeneration* of Germans born in, or growing up in, a reunited Germany" (Sark, 2012 p. 257). The beginning of the era of the "new" Germany commenced with a symbolic fall of one thousand oversized dominos positioned in the same place of the former Berlin Wall, starting at *Potsdamer Platz* all the way to the *Reichstag* (Sark, 2012); along with the German Historical Museum's exhibition, similar to the "What is Germany exhibition" displaying 1000-year history of Germany, which calls for "critical self-awareness" and "self-affirmation" (Ottomeyer, 2006 p. 172). In addition Sark (2012) points out that the Bundespräsident Köhler, initiated the German government's self-reflexive identity formation campaign, symbolically called *Land der*

Ideen (Land of ideas), which included the "Walk of ideas", displaying symbols of Germanness all around the capital in order to reinvent German identity in bringing back preexisting symbols of identity such as *Weltoffenheit* (cosmopolitanism), *Ordnung* (order as opposed to chaos also organization), *Sprache und Bildung* (German language and education), *Geschäftstüchtigkeit* (industriousness & entrepreneurial spirit) , kritische Selbstbetrachtung (critical self-awareness also remembrance) and *Freiheit* (freedom). This public display of symbols of identity, helps the inhabitants of the "the land of ideas" to believe that they represent the new Germany "neither East nor West, neither Nazi nor socialist, communist, or capitalist: not divided, but new" (Sark, 2012 p. 261). The big question of what is Germanness was strategically presented through symbolism with the help of visual presentation. The answers neither mirrored racial, regional, or national oneness but suggested the above-mentioned symbols of identity e.g. cosmopolitanism, order, language and education, industriousness, remembrance and freedom to make up Germanness.

"The Berlin campaign contained a boulevard of six large sculptures, symbolizing German cultural, technological, medical, and scientific achievements: a gigantic stack of books with the names of Goethe, Schiller, Hesse, and other notable writers, strategically placed at Bebelplatz, across from the Humboldt University – the very place where the Nazi book-burning took place; musical notes at the *Gendarmenmarkt* in front of Schinkel's concert hall; Einstein's formula $E = mc2$ in front of the *Altes Museum*; a large aspirin pill at the *Reichstag*; enormous soccer shoes at the *Hauptbahnhof*; and an oversized car at the Brandenburg Gate " (Sark, 2012 p. 261).

Further to the "Walk of Ideas" serves the German Historical Museum, which represents a place of critical self-awareness and visual remembrance in which since 2006, several thousand historical artefacts, of which the most difficult German epoch feature items of the Third Reich, serve as objects in which history crystallises itself (Sark, 2012). It is through strategic self-presentation of symbols of identity that the "new" Germany started the process of reinventing itself again, to find a balance between remembrances and shaping its future in bearing its history in mind. Turner (2006) remarked "We are on our way to separate from German history up until 1945 and the country afterwards. Let me exaggerate a little: just like the Swedish and the Vikings and the Italians and the Romans" (p.29). Contemporary Germany no longer represents a country of crimes against humanity, however the new Germany presents itself as cosmopolitan and the reinvented German identity involves a multicultural nature, which is both a product and agent of change, which allows Germans to overcome their history, thus strategic changes of self-presentation of symbolism in identity constructions continue to transform the "new" Germany and its laws.

Germanness in the context of citizenship education

Ortloff (2009) explored the formation of Germanness through a study on German citizenship education because she is a firm believer that citizenship must be defined not only as political policy, but also as an educational practice. Ortloff conducted 58 interviews with teachers at the *Hauptschule* and the *Realschule* in Bavaria. The *Hauptschule* and the *Realschule* are two of the offered secondary schools to which students transfer after completing elementary school. Elementary school generally runs through to the fourth grade, which in most cases has followed a three-year preschool called *Kindergarten* . In using mean-field analysis, Ortloff was able to establish the entire range of possible, as well as less possible, meanings for the interviewees' answers.

Ortloff (2009) suggested that ethnoculturalism is the main paradigm used in citizenship education as the most prevalent way to clarify German citizenship: 'Ethnoculturalism is invoked by the teachers as a way of explaining German citizenship as something historic and based on a shared ancestry. Citizenship and belonging are linked directly to an essential notion of Germanness' (p.194). The notion that being German is something ontological—one is German, one cannot become German— is pointed out in her research in various ways: 'Germanness is a state of being or through explaining the idea of *Heimat* as accessible only to Germans' (p.196). This study challenges her interpretations and conclusions drawn and points out the influence symbols of identity have on what Ortloff calls state of being. From my own citizenship education experiences, the incorporation of symbolism, especially traditional music, is another aspect that contributes to Germanness because music and its application, especially through singing, are used to achieve unity, starting from an early age. For example, in *Kindergarten*, children are taught to sit on small chairs in a big circle and sing, listen to stories and craft things together, which triggers the effect of happiness within the group through unity. From this I can infer the inclusiveness symbols of identity have on Germanness regardless of Ortloff's believe for it to be exclusive. According to the *Bundeszentrale für politische Bildung* (Federal Agency for Civic Education) roughly every fifth German citizen has a migration background, which accounts for 20,3 per cent of the entire population (www.bpb.de). Thus the transforming meaning of symbols representing and shaping German identity, regardless of blood ties; contribute to contemporary Germanness in the "new" Germany.

Ortloff's study identified a clear pattern of consistently foregrounding the concept of remembrance and critical self-awareness as a reason why no one except Germans by blood can be German. From this she concludes that shared memories, tragedies and victories contribute to the formation of Germanness: 'One must say: you are not guilty, you were born much later, you have not done anything. But you will forever, as long as there are Germans, have to help carry this package' (Ortloff, 2009:p.197). In hypothesizing that only a German can feel the guilt of being German, the argument touches upon Germanness as a concept, which is not confined to a specific geographic area, but to a collective emotion, the so-called awareness of shared remembrance and critical self-awareness 'The idea of shame about being German was often cited as a key to raising good German citizens, but it was likewise explained that non-Germans could not understand this guilt and should not even be expected to' (Ortloff, 2009:p.197). In essence, this idea itself enacts the temporal nature of Germanness. Cornwall and Stoddard (2001) supported Ortloff's expression of temporality, which is not viewed and interpreted as a lack of a special relationship with a designated area, but rather as the concept of Germanness surpassing place through time. Cornwall and Stoddard's interpretation is that Germanness is passed on from generation to generation regardless of country and continent. Therefore, Germanness resists physical demarcations and gets passed through symbols of identity. "I inherited this feeling ... I am not tied to the place and cannot pass on this sense of belonging to a place ... it is like this for us Germans; it is not about where one is, but about the feeling of home and the creation of homeland" (Ortloff, 2009 p.198). The symbol of remembrance and critical self-awareness as part of the reinvention of Germanness expressed through symbolism in the *Land der Ideen* campaign, does not just emphasise the past e.g. the Third Reich and the division of the nation but reminds citizens to bare the past in mind when shaping the present and the future.

This leads to the debatably most well known concept of explaining Germanness so called Blut (blood ties). Even though the *Blut* concept has an extensive discourse history (see Moore 2005, pp.42-44), the recent rectification of law made it possible to become German regardless of blood ties, however through the essential expression of symbols of identity e.g. industriousness, language and education. This major change in the legal perspective of what is required to obtain German citizenship was long discussed by the German government before they changed the constitution (Bauder, 2008). However, the *Blut* discourse is still relevant to this study because the two national identities Korean and German will be compared in the study. Thus, *Blut* does not define a single way of being German, but has different connotations under the German continuum, the coherent web of Germanness, in which adjacent symbols of identity are not noticeably different from each other, but the extremes are rather distinct.

Overall, Ortloff's interview responses show a clear pattern of numerously repeated attributes in citizenship education that are meant to establish the essence of Germanness or, in other words, which symbols of identity have to be internalized in order to attempt to call oneself German. Politeness, reliability, punctuality, the ability to follow through, appreciation for education, being industrious, quality in speech and behaviour, an emphasis on the 'we' without self-praise referring to a group shaping the German nation and respecting or implementing Christian values, presumably defined by the *Landeskirche* (state church) are terms that were independently present in most interviews and can therefore be considered to contribute towards a definition of Germanness (Ortloff, 2009).

References to everyday situations were given to visualize the importance of these view-overlapping values that cohesively support each other's purposes, for example, 'And when there are two to choose from when someone has to be let go, the one who is always late is going to be the one fired' (Ortloff, 2009:p.201). Ortloff categorized the notion of symbols of Germanness —in the above list of terms, punctuality—as a concept that has to be absorbed into flesh and blood to be efficient, as something predominantly German. Further examples could be given for every single characteristic.

Most of the time, interviewees repeated references to industriousness, which is a particularly important value because it is a quality that is essential to understanding or embracing German identity. Immigrants in various stages of becoming Germans, who embrace as many of these values as possible will have very few problems living among Germans. Romanian-Germans are the best example to demonstrate successful integration:

> Well they are adjusted [*angepast*]. They are industrious and involved and there is great pressure from the parents that children do well … first of all, the native language [German] is simply spoken better than by other immigrant groups … they are very industrious and they build their own houses in the shortest amount of time because they work together. (Ortloff, 2009:p.2002).

From this we can infer that symbols of identity as seen in the case above (language and education, industriousness and *Ordnung*) and the expression of such thorough strategic self-presentation enact the reinvented notion of Germanness in the "new" Germany.

Germanness in the context of un-Germanness

Judson (1993) described the evolution of Germanness as a construct of identity that became increasingly imagined as something set, ontological and notably trans-historical by the 1880s, in contrast to its previous characteristic, which defined national identity as contingent and changeable, a construct made up of symbols applied through strategic self-presentation.

The formation of a distinct German national identity was encouraged by geographical peripheral nationalists such as Lippert (1882), who reminded German speakers in Austria to focus and reflect continuously on differences that separated them from Czechs. 'In time, German speakers would come to see these incidental differences as fundamental to their identity, and would gain clearer sense of their own Germanness' (Judson, 1993:48). Studying Germanness by distinguishing differences offered individuals the chance to select their preferred identity in embracing shared symbols of identity and thought:

> German identity corresponded to the cultivation of liberal bourgeois cultural values like education freedom and enlightenment. By this standard, German identity was available to anyone who chose to

adopt those higher cultural values. In theory at least, individuals from any background, from Jews to Slavs, could attain a German identity through education and acculturation (Judson, 1993:page unknown).

Furthermore, Schwarz's (2003), similar to Lippert (1882) took the approach to examining Germanness by defining un-Germanness and thus followed the model of studying identity by establishing differences. Germany's citizenship laws have traditionally been constituted on the idea of *jus sanguinis*, in other words, the law of blood. Contemporary German citizenship is now determined by place of birth and *jus sanguinis* has therefore been amended. Through this change of law, the German government has been forced to assess what is required to be German. Hence, a *Leitkultur* (leading or core culture) has been printed to prevent the creation of parallel cultures within an existing what I term identity setting through the change of law. Schwarz's media research is based on roughly 1,600 newspaper articles from reputable Australian and German newspapers from January 1996 to December 2003 in which the terms 'un-Australian' and *Leitkultur* were found. Her major findings suggested that Germanness is viewed as adjusting to German codes of conduct, abiding by German laws and showing respect for German traditions. Her own research allowed her to establish a definition of *Leitkultur*: 'When asked to define *Leitkultur*, most supporters of the term named German laws, constitution and the German language, as well as— although to a lesser extent—Western-European values' (p.218).

Her analysis has shown that the change of law triggered a change in expressing what being German means. Well-known personalities quoted in her analysis such as Freidrich Merz and Jörg Schönbohm underlined that Germanness is constituted through national unity and that parallel societies whose cultural imprints conflict with the *Leitkultur* are a potential threat to the existing national identity. According to Schwarz, 'these speakers are able to communicate a longing for social cohesion and unity, as well as their fear of the loss of this unity' (p.217).

Furthermore, Schneider (2001) conducted some empirical research in the field of discursive representations of German identity. His study analysed how Germanness is constructed and communicated through public and everyday discourses. His research confirmed the importance of the prominent role of 'the Other' for reassuring German self-definitions. Schneider continued by evaluating the strategic pathways and possibilities that 'the Other' may peruse as a result of being subjected to being fundamentally unique compared with the collective German identity. Schneider argued that the most central category of 'the Other' in German self-definitions are immigrants in various stages, who are unwilling to integrate and contribute towards German society and resisting to adhere to essentials such as overcoming language barriers and comprehending as well as respecting cultural expectations.

From this section we may infer that contemporary Germanness in the context of un-Germanness corresponds much to its early meaning prior to the 1880s when German identity was accessible to individuals from any background from Jews to Slavs who, strategically chose to present themselves with higher cultural values, attained through education and acculturation. Much like back then do symbols of German identity today correspond to what Judson (1993) termed education and acculturation, seen in Schwarz (2003) and Schneider (2001), who stress the importance of symbols such as language and education, *Ordnung* in the legal context and the overall willingness to present oneself with symbols of German identity.

Germanness in the context of cultural analysis during the Cold War

Tinsley and Woloshin (1974) analysed Germanness by comparing German and American perceptions of human nature, social relations, humans and nature, time and space. The general trend of their cultural analysis showed that the majority of comparative culture studies have a collective versus individual and Western versus non-Western focus. Tinsley and Woloshin's comparative study of two Western cultures showed that it is essential to identify the context of behaviour and the contingencies of action before prescriptions and proscriptions for specific acts can be given. Ultimately, their findings were that Germanness and Americanness have little in common and that one has to be careful when using the term Western. This is particularly relevant to this study, as there seems to be a trend, which assumes the term Western with Americanness, especially in the literature regarding comparative Korean studies discourses.

Human nature in Germanness as identified by Tinsley and Woloshin (1974) is the individual's responsibility to know his or her purpose in the universal and social order, to achieve his or her duties correctly and professionally, and to preserve this order, which is inevitable to make the entity's being possible. The authors observed that:

> The German unconsciously assumes that he and his fellow men are
> integral parts of the universal order, which functions in accordance
> with universal laws of nature. The society and the individual are simply
> aspects of the universal order without which neither could exist, and
> the society is an intermediate order between the microcosm of the
> individual and the macrocosm of the universe' (p.126).

From this they conclude and stress that German identity is based on the symbol of *Ordnung* and logic, which as pointed out by Stefan Kisielewski (1965) marks German identity to be collective. Furthermore, Kisielewski stresses the sense of belonging to the group and its roots within Germanness much like Schwarz (2003), however in an industrious context:

> The German has a pronounced feeling of belonging to the whole; he
> derives gratification and satisfies his ambition from the fact that he
> is a small but indispensable cog in a precisely functioning machine.
> Work in a limited area of production gives him as much satisfaction
> as a position of leadership and arouses no bitterness as it does among
> Poles. (Kisielewski in Tinsley & Woloshin, 1974:pp.126–127)

We can infer from what he says that prevalent symbols of identity give actors the chance to strategically present themselves with symbols of identity that support a sense of belonging.

Furthermore contributing to the symbol of *Ordnung* is the predictability of *Ordnung* in quality and trustworthiness. Both are two important components of Germanness because they are highly valued character traits of the *Ordnung* symbol, especially in relation to honesty in money matters and expressing one's opinion free from external influences, as well as predictability. According to Tinsley & Woloshin (1974), 'The ideal person is one who can be relied on to do what is expected of him and whose behaviour is predictable, steady, and not much influenced by the opinions of others or by opportunity' (p.127).

The symbol of language and education adds to these components. The Germanic term *Bildung*, is very important in the concept of the educated person, who embodies quality and trustworthiness. The term *gebildeter Mensch* (educated person) stems from the German verb *bilden*, which is best translated as 'to form'. Therefore, the entire concept of education is the aim to form young people and their character and will to become responsible. Tinsley & Woloshin (1974) observed that:

> School work is not only a means for the child to learn facts; it is also supposed to train him to responsibility and a sense of duty. The German ideal is maturity, as opposed to the American ideal of youth. (p.127)

Tinsley and Woloshin (1974) categorized humanity as an acquired characteristic in German culture, and hence in the German identity. Humanity is perceived as being a result of training and education. It is assumed that the higher the level of education, the greater the implied humanity. In other Western identity contexts, education fulfils different purposes in fostering national identity. For example, in American culture:

> Education is not considered so much a means for inculcating 'human qualities' as it is a means for obtaining money and material comforts—a process which may even involve learning to suppress certain aspects of 'humanness', as witness the rather common American belief that politicians are 'crooked', lawyers are 'shysters', and businessmen are avaricious and grasping 'Scrooges' who 'exploit' their employees, 'swindle' their customers, and would 'sell their grandmothers to make a fast buck'. (Tinsley & Woloshin, 1974:p.127).

From this we may infer that acculturation and embracing symbols such as language and education as seen prior to the Cold War period (see Judson 1993) and throughout contribute to the understanding of Germanness in the "new" Germany as defined in this study.

Profession and person are closely linked within the notion of Germanness. Changes of profession are rare; Germans are generally proud to be a specialist within their field of profession (ibid). The German word *Beruf* has a rather positive connotation because it evokes fulfilment within itself and implies that a person is meant to practise a certain profession. Germans are therefore more likely to identify themselves immediately with their social roles and duties. For example:

> If one has attained the title of Dr., regardless of discipline, he has simultaneously achieved social prestige. Titles appear on announcements of engagements and weddings, in obituaries, on calling cards, return addresses on envelopes, social invitations, and

even on grave markers as an eternal monument to the academic and the social success of the decreased. (Tinsley & Woloshin, 1974:p.128).

Social status is important within Germanness, as is the selection of friends and acquaintances. Friends in the German understanding are moderately few and intimate. According to Tinsley and Woloshin (1974), Germans prefer their friends and close acquaintances to be almost exclusively from their own social and educational background. Generally speaking, it is hypothesized that once Germans have graduated from *Gymnasium* (grammar school) or university, it is very unlikely that they will maintain contact with any classmates who went on to attend the *Hauptschule*. This is often due to a lack of mutual interests and utterly dissimilar social functions. In addition, it is worth noting that Germans tend to like or dislike an entire individual. Tinsley & Woloshin noted that:

> Americans tend to apply the term friend indiscriminately to anyone with whom they have exchanged personal data and opinions on several occasions. This tendency makes any comparison with German culture difficult since the American word 'friend' cannot be applied to the German concept *Freund,* and it is all but impossible to differentiate between friend and acquaintance in contemporary American usage. (p.129)

Germanness becomes visible through Germany's vertically structured society. Social interaction in the German identity context is grounded upon a reasonably formal scheme of behavioural arrangements, and, for the most part, accepts a vertically structured society:

> Respect for others is based upon their knowledge and practice of the behavioural patters appropriate to their function as indicated by title, vocation, education, and often even by dress, speech, or attitude. Stratification is vertical, and German, like many other languages, requires some degree of knowledge of the social status of the other person before the appropriate form of address can be chosen. (Tinsley & Woloshin, 1974:p.129).

From this they conclude that there exists a strong correlation between social roles, professions and the respect granted to individuals within the German identity context, thus such correlation furthermore gives meaning to the *Ordnung* symbol.

The German individual is seen as a nature lover and born conservationist, who must function as part of nature:

> There is a feeling that man is at his best when he is in harmony with nature, and he must return to nature periodically to recuperate from the physical and mental stresses imposed by city life. Anything 'natural' is better and healthier than something made by or adulterated by man, and labels on many food products proudly proclaim that they are naturrein and contain no additives' (Tinsley & Woloshin, 1974:p.130).

Germanness is heavily influenced and shaped by time and the concept of time. The German sense of the value of time is very strong, and German punctuality in all situations has universally been recognized as one of the most consistent identity stereotypes. German identity is indisputably oriented to the present and the near future, but a much stronger consciousness of the past is rooted within Germanness compared with other national characters. Tinsley and Woloshin (1974) traced this back to the formal structure of the culture, which tends to raise behavioural patterns to the status of tradition and does not incorporate alterations easily. Germans have a general knowledge of and pride in their historical heritage and a realization of that shapes their present. This realization stimulates a solid appreciation of continuity within Germanness and an affinity to see current situations in relation to longer periods. Tinsley and Woloshin explained that:

> Births, birthdays, the first day of school, confirmations, graduations, engagements, marriages, wedding anniversaries, and deaths are family often community concerns which are, for the most part, formally recognised and celebrated as important time-posts along the path of life which itself is considered only a section of the longer road from eternity to eternity. Each of these individual time-events is important not only for the individual but also for the community; each marks a higher level of maturity and responsibility for the functioning member of the culture. (p.131)

Even though Tinsley and Woloshin traced the concept of time, especially a much stronger consciousness of the past compared to other identity contexts, back to the formal structure of Germanness; I may infer from their conclusions that such consciousness relates to the symbol of remembrance and critical self-awareness as portrayed by the "walk of ideas" in the "new" Germany.

Time and the division of time that mirror the structured notion of Germanness furthermore mark the symbol of *Ordnung*. The day is not divided into just daylight and darkness; there are eight periods of the day, which all use different greetings. Further, certain periods are reserved for traditional activities, for example, a hot meal at lunchtime.

Additionally, space has been a limited commodity in Germany; hence, it has been utilized as efficiently as possible. Germanness and space are closely intertwined with the German's consistent, strong sense of belonging to a group, calling for shared symbol of identity or as Schwarz (2003) terms it a *Leitkultur* that allows actors to present themselves with symbols of identity strategically, in order to achieve a sense of belonging. The above becomes apparent in the constellation of olden day farmhouses: 'Originally with the need for mutual assistance and protection as well as space limitations farm houses were grouped into villages, and the people "commuted" to their outlying fields' (Tinsley & Woloshin, 1974:p.134). This visualizes the collectiveness in German identity, embedded in their architectural style and preference of living in contrast to other Western nations, which resemble a more individualist approach. According to Tinsley & Woloshin:

> American farmhouses have almost invariably been located on and preferably near the centre of the farmer's land. When the frontier farmer 'could see the smoke from his nearest neighbour's chimney,' he felt crowded and began to think of moving. (p.135)

This metaphoric isolation of the American farm shows the notion of independence and individuality in America's individualist culture.

An overall tendency of symbols such as *Ordnung*, language and education, remembrance and critical self-awareness, which reflect the "new" Germany's symbols of the reinvented self-presentation, can be identified in Tinsley & Woloshin's cultural analysis. Most of Tinsley & Woloshin's (1974) analysis of Germanness corresponds to the reinvented symbolism of the "new" Germany's self-presentation, especially the concept of *Ordnung,* which consistently reoccurs in one way or another. While a deeper discussion of *Ordnung* may be found in Hoecklin (1996; Moore 2005, pp. 45-46), it is worth noting that the *Ordnung* symbol along with language and education as well as remembrance and critical self-awareness are the linchpin in all the German does or attempts to do, as outlined earlier. It is significant that the term *Ordung* does not have only one translation—'order opposed to chaos'; it also refers to a wider concept, as noted by Tinsley and Woloshin, including cleanliness, structure and morality (see also Hoecklin, 1996:pp.26, 36). *Ordnung* is taught from a very young age and is even prevalent in children's rhymes: '*Ordnung muss sein, das weisst man schon von klein.*' (Bornemann, 1992:p.8 cited in Moore 2005, p. 45) (There must be order; one already knows that when one is little.) The prominent features noted by Tinsley and Woloshin (1974) are symbols which all may be found in the notion of the reinvented Germanness presented through the display of symbolism in the "Walk of Ideas". Therefore, most appointed symbols of German identity are *Ordnung*-related discourse notions, which stress the appreciation of structure and rational organisation within Germanness.

In sum Germanness and its transformation and renegotiations in the "new" Germany will continue to shape contemporary German identity and therefore symbols of national character. Events such as the 2006 World Cup and the twentieth anniversary of the fall of the Berlin Wall, as well as the paradigm shift in law have had an important effect on the German identity discourse. The Goffmanian perspective in this study draws on an interactive account how causes and consequences of expressed symbols of German identity are addressed and how symbols of national identity may construct strategic identity performances in which actors display symbols, for instance, *nunchi* in order to fulfil role expectations to work and manage across borders and identities.

Korea's Contemporary Identity – Koreanness

The concept of national identity has progressed during the last half century within the Korean social studies curriculum. There have been seven curriculum versions since the syllabus period was released under the American military administration from 1946 to 1954. The Korean understanding of teaching national identity as part of the Korean curriculum draws on the Korean notion that to be a citizen is not only to be a member of a state and fulfil allocated rights and duties for the state but also to become involved in community affairs.

Kim (2004) examined all seven curriculums and filtered out what the Korean national identity stands for according to the Korean social studies curriculum:

> The problem is that the identity, especially national identity, is not innate but must be developed. It is important to note that the most effective means to raise this issue would be through education. Therefore, when we want to grasp the characteristics of national identity of one nation, the most effective way we can use would be the examination of a nation's curriculum. (p.1)

Kim stressed Korea's long history and in Kim's perspective its "unique national identity" (p.5), which, because of religious and philosophical ideologies, perceives the nation as an extended form of family. Nevertheless, rapidly changing circumstances and the strong effects of globalization have been changing Korea's initial national character, and sent the nation on a journey to reinvent its national identity. The latest curriculum, which was introduced in 2000, includes all the characteristics a good Korean should follow:

> The well-educated Korean citizen promoted by this curriculum is defined as a person who seeks to develop his/her own individuality on the basis of well-rounded and wholesome development; a person who demonstrates creative ability on the basis of solid grounding in basic knowledge and skills; a person who explores career paths on the basis of broad intellectual knowledge and skills in diverse academic disciplines; a person who creates new values on the basis of understanding the national culture; and a person who contributes to the developments of the community where he/she lives, on the basis of democratic citizenship. (Kim, 2004:p.5)

The ethics part of the sixth curriculum explicitly discusses national identity and three essential conditions, which according to the curriculum's textbook form the basis of the ideal Korea. To form an ideally developed nation, each Korean has to internalize the strong national identity and the appreciation of liberty, equality and responsibility along with three conditions: to be a democratic society, to be a welfare state and to be a nation in which its people feel strong coherence to each other (Kim, 2004). According to Kim (2004), Korean people carry pride in their predominantly homogeneous society and their preservation of Korean blood, which also becomes apparent in Korea's contemporary law. Kim noted that:

> Actually, among Koreans, it is proudly said that Korea is one of the
> few nations in which single-blooded people have dwelt on the same
> land, and kept their own culture for a long time. This allows Korean
> people to have a unique national identity. (p.5)

As a result, the Korean national identity unconsciously assumes that it includes national identity as well as ethnic identity: 'So for Koreans, national identity is the same as ethnic identity' (Kim, 2004:p.5). Nevertheless, it is worth mentioning that Korean nationalism is transforming into the concept of 'open nationalism', which does not include other nations or people, but fosters world peace and happiness outwardly at the same time as it enhances Korean national solidarity and prosperity inwardly (Kim, 2004).

Yim (2002) analysed the challenges of Korean cultural policy to resolve the issue of cultural identity that has been on-going since the establishment of the first republic in 1948. Yim's discussion foregrounds, that cultural identity has been the main challenge in the evolution of Korean cultural policy. Yim stressed the instrumental significance of identity in Korea, which serves the nation's economic development and social cohesion. Traditional Korean culture has been central to the argument of what Korean identity is; thus, it is important to mention the characteristics of traditional Korean culture. According to Yim:

> One of Korea's most striking characteristics has been its long term
> and continuous existence as a unified country. In spite of numerous
> invasions and occupations, the Koreans have remained remarkably
> homogeneous, and have been termed *Han minjok* (meaning "Great
> Han Race" in a Nazism context). (p.38)

In addition to the mainly single-blooded identity is the ruling ideology of the Choson dynasty—the last dynasty that ruled over 500 years from 1392 through to the start of the Japanese colonial rule in 1910. The last dynasty embraced Korea's unique interpretation of Confucianism: 'The Choson dynasty emphasized humanity, ethical morality and spiritual self-cultivation and furthermore valued spiritual over material life ... virtue, harmony, faithfulness, propriety, righteousness' (Yim, 2002:p.38).

Yim (2002) argued that this idealistic representation of the Korean identity, in terms of its characteristics rather than its blood, has been heavily influenced by colonialism and occupation: 'Firstly, the problem of cultural identity is caused by the experience of Japanese colonialism, which sought to eradicate and distort Korean cultural identity by the enforcement of cultural assimilation policy at the end of the Japanese colonial period' (p.39). The division of the country and international interventions mainly caused by North America have contributed to a heavy shift away from the traditional Korean identity:

> Although the Korean people were ethnically and linguistically homogeneous before the division, the last 55 years have witnessed growing differences and heterogeneity between South and North Korea. These differences have taken place in the whole area of society, including language, culture and the arts. While South Korea was founded on the basis of democracy and capitalism, North Korea came to be dominated by the principle of communism and socialism. (Yim, 2002 p.39).

Yim's (2002) third aspect is the influence of North America, which is held responsible for the gradual loss of traditional Korean characteristics. Yim highlighted the problematic and distinguished what he referred to as Western culture as opposed to specifically traditional Korean culture:

> From the Korean point of view, it has been argued that Western popular culture tends to be synonymous with commercialism, materialism, violence and sensuality as compared with the Korean traditional culture … What was worse, the swift pace of modernization tended to increase extreme individualism and hedonism. (p. 39)

In the framework of cultural policy, which can be considered the representation of the core culture, the issue of cultural identity has been reinterpreted and organized differently according to changes in the government, fiscal and sociocultural environments in which cultural policy has been formulated and implemented. Therefore, the issue of cultural identity remains influential in shaping national identity policy. In contemporary Korea, the influence of cultural nationalism, with traditional Korean identity at its core, strengthened the modern Korean identity context. This formation was only possible because of historical experiences of colonial imposed views and the absorption of Western culture, which made the familiar strange and therefore special and unique again. Moreover, the purposive construction of the cultural identity after the formation of the first republic in 1948, through the state-led intervention of cultural policy, was mainly based on traditional Korean values: 'Traditional culture was mobilized as a strong instrument for anti-communism, state-led economic development strategy and the political legitimacy of Park's government' (Yim, 2002 p.47).

Park and Chang (2005) evaluated the perspective of the Korean identity using a sample of 1,000 individuals aged over 20 selected by a random sampling method and conducted through a South Korean non-governmental organization called the Committee on Overseas Korean Network. Their research revolved around the debate of mystified notions of national/legal/ethnic identities, using the provided survey data supplemented by qualitative interviews. Park and Chang tried to define the relationship between the South Korean government's determination to define Korean identity legally and the Korean diasporic community's challenge grounded in ethnic homogeneity. In particular, this study analysed the controversies of the *Overseas Korean Act* in a broader geopolitical, historic and economic context with regard to the (dis)connection and tension between national and ethnic identities and the question of redefining and negotiating such identities in an era of globalization. Park and Chang's results show a strong trend of ethnic affiliation, and hence blood affiliation, despite (im)migration and intermarriages. They indicated that the ethnic homogeneity in and without the nation state has rarely been challenged: 'In fact, Korea is acknowledged as one of the few countries whose ethnic makeup is extremely homogeneous. Thus, Koreans both in Korea and abroad firmly believe in the "oneness"' of the Korean people, regardless of their residence' (Park & Chang, 2005:p.8). Some interesting interpretations can be drawn from their findings. Although overseas Koreans are generally referred to as *tongp'o* and South Korean respondents subjectively include or exclude overseas Koreans, these opinions were almost coexisting with the *Overseas Korean Act*:

> For instance, the groups included in the OKA—Korean-Americans and pro–South Korea Korean residents in Japan—are regarded as tongp'o by a greater number of Koreans (92 percent and 83.2 percent, respectively), compared to their excluded counterparts, including Korean Chinese (76.8 percent), Korean Russians (65.7 percent), and pro–North Korean residents in Japan (52.2 percent) (Park & Chang, 2005:p.11).

These figures show that the legal inclusion/exclusion is not only a result of a complex interaction of political and economic influences, but also suggests the pervasive emotional and psychological attachment and detachment between South Koreans living in South Korea and overseas Koreans. Park and Chang's study has shown that blood ties are still the dominant factor that determines Koreanness in terms of identities: 'Besides the significance of ancestral heritage, we can infer from this division that South Koreans seem automatically to assume overseas Koreans' full-bloodedness. A similar attitude towards heritage is found in the evaluation of half-blooded Koreans and Korean adoptees' (Park & Chang, 2005 p.13).

Koreanness and Goffmanian theory propose an emotion-management perspective as a lens through which to inspect the self, interaction and structure. Koreanness, it is argued, can be and often is subject to acts of management. The individual often works on inducing or inhibiting feelings so as to render them appropriate to identity. The Goffmanian perspective draws on an interactive account of symbols of identity such as *nunchi*. It allows us to inspect the relation among emotive experience, emotion management, feeling rules and ideology of identity. *Nunchi* is seen as the side of national ideology that deals with feeling rules. The management of the incorporation of the self as a performance is the type of work it takes to cope with feeling rules hence *nunchi*.

.

Conclusion

In conclusion, shared histories of war and division as well as military occupation have shaped both Germany and South Korea and forced them to determine what it means to be German and South Korean. Germany has dealt with this question several times in history (Bruhn, 1994; Elias, 1996), and the nation recently rectified its laws to offer post-reunified Germany the chance to return to its roots (Schwarz, 2003). In contrast, Korea has witnessed growing differences and heterogeneity between South and North Korea even though all Koreans were ethnically and linguistically homogeneous before the division. These differences have taken place in the whole area of society, including language, culture and the arts. Whereas South Korea was founded on the basis of democracy and capitalism, North Korea came to be dominated by the principles of communism and socialism (Yim, 2002).

The change of law triggered a change in expressing what being German means. Germanness is constituted through unity in the use of symbols of identity, resulting in one identity context; parallel societies whose cultural imprints clash with the *Leitkultur* are therefore a potential threat to the newly established German identity (Schwarz, 2003). The current definition of Germanness touches on the perception of the late eighteenth century that anyone can obtain German identity, as described by Judson (1993) by embracing its shared values and thought. Contemporary German identity thus corresponds to the strategic self-presentation of symbols of identity such as, cosmopolitanism, *Ordnung*, language and education, industriousness, remembrance and critical self-awareness and freedom. By this standard, German identity is available to anyone who choses to respect, acknowledge, adopt and present himself/herself with such symbols. In theory at least, individuals from any background, are able to attain a German identity through the strategic self-presentation of the symbols of the "new" Germany and its identity.

In contrast to Germanness and Germany's citizenship laws, despite shared histories of war and division, those of Korea still follow *jus sanguinis*, the law of blood. Park and Chang's (2005) study revealed a strong trend of ethnic affiliation, and hence blood affiliation, despite (im) migration and intermarriages. From this they conclude that the ethnic homogeneity within and outside the borders of the nation state has rarely been challenged: 'In fact, Korea is acknowledged as one of the few countries whose ethnic makeup is extremely homogeneous. Thus, Koreans both in Korea and abroad firmly believe in the "oneness" of the Korean people, regardless of their residence' (Park & Chang, 2005:p.8). According to Kim (2004), Korean people carry pride in the symbol of blood ties in their predominantly homogeneous society and their preservation of the Korean blood, which also becomes apparent in Korea's contemporary law:

> Actually, among Koreans, it is proudly said that Korea is one of the few nations in which single-blooded people have dwelt on the same land, and kept their own culture for a long time. This allows Korean people to have a unique national identity. (Kim, 2004:p.5)

As a result, the Korean national identity unconsciously assumes that it includes national identity as well as ethnic identity, 'so for Koreans, national identity is the same as ethnic identity' (Kim, 2004 p.5).

Korea's assumed oneness based on the symbol of blood ties, which entails the unconscious assumption that national, cultural and ethnic identity are the same, causes the country a great deal of problems because Koreans believe that they were born with distinct symbols of identity that are all rooted in the symbol of blood ties, as opposed to German identity, which believes that Germanness may be learnt, yet even legally acquired through the strategic self-presentation of symbols of German identity as outlined above (Judson, 1993; Schwarz, 2003). However, both identity contexts are based on strong national symbols that determine everything the German or Korean does. Shared perception of collectivism exists within both identities; however, these perceptions follow different interpretations. Koreanness assumes that Korean symbols of identity are only available to ethnic Koreans who share the same national as well as ethnic identity. From this I can infer that Koreans assume that non-Koreans cannot obtain Korean identity by expressing a strong set of symbols of identity of which *nunchi* takes a large share because of the lack of being ethnic Korean. Thus, to be Korean is to belong to a particular national and ethnical group, presenting oneself using significant symbols of identity, such as blood ties. Consequently, to be Korean is to belong to a single entity, within or outside the national borders, embracing symbols of Koreanness that are thought to be exclusively Korean, e.g. *nunchi*.

Korean Identity and Business

Introduction

Numerous, arguably negative international interventions, 40 years of Japanese colonial rule, the separation of the country by the United States and the Soviet Union at the end of World War Two and several suppressive regimes have formed the modern history of Korea and shaped the contemporary Korean peninsula and thus Korean identity and its business practices (Lee, 1987).

The 1980s were highly significant in terms of the emergence of new industrialized countries, especially in East Asia. Korea skyrocketed from nearly nothing to being a global player in the world's economy. Some scholars refer to the twenty-first century as the Asia-Pacific century (Tung, 1994). Ever since the Second World War, Korea has been on the rise and some of its *chaebols* (see below) have emerged as major competitors in world markets (for comparison to the *zaibatsu* and *keiretsu* see Bhappu, 2000). This section will examine the character of the general Korean management style and its symbols of identity such as *chaebols*, Confucianism and *nunchi*, in analysing pre-existing literature. Scholarly work provides an ideal platform to establish a better understanding of how the past has shaped the present and might influence the future of Koreanness and its business practices in the context of international business.

Chaebols as a symbol of Koreanness and business practices

Choi and Cowing (1999) examined the relationship between group affiliation and firm behaviour in the case of Korean firms. Many propriety Korean companies are members of a larger business group, which in Korean is referred to as the *chaebol*. As indicated by Choi and Gowing, '*chaebols* are exclusive business groups of formally independent firms whose top management is centered in the hands of one person or family' (p.197)

A large *chaebol* usually includes between 40 and 50 individual firms, including financial institutions, which are operated by the founder family. Even though a Korean *chaebol* consists of many legally independent entities, it is run as if it were a single entity company. *Chaebols* are highly spread across many industries, such as electronics, construction equipment, chemicals, cars, shipbuilding and financial services. Because *chaebols* are diversified, they can help each other out of business hardships and hence reduce risk (Cho, 1995).

Wilkinson (1996) critically compared business structures in East Asian 'miracle' economies, using Korea, Japan and Taiwan as his major examples. Wilkinson outlined the culturists' perspective, which is fostered by pre-modern belief systems, in contrast to the institutionalists' perspective, which is mainly supported by pre-modern traditions and developing 'institutional environments'. It is suggested that Korea's economic growth was interlinked with the update of its old Confucian thoughts. According to Wilkinson, 'the East Asian economies were able to develop successful capitalism only when they began to throw off the shackles of Confucianism' (p.442).

The Korean *chaebol*, the Japanese *kaisha* and the Taiwanese business structure are formed differently in important respects. From this I infer that if any relations between Confucianism and the establishment of organizational forms exist, either three different compositions of Confucianism exist or Confucianism provides three different value systems, according to the selected country. Consequently, Wilkinson (1996) argues that 'either way, the culturist argument, in itself, becomes next to useless in explaining East Asian business structures' (p.427); 'characteristic business structures in Japan, Korea and Taiwan, for instance, do exhibit some significant differences despite some common cultural characteristics' (pp.427–428).

Wilkinson (1996) argued that Korean companies enact a patrimonial logic, in contrast to Japanese companies, which enact communitarian logic, and Taiwanese companies, which follow patrilineal logic. Hence, Korean *chaebols* rarely cooperate with each other. Relationships between employers and employees are less paternalistic and more authoritarian than in Japan; further, authority is highly centralized within the founder's family. *Chaebols* use particular authority practices that were inherited from patterns of authority and subordination from pre-modern Korea and its history of invaders and colonial rule. Management practices in Korean MNCs are held to derive from the legitimizing strategy of the post-war government. On-going competition within *chaebols* reflects the competition of the *yangban* elite.

Wilkinson (1996) noted that business structures such as Korean business structures reflect social rules, which have the power of understanding and approval in the community. Wilkinson stressed that it is too simple to draw casual links between culture and institutional environments and modern business practices. He criticized the implementation of the past in the present. His emphasis foregrounds the differences in interests and values within populations. As Wilkinson observed, 'What could be more appealing to an employer than to be told that his behaviour is a re-enactment of a great historical tradition? It's OK, he's Confucian!; It's OK, his father was a slave-owner!' (p.442).

Glover and Wilkinson (2006) explored the factors that served to remove an adopted strategy of quality management within a multinational Korean-owned British subsidiary. They identified three major differences at the external organizational, intra-organizational and internal organizational workplace levels. The two different managing styles studied showed the notion of the "negotiated process" where multiple actors compete over "the interpretation of the management practice's meaning and function" (p.4). Their study emphasizes the differences in micro-organizational dynamics in Korean and British management styles.

Glover and Wilkinson (2006) agree with Wilkinson's (1996) approach that Confucian culture and the related countries cannot be thrown into one big melting pot: 'One could not talk of a unique model of Asian HRM. This suggests that one cannot merely "lump together" the Asian tigers and assume for example, that management approaches in Japanese-owned MNCs are likely to mirror those within Korean-owned' (p.10). Further, they reinforce Wilkinson's argument that the Korean *chaebol*-dominated economy has historically received strong support from the post-war government and take it further by arguing that the growth and diversification of the *chaebols* was influenced by the state's requirements, serving the state in developing chemical and engineering production because of the North Korean military threats in the 1970s.

Glover and Wilkinson (2006) outlined the evolutionary changes in Korean management styles from a typically authoritarian approach to a more modern one, explaining that 'the traditional approach to management in the *chaebols* was typified by scientific management with jobs broken down into narrowly defined tasks, workers were closely supervised and an authoritarian management style tended to prevail' (p.12). The new Korean MNCs' management styles, according to Glover and Wilkinson, are more likely to implement a low-trust/low-investment approach within developing countries and a rather high-trust approach within more advanced countries. Another aspect that the authors stressed is that human recourses are one of the crucial factors to guarantee organizational success in Korean MNCs. Hence; the new implementations in the Korean MNCs' management style are influenced by high-performance work systems. The authors observe that 'Korean companies have been experimenting with Western-influenced high-performance work systems, including an emphasis on training and development, appraisals, empowerment, pay-for performance, flat structures, team systems and flexibility' (p.13) The new approach is unlike the traditional one in which rewards where purely based on seniority and bonuses were more or less linked to the MNC's overall performance, nevertheless the traditional approach is still the prevailing one. The authors' findings have shown that the adoption of some new management aspects have transformed the individual ability to think; hence, it allows employees to engage in a slightly more autonomous decision-making process and involvement, even though just to a small extend.

Morden and Bowels (1998) outlined the change in Korean management style and national character from the Yi Dynasty in 1392 to the Japanese rule that annexed Korea in 1910 to today. They described the South Korean national character as not easily forgiving in terms of personal and national pride and not embarrassed to release its feeling in an energetic manner. Morden and Bowels' general approach to explain the Korean management style and national character does not differ much in terms of methodology from most studies because they compare and establish overlaps and differences between the Japanese and Korean styles of management. Their study also includes a comparative analysis between France and Korea and some minor references to the Germans and their working practices and relations: 'Korean corporations have never had the sense of managerial paternalism (*amae*) that exists in Japan or Germany, with (their) extensively... developed welfare for employees' (p.320). They argued that the cultural diversity in terms of religion and philosophy in South Korea makes it different from most other East Asian nations: 'The very strong Christian influence in the twentieth century... Korea is the only country in East Asia that has a significant Christian population' (p.317). Korean managerial characters are described as self-confident, patient, respectful, tolerant and determined to negotiate with a moderate but persistent aggression that can often lead to win–lose results and explained that 'the taipans of Korea and their business culture are said to be the world's toughest' (p.319). The authors argued that all comparative management studies agree on a unified authoritarian management style, which is rooted within Korea's history and traditions:

> Virtually all comparative studies of Korean management (have indicated) that Korean businesses tend to be run in a hierarchical, authoritarian and centralized manner.... This was particularly true of... *chaebol* still run by founding entrepreneurs, who insisted on making all major management decisions personally. (p.320)

Morden and Bowels (1998) described the official *kyul-jae* procedure, which has to be followed to obtain approval for new projects. The process includes receiving several stamps from managers at the very senior level. In some companies, the number of stamps required is as high as 21, which prolongs the approval process. This is subject to change: 'The Samsung group in the past used a process of 21 chops, which took several months to get a project approved. After *Kun Hee Lee* took over the group, he demanded that these 21 chops be cut down to three' (Morden & Bowels, 1998:p.321). Although the authors support the top–down authoritarian management and decision-making style, they argued that Korean management is also heavily influenced by two key Korean values, *inwah* (harmony) and *nunchi* (emotional intelligence):

> *Inwah,* which is defined as harmony and is similar to the Japanese *wa* … emphasizes harmony between unequals in rank, power and prestige … Korean managers cherish good interpersonal relationships with their subordinates and try to keep the needs and feelings … of subordinates in mind. (p.321)

Another aspect is the high risk of generating misunderstanding in Korean companies because of very general directives made by superiors followed by hesitant responses to ask for clarification to avoid potential humiliation or loss of face: 'The superior's preference for communicating in general terms, combined with a relatively large power distance, comprises a major source of misunderstanding in Korean companies' (Morden & Bowels, 1998:pp. 331–332). However, good personal relations, which can be achieved through similar affiliations may help to overcome hierarchical barriers and enhance a more effective communication strategy. Morden and Bowels (1998) noted that South Koreans act rather hesitant, shy and reluctant in formal work-related settings, in which a hierarchy exists, in contrast to informal settings, which mainly take place in a smaller group or on a one-to-one basis: ' Koreans are … good at communication on informal occasions, especially on a one-to-one basis with a superior. There are many opportunities for informal communication between superiors and subordinates; sophisticated superiors will constantly make such opportunities available' (p.332). These informal occasions are considered of high importance to build up trust and mutual understanding and mainly take on the form of company dinners and drinking sessions.

Chun (2009) empirically examined Korean MNCs' preferences in ownership structure. His quantitative research approach in using the *Overseas Direct Investment Statistics Yearbook* allowed him to establish several graphs that considered independent variables, including the black market, the resource-based sector, research and development intensity, economic growth, educational level, infrastructure, restrictions on foreign direct investment (FDI), dummy variables and sociocultural distance. The findings were that the ownership structure is highly related to host countries' economic growth: 'MNFs equity participation in its affiliates is lower in fast growing countries than in slow growing host countries' (Chun, 2009:p.34). Another aspect is the host country's level of education, which is inversely related to Korean MNCs' equity participation. MNCs tend to hold a lower equity share and depend more on the local partner when the sociocultural distance level is high. In addition, Korean MNCs tend to share control rights to a higher extent if the sociocultural distance level is higher: 'The greater the sociocultural difference between Korea and the host country, the more the Korean MNF tends to share control rights' (Chun, 2009:p.34).

Erramilli, Srivastava and Kim (1999) applied an internationalization theory developed by Uppsala scholars to explain Korean MNCs' country selection for FDI. The study's results varied from initial FDI to later entries of FDI, which are described as more mature: 'Time and its associated learning effects have apparently resulted in reduced uncertainty, greater self-confidence and bolder investment decisions' (p.43). Further, they found that ownership patterns have changed according to time as well: ' Minority joint ventures represented the preferred modes of entry during the early years of overseas expansion, but majority joint ventures and wholly-owned subsidiaries became the norm in later years' (p.42).

In sum *Chaebols* are a symbol of Koreanness, as their management practises are legitimised by the post war government, thus business structures and practises, which are granted the power of total acceptance and understanding in society represent Korean identity (Wilkinson 1996). The on-going competition within *chaebols*, reflects strategic *nunchi* presentations in which actors aim for ideal self-presentations to achieve their goals in instilling harmony in a hierarchical, authoritarian and highly centralised identity setting.

Confucianism: an identity symbol of Koreanness

Lee and Trim (2008) discussed the differences and similarities between Korean and Japanese businesspeople with a strong focus on culture, using Buddhism and Confucianism as the main cultural elements of national identity. According to Lee and Trim, the major differences between Japanese and Koreans occurred because Confucianism and Buddhism were introduced at different epochs of history in each nation. These differences become apparent in corporate identity, organizational behaviour and two unique management styles: 'Confucianism and Buddhism have influenced Japanese and Korean people and their characteristics, and to some degree is responsible for the management models that have evolved and which are evident in Japanese and Korean organizations today' (pp.63–64). Lee and Trim included self-control, self-cultivation, filial piety, virtues and loyalty as typical Korean characteristics, which can be traced back to the school of Confucian thought. They argued that the acceptance of Confucian teaching, hence the characteristics listed above, legitimize and contribute towards Korea's place to be positioned in an organization-society context. Buddhist elements support this model along with Confucianism. The Eightfold Path, which defines Buddhism and its' three divisions—wisdom, mental culture and morality—are mirrored in the Korean management style. Lee and Trim noted that Japan and Korea's identities are separate and far away from China's cultural identity. The study found that big businesses—*chaebols* in Korea—are heavily influenced and shaped by society's acceptance of Confucian thought and the implications, which affect the Korean management style: 'It can be suggested that the key difference between the two countries is that Korea embraced Buddhism in a religious context as did Japan, but Korea embraced Confucianism in both a political and social context' (p.66).

Moreover, Lee and Trim (2008) pointed out that both Japanese and Koreans use respect, modesty and politeness as their major guidelines when dealing with others; according to the authors, they are embedded in each cultural value system. They describe the overall approach for the Japanese as determined and, for the Koreans, rather patient: 'Korean people are influenced by the concept of mutuality, whereas Japanese people are more concerned with achieving a goal' (p.66). Lee and Trim found that, because of the heavy Confucian and Buddhist influence in contemporary Korean society, value creation and a commitment to satisfy customers' needs, along with creativity, harmony and a focus on family-oriented HR management, are characteristics of Korean companies. In addition to attentiveness, competitiveness and the ability to think as an individual if need be, Korean employees differ from Japanese employees in their contemporary working approach in that they are sometimes in certain situations able to think and provide constructive criticism to superiors:

> Korean employees pay attention to building relationships possibly,
> through imparting knowledge and information ... Korean employees

are keen to achieve a satisfactory result and consider mutuality as it underpins the relationship building process ... Korean employees do on occasions act as individuals and this contrasts with the way Japanese employees think and operate ...[in] Korean organizations, employees may decide to challenge those above them in the hierarchy. (p.67)

Lee and Trim's (2008) findings also reveal the secrets of recruitment policy of Korean companies and its main components, *yon-go* and *gong-che*: '*Yong-go* is based on Confucius' thought and refers to the network(s) that the individual belongs to and *Gong-che*, is the visible employment system' (p.76).

Generally, Lee and Trim's (2008) literature analysis and studies show that managers in Korean organizations have effective control through strong affiliations with all parties involved, which provides internal certainty. The prevalent value system among Korean staff helps organizations to nurture the corporations' needs. Corporate aims and future development often overlap with governmental aims and objectives.

Lee and Trim's (2008) argument that contemporary Korea's management style is fully based on history and culture (Buddhism and Confucianism) completely marginalizes Morden and Bowels' (1998) perspective that Christianity has a strong influence on Korean society. Lee and Trim's approach of comparing Korea with Japan does not legitimize the marginalization of Christianity because Korea is the only country in East Asia where Christians are not a minority. In the cultural and religious context used by Lee and Trim, the marginalization of Christianity might have had a considerable effect on their findings.

Dacin, Hitt and Levitas (1997) argued that Korean managers are less egocentric compared with American managers. The authors drew comparisons between Korean and American managers and their expectations in international business alliances. They found that Korean managers have a stronger long-term orientation than American managers. In addition, their distinct ownership preference supports this finding: 'The concentration of family ownership in the *Chaebols* encourages a longer-run orientation by Korean executives' (p.9). Further, they stressed that Korean managers have the ability to quickly adjust to different environments and cater to specific parties' needs: 'By working in *Chaebol* networks and their linkages to the system of state government, Korean managers have developed internal capabilities for networking' (p.8).

When Korean firms build alliances with international partners, their focus is on constructing mutually beneficial relationships through information sharing and exchange of skills: 'Korean executives are specifically searching for partners that have technical capabilities or marketing know-how that their firm may not possess but wishes to learn' (Dacin, Hill & Levitas, 1997:p.11).

Dacin, Hitt and Levitas's (1997) comparison of Korean and American managers suggests that American managers are more egocentric than Korean managers, which contrasts with the findings of Morden and Bowels (1998), who classified Korea's managers as taipans and their associated management style as the toughest in the world. Lee and Trim (2008), also foregrounded that Japanese managers are more concerned with achieving a set goal compared with Korean managers.

Ha (2007) argued that state-led industrialization affected social changes. In contrast to predictable sociological findings, Ha asserted that industrialization in Korea nurtured the rise of neofamilism, which is defined as the unintended reinforcement of regional ties, blood and networks, for example, university alumni. Ha's discovery that neofamilism arose in correlation with the state differs from Lee and Trim's (2008) argument that Confucianism is responsible for Korea's neofamilism, especially in the workplace.

Kim (2003) collected qualitative data through document analysis along with intensive interviews to explore global public relations in the context of Confucianism in Korean MNCs. Kim argued that Korea has been affected by Confucianism more strongly than any other country in the world, including China and other countries that embrace Confucianism. In terms of Confucianism and Korean MNCs' management style, Kim presented evidence, gathered from female employees, that Korea has a rather male-centred culture hence identity. He emphasized that a *chaebol* chairman takes on a rather patriarchal role with absolute control, which he linked to the Confucian tradition in Korea. Kim stressed certain gender expectations within *chaebols*, which he also linked to Confucian traditions in Korea. According to one of the female employees interviewed for the study, 'The management expects me to do the same amount of work as male workers do. But I feel, at the same time, our company asks me to behave as a woman' (p.88).

In summary, a major discourse has emerged on how the current Korean management style came into existence and where its contemporary elements originated. A persistent thread of a unified authoritarian management style is present in most scholarly work, but modern adjustments and improvements have not been fully discovered. As Wilkinson (1996) indicated, it is too simple to use Confucianism as the core argument to explain and justify everything. It is essential to identify Korea's unique Confucianism and identity implications before considering the cultural argument in more depth. From the general trend above I can however infer that Confucianism identifies as a Korean symbol of identity underpinning management practices in Korean identity settings.

In sum, from what the literature concludes has Confucianism affected Korea more than any other nation in the world. Thus Confucianism takes on an important role as a symbol of Koreanness in Korean identity overall but specifically in Korea's corporate identity, organizational behaviour and management style. The Korean management style enforced by *Chaebols*, which embrace Confucian style control that permits chairmen to take a patriarchal role with absolute control, shaped Koreanness through Korean society's acceptance of Confucian thought in a political and social context opposed to a merely philosophical and ethical context. Confucianism at its core demands harmony and mutuality which actors strategically are meant to attend to in competitive settings such as *Chaebols* in satisfying others through the use of *nunchi* to create harmony and to build and maintain mutually beneficial relationships. Confucian thought in Korea's political and social context primarily demands harmony, filial piety and self-control; all such teachings correspond and correlate to aspects of the *nunchi* symbol. I shall now move on to discuss *nunchi* as a symbol of Koreanness in business.

Nunchi as a symbol of Koreanness in business

Nunchi is an important aspect in the Korean identity context; it heavily influences the way business is conducted in South Korea and is interlinked with *kibun*. *Kibun* does not have a direct English translation; it refers to a feeling of balance and good behaviour or state of mind (Chaney & Martin, 2011). It is essential to maintain persistently an environment of stable *kibun* in private and corporate life. People are expected to maintain their own as well as others' *kibun*, which implies that the ability to practise *nunchi* well is important to perform successfully in Korea's corporate world (Southerton, 2008). *Nunchi* involves paying attention to others' non-verbal and body language as well as the tones of what is being said; in other words, it is the ability to regulate another person's *kibun* using the eye (Southerton, 2008).

A further key aspect in the way business is conducted in Korea, which is closely related to *nunchi*, is *inhwa*, which translates as 'harmony'. In a collectivist society, agreement is a significant component in endorsing and sustaining harmony. In the business world, *inhwa* requires employees to be loyal to their superiors and superiors to take care of their employees; this can only be assured if both parties practise *nunchi* (Alston, 1989; Chen, 1995; Mensik, Grainger & Chatterjee, 1999). This concept of using *nunchi* to preserve inhwa is consistent with *kibun*. Koreans do not like to hear bad news and thus wait until the very last moment to deliver it to maintain the recipient's *kibun* for as long as possible, especially at work (Alston, 1989). *Inhwa* is the most desirable state in the community or at work (Chang, 1983). As an important way to achieve harmony-oriented leadership, Korean managers practise *nunchi* to ensure *inhwa* (Chen, 1995; Kim, Sohn & Wall, 1999; Song & Meek, 1998). Additionally, *yon-go*, which translates as 'relation-based behaviour', is an important driver in Korean management (Chung et al, 1997) for building strong bonds between people (Mensik, Grainger & Chatterjee, 1999). A strong sense of belonging promotes *inhwa* within a corporation (Chung et al, 1997), strengthening trust among colleagues through the use of *nunchi* (Lee, 1998a). The Korean term *jung*, which has its origins in Confucian philosophy, entails all seven emotions of humanity as defined in Confucianism (Chung, 1995; Lee, 2001a, 2001b). *Jung* is an unconsciously formed emotional bond, which arises through contact over time (Kim, 1993). *Jung* is the fundamental base of Korean relationships (Lim, 1993). The rich existence of *jung* in Korean society stimulates a management style that narrows the line between corporate and private life. Personalized relationships are a central measure of HRM practices in Korean companies (Paik & Sohn, 1998). *Jung* leads to strong feelings of collective identity, or *woori*, among company members (Yum, 1994). As *jung* grows through the use of *nunchi*, *woori* becomes stronger and the instrumental, work-related complexion of relationships within the group changes to a more affective basis (Ibarra & Andrews, 1993). It also has an effect on the flow of information, influence and solidarity available to members (Adler & Kwon, 2002), facilitating learning and the complex managerial routines in Korean companies.

Conclusion

The Korean management approach along with symbols of identity that define Germanness and Koreannss provide the context for the study of *nunchi* in strategic self-presentations of *HanaEins* members. German MNCs in Seoul, which are by means of communication, trade and business practices connected to both Germanness and Koreanness, offer insights into *HanaEins* members' strategic self-presentation of *nunchi* in a context much influenced by the Korean management style and business practises of *Chaebols*. National identities such as Germanness and Koreanness are defined and given meaning to by symbols of identity, such as *nunchi*, which when working across borders and identities are exposed to various international interpretations that are influenced by management styles and business practices and are therefore subject to recontextualisation.

HanaEins members, as well as German MNCs in Korea therefore transform and get transformed on a daily basis as they negotiate, add to and take from management styles and symbols of identity and thus create transnational meaning for management practices worldwide. Consequently one cannot address *nunchi* as solitary, fixed symbol, exclusive to Korean identity, but rather as involved, not only with *HanaEins* members, but with several distinct transnational entities, their connectionas and motivations.

Chapter 3

Methodology:

From my desk to Seoul and back:

the journey of my research

Introduction

The research carried out for this book is an ethnographic study looking at transnational German businesspeople working and living in Seoul and how they strategically work and manage across borders and identities in MNCs.

While there is a growing interest understanding the relevance of *nunchi* practices (see Yi and Jezewski, 2000; Lee-Peuker, 2004; Chung and Gale, 2008; Kang, 2000; Scherpinski-Lee, 2011, Blackhall et al., 2001; Stowell, 2003; Meurant date unknown) and how it matters in business studies. There seems to be no consensus on what constitutes *nunchi*. In fact some scholars classify it as "innate" (Kang 2000) while others limit it to non-verbal communication (Yi and Jezewski 2000; Chung and Gale 2008).

Although these current studies offer somewhat of an understanding of what *nunchi* is they reveal little about how it is incorporated into strategic self-presentations. With few examples such as Scherpinski-Lee (2011) and to some extent Lee-Peuker's (2004) work on how *nunchi* is applied in business contexts. Given this gap in the *nunchi* discourse, this study looks at *nunchi* and how it is incorporated into strategic self-presentations of transnational businesspeople. It is to note that my work does not aim to establish a somewhat of a '*nunchi* formula', however it seeks to understand how transnational businesspeople incorporate *nunchi* into their strategic identity presentations and how they give meaning to these practises in re-contextualising symbols of identity such as *nunchi* through their everyday activities at work and in the private sphere. In doing so it looks at how meaning gets transferred and transformed from one identity context to another.

As previously discussed in chapter one, the main aim of my research is to explore *nunchi* and identity in transnational settings in which the process of re-contextualisation of symbols of identity from one identity specific setting to another takes place.

My interest in researching this topic goes way back and is due to being a transnational German, who always lived with and around Koreans in Germany, China and what I call 'Asia town' in Sydney, an area consisting of two blocks centred around World Square, which is home to the Korean, Chinese and Thai enclave of Sydney. This experience motivated me to investigate how transnational businesspeople incorporate or do not incorporate re-contextualised symbols of identity into their strategic self-presentations.

The intention of the data collection in this study is to capture the identity related meanings and ordinary activities of informants in everyday life in the real world, for example, at work. This includes complex networks with messy and probable elusive effects. Therefore, I have not chosen to use a deductive research approach, which assumes that 'one step follows the other in a clear, logical sequence' (Bryman & Bell, 2011, p. 11). However for this study an ethnographic approach (Fetterman 1998) has been chosen, to allow unspoken, non-linear at times 'messy' methodological considerations (Law 2004), which I believe, are more appropriate for exploring the meanings of *nunchi*.

The ultimate goal was to collect data in a way, which allows the researcher to deploy reflexivity as a tool. Reflexivity is extremely important in data collection because the researcher is working alone and cannot be everywhere at the same time. Reliability and validity go hand in hand. Reliability can be assured because the researcher will be consistent, and any other researcher who has the same starting-point condition would find similar results. Validity is better-achieved using ethnography compared with questionnaires, which often lack validity because participants may lie or give answers that are desired (Schensul, Schensul & LeCompte, 1999). Furthermore, ethnography relies a great deal on up-close, personal experiences. Participation, rather than observation alone, is integral to success; therefore, my own experiences, relationships and longitudinal participation contributed significantly, in order to accomplish a neutral observation (Alvesson & Sköldberg, 2009). Interpretation of the symbols of identity derived from the pre-existing literature, formal and informal interviews and personal experiences that examine the effect of *nunchi* in transnational settings in MNCs between Koreans and Germans and their strategic self-presentation skills between the two identity contexts.

My research approach addresses the discursive, complex nature of the field, and is appropriate due to the limitation of extant research on *nunchi* and identity. In fact my research journey has been an explanatory search, in order to explain how I conducted my data collection to "make sense of, or interpret, phenomena in terms of meanings people bring to them" (Denzin & Lincoln, 2003 p.5) I will first discuss ethnography and the research paradigm. Followed by a review of the pilot study, which had effects on my work, followed by the research process, including ethical considerations and lastly the analysis and interpretation.

The research paradigm

The following section will discuss the research paradigm chosen for my work as the ethnographic research process is described as rather messy (Jullien 2004; Law 2004).

This research adopts an interpretive (Conger 1998; Grint 2000) paradigm because it is argued that organisations and their associated activities are constructed by human and non-human actors and perceived differently by individuals, thus it is desired to attempt understanding the realities constructed by others (Czarniawska-Joerges 1993). A paradigm defines a set of beliefs which make plain the nature of how the world is, how an individual fits into it and how the networks between the world and its numerous parts function (Guba, Lynham & Lincoln 1998). Thus the oppositional paradigms such as deductive and inductive approaches, positivism and interpretivism, objectivism and constructivism, quantitative and qualitative research strategies follow different ontological and epistemological rules (Bryman & Bell, 2011). Or in other words the nature of what is considered knowledge and the meaning of truth and how it can be studied are different (Duberley, Johnson and Cassell, 2012).

Ontology concerns itself with the essence of a phenomena and the complexion of existence, it discusses if a phenomenon exists independently of what we know, or if what we claim to be real is the result of what we know and perceive (Duberley et al., 2012). Instead of declaring that social phenomena and their meanings occur independent of actors, constructionism, as an ontological stance is taken in this study, which denotes that phenomena are not only produced through human interaction but they are constantly changing entities (Bryman & Bell, 2011). The ontological assumptions of the interpretive paradigm imply that there might be more than one reality, hence it assumes the coexistence of several possible realities and believes in the world and in this case amongst *HanaEins* members. As many scholars pointed out, that the most profound recognition in organisational studies is that much of the world we live in and engage with is essentially constructed through specific contexts that people interact with and therefore give different meanings to their interactions within different contexts and the world (Berger & Luckmann, 1966; Weick, 1979). Studying such construction processes implies that I focus more on the means by which *HanaEins* members go about constructing and understanding their realities and less on the number of frequency of measurable occurrences (Cunliffe, 2008; Geertz 1988). According to this ontological understanding, this interpretive ethnographic business research aims to analyse *HanaEins* members in their natural context according to how they construct their realities rather than from the ethnographer's perspective (Denzin and Lincoln, 2003).

In interpretive studies the epistemological belief assumes and aims to understand single facets that make a phenomenon such as meanings and experiences, which are ever shifting entities according to contexts and time (Sandberg, 2005). Thus understanding is neither static nor complete because it is subject to the researcher's interpretations drawn form the analysis (Sanberg, 2005). Hence ethnographers are often challenged to justify the generalizability of their research. However ethnography does offer unique contributions in the form of deep understanding of organisations, through multiple perspectives that provide insights into the description of human interactions, rituals and processes in everyday life (Fine, Morrill, & Surianarain, 2009).

While these ontological and epistemological assumptions are generally common in interpretative organisational research, there are distinct theoretical positions regarding triangulation of methods. Triangulation is viewed as common practise, however ethnography naturally includes multiple research methods (Brewer, 2004; Alvesson and Deetz, 2000: 75-76), such approach is considered inherent in qualitative research in order to elucidate a deep understanding of the phenomenon (Flick, 2002). Nevertheless, triangulation responds to quantitative methods assuming the existence of "the objective truth". Additionally Flick (2002) points out that "triangulation is not a tool or strategy of validation, but an alternative to validation" (p.227). Thus, the combination of various research methods, perspectives and empirical data is considered to be a strategy, which facilitates rigor, depth and richness to the inquiry (Denzin & Lincoln, 2005; Flick, 2002). This is called the 'crystallisation process' implied by Richardson and St. Pierre (2005), who argue that it should be the focus of qualitative inquiry opposed to triangulation. Narrating similar accounts form different perspectives is termed crystallization process, as "there is no one correct telling, each telling, like light hitting a crystal, reflects a different perspective on the incident", (Denzin and Lincoln, 2005 p. 6).

In sum ethnography can approach generalizability from a different perspective. It tends to supply a "theoretical" generalization that is "suggesting new interpretations and concepts or re-examining earlier concepts or interpretations in new and innovative ways", (Orum, Feagin, & Sjoberg, 1991, p. 13). Additionally, ethnography adds to the "naturalistic" generalizability given that it mirrors readers' realities in presenting credible, convincing and at times unexpected findings (Fine et al., 2009; Lincoln & Guba, 1985; Stake, 1978).

Therefore the ethnography written for this book follows these interpretive and reflexive paradigm principles, hence the aim for deeper and richer insights of the complex notions of constructing the realities of *HanaEins* members, rather than attempting to validate those.

Ethnography in Organisational and Business Studies

As Watson argues, ethnography should not be simplified or reduced to merely being a data collection method, however it should be considered as a way of conducting research, which encourages researchers to uphold a positive attitude towards, an exploratory research journey (2011). Willis and Trondman (2002 p. 394) answered the question what ethnography is in their *Manifesto for Ethnography* as followed, "most important, it is a family of methods involving direct and sustained social contact with agents and of richly writing up the encounter, respecting, recording, representing at least partly in its own terms the irreducibility of human experience." Fetterman (2009) refers to ethnography as 'a way of life' and Humphreys, Brown, & Hatch, denote it as a fundamentally creative, exploratory and interpretive process (2003). In an organizational context Watson explains that "ethnography is not a research method, but a way of writing about and analysing social life", with the aim to investigate "the realities of how things work" in organizations and management practices (p.202). Indeed Brewer (2000) points out that ethnography defines "the study of people in naturally occurring settings or 'fields' by means of methods which capture their social meanings and ordinary activities, involving the researcher participating directly in the setting, if not also the activities, in order to collect data in a systematic manner but without meaning being imposed on them externally" (p.10) see also Hackley (2003: 129).

Thus this ethnography investigates the realities of *HanaEins* members in their naturally occurring setting, in which I immersed myself through direct observation and participation to then present the complexities of *HanaEins* members' experiences.

Furthermore when viewed from the culturally holistic perspective as discussed by Watson (2012), ethnography is "a genre of social science writing which draws upon the writer's close observation of and involvement with people in a particular social setting and relates the words spoken and the practices observed or experienced to the overall cultural framework within which they occurred" (p. 2). Indeed such rich and detailed accounts of lived experiences derive "from the inside" which make "some kind of voice to those who live their conditions of existence possible to be heard (Willis & Trondman 2000 p.7), therefore ethnography's purpose is narrating a "rigorous, and authentic story" (Fetterman 2009), which instead of addressing what do I see these people doing, addresses what these people see themselves doing (Spradley 1980; McCurdy & Spradley 1972). Wolcott (1999) reinforced this in metaphorically terming it "ethnography is a way of seeing through the lens of culture" (p.47). Watson (2008) furthermore points out that ethnography; "a written account of cultural life of a social group, organisation or community which may focus on a particular aspect of life in that setting" is dissimilar from participant observation defined as "writing" (p.100).

As a concept "in motion" (Van Maanen 2006 p.15) even though there is some general agreement over the characteristics which most contemporary definitions of ethnography entail (O'Reilly 2009) such as the prevention of technical jargon usage and the preference of a somewhat descriptive writing in comparison to other forms of social science writing, and the stress on empirical work (Van Maanen 2006), ethnography does "not always mean exactly the same to all social scientists at all times or under all circumstances" (Atkinson, Coffey, Delamont, Lofland, & Lofland, 2001, p. 5). In this study's ethnography rich and rigorous detailed accounts of *HanaEins* members' lived realities are presented in a way addressing what *HanaEins* members see themselves doing, through my own insider position in the field, which makes it possible to give voice to *HanaEins* members' *nunchi* experiences as a particular aspect in the setting of *HanaEins* Seoul.

To further unpack ethnography as an academic discipline its etymology might be considered. The term ethnography stems from the Greek words *ethnos*, which translates to nation or culture and *graphein*, which translates to writing (Huang 2002), this classifies the development of ethnography as writing reflexive accounts known through fieldwork (Marcus 2007). As a result, ethnography is a research method commonly used in social and cultural anthropology and also albeit less often in sociology, history, economics and others. Anthropology is correlated with the study of indigenous cultures and tribes. As an outlet of anthropology, ethnography directly engages with experiencing a culture. Researchers are meant to learn the language and spend a decent amount of time immersed in the culture as a so-called local (Brunner and Turner, 1986; Levi-Strauss, 1963; Malinowski, 1979).

Although "culture" appears to be the most widespread ethnographic notion, exploring a social group's behaviours, customs, ideas, beliefs, jokes and language (Hackley 2003) it is furthermore believed that ethnography contributes to the enlightenment and richness of cultural interpretation (Harris, 1968; O'Reilly, 2009; Strauss & Quinn, 1997).

Since the 1920 ethnographic research has been on the rise (Roethlisberger & Dickson, 1939), the popular yet broad term "organizational culture" (Pettigrew

1979) has been used by scholars and practitioners, which led on to the argument that ethnographic research might better help to research sociological processes that people rely on to make sense of their world and organizational lives, opposed to more quantitative research (Kunda & Van Maanen 1999; Van Maanen 1979). Therefore ethnographers are required to get close enough and participate in the lives of organizational members to develop an outsider – insider perspective; that is to say, an outsider must become a provisional insider to see how the realities of the shared world of the group are constructed (Flucher & Davidson 2007). Consequently, understanding those denotations, which are fostered through these customs in organizations are quite subtle and sometimes expressed through "winks and blinks' as Fetterman (2009) terms it. To do so, a close association with the setting is needed (Brewer 2000).

Writing comprehensive reports of organizational life is a well-established practice, as others have also stated (e.g. Morril and Fine, 1997). Prominent among these reports are the Hawthorne studies, which focused on informal interactions in organizations, of the 1920s and the 1930s and Elton Mayo's implementation of anthropological field approaches (Mayo, 1933), as well as innovative, in depth studies Published from the late 1940s to the early 1960s of the 'informal organization' and the bureaucratic 'underlife' (Goffman, 1961). Amongst the latter are classic studies by Whyte (1948), Selznick (1949), Gouldner (1954), Blau (1955), Dalton (1959), Goffman (1983/1959) and Kaufman (1960). These scholars enhanced the field of organizational studies by presenting some of the limitations of theories showing formal bureaucratic organizational forms as competently operative machines, taking into view the 'irrationalities' of behind-the-scenes politics and other practices occurring in organizational 'back regions' (Goffman 1983/1959). Therefore, ethnography's value is, first, that it permits researchers to comprehend the actions of organizations, by extracting the dwelt experiences that trigger ideal, typical explanations of work (Barley, 1996; Chapman, 1997:pp.15, 21; Morris et al., 1999:pp.781–782).

Ethnographic research has been evolving since and in different variations (Alvesson, 2009; Boje & Tyler, 2009; Pink, 2007). Denzin (1997) points out that deep understanding of context may be achieved through reflexive description of the ethnographer's position in the field. The way the ethnographic account is written for this book necessitates reflexivity to offer a richer description, which results in the inclusion of different voices, specifically those of the ethnographer and the participants' (Charmaz & Mitchell 1997; Ybema et al., 2009).

Reflexivity as defined by Peregrine Schwartz-Shea and Dvora Yanow (2009), indicates that the researcher recognises himself as "the means, the instrument, through which the research (as well as its reporting) is produced. Researchers' demographic identities (gender, race, sexuality, social class, nationality and other components), manifested in dress, accent, physiognomy, and other elements of nonverbal communication, and other aspects of their phenomenological backgrounds (education, training, upbringing, and other elements of lived experience carried internally), the contribute to a 'positionality' that can affect not only the character of the interactions and research questions posed, but also access to research sites and persons in them and the kinds of data co-generated with research participants" (Schwartz-Shea & Yanow, 2009 cited in Yebema et al., 2009 p. 60).

Reflexive writing is fundamental to my study because as Richardson (2000) points out, it offers a way to find out about oneself and the researched topic. It is within the writing process and re-writing process that the author allows a dialogue between his voice and his participants' voices. Such dialogue between the two is created through the act of representing the portrayed phenomenon in reorganizing and reviewing the accounts presented (Denzin 2000). Such process allows the ethnographer to place himself in the field and therefore the representation of lived experiences becomes an interplay of both the ethnographer and participants' voices (Denzin, 2000). Although ethnography in organisational studies has only gained recognition since the 1970s (Baba 1998) its value in making the "familiar strange" as described by Agar (1996) means leaving behind a common-sense or instinctive understanding of the societal world to obtain comprehension of the profounder incentives, relationships, tactics and narrations underlying collective mind-sets, interaction and behaviour. Therefore the ethnographic account in this book deals with these interpretive and reflexive ideas in order to provide richer understandings of the complex processes of *nunchi* in strategic self-presentation. Moore (2005) emphasizes, " the relative scarcity of ethnographic studies of business, plus the qualitative, experiential aspects of ethnomethodology, suggest that new insights…can be gained through adopting this particular method" (p.10). Therefore, an ethnographic approach has been pursued for this study to gain new insights on *nunchi* and identity in business studies.

Recruiting *HanaEins* members for formal Interviews

One of the reasons I had no significant problems finding informants for my study was the fact that I managed to keep my ethnographic role away from them for a very long time in having been either a Korea University student or their bartender. Even though holding back my role as an ethnographer at work for so long made me really nervous and stressed at times, later on I realized that the time spent on the first stage was needed to identify the desired gatekeeper and build up close relationships with informants. In having let my informants getting to know me as one of them and not as a researcher, I attempted to take away fears and prejudices that *HanaEins* members might have had against me being a researcher. Indeed, informants later on reported that, "If I would have known from the very start that you were doing this for your study I would have felt judged" because as someone else noted, "I am afraid I cannot articulate myself well." Indeed, some informants were worried about not giving the right responses or not being good enough to be part of an academic study. Also some of them invited me to interview them at their houses and admitted that they would not have felt comfortable inviting a researcher to their home previously, however because they perceived me as one of them they overcame these feelings of discomfort. Others preferred to be interviewed in one of the VIP rooms at the German Pub because, "we miss having you there and associate you with this environment" or they felt "freer while sharing some beer" albeit being recorded. I was very lucky that my main gatekeeper, although I did not work for the pub anymore during my time conducting recorded interviews, still let me use one of the two VIP rooms at the Pub free of charge to meet and interview my informants. The location was moderately quiet, which made the recordings easier to transcribe.

An overview of the interview

This paragraph will provide an overview of the interview as a qualitative method in management and organizational studies. Neo-positivism and romanticism both represent different perceptions of the ideal interview. Interviewing is a complex social activity that calls for vigilant, concentrated and suspicious reflection. Thus, greater weight should be given to theoretical thoughts, especially as ways to contextualize the predominant focus on methodological procedure (Lindlof & Taylor, 2002a,b). This section is concerned with cultivating conscious reflection on greater epistemological, dogmatic and procedural problems, comparing neo-positivism and romanticism in magnifying the range through which these problems can be approached. Alvesson and Ashcraft in Symon & Cassell (2012) classify neo-positivism as a modified oral survey instrument through which softer forms of objective and generalizable knowledge can be discovered. Romanticism represents interviews in the form of an authentic dialogue that can draw out (inner) subjective knowledge through attempting a relationship, according to Alvesson and Ashcraft. I conducted both recorded and ethnographic (romantic) interviews, which were informal, unrecorded discussions held with workers in the pub, my German guests, my student and while working or in social settings e.g. at church, embassy and German chamber of commerce parties and of course German festivals and cultural events such as *Oktoberfest*, *Weihnachtsmarkt* at the German school (Christmas market), *Grippenspiel* at the German Church (nativity play) *Fasching* (A Carnival to scare the winter away), significant soccer games like the world cup and events organized by the German club. This approach was chosen because ethnographers bring with them to the field, as well as their literature, an assertiveness of wonder, a sincerity to the potential for the unfolding of surprises in the field (Yebema et al. 2009; Kamsteeg & Wels, 2004). Along with an ability for improvising as observational or interview opportunities demand and for being less dependent on interview schedules and closed-ended questions, and a theoretical creativity that links observations to interpretations (Humphreys, Brown and Hatch, 2003).

Researchers who practise the neo-positivist approach predictably claim to extract what is supposedly 'actually' out there by strictly following their research procedure and collecting pertinent responses, while diminishing researcher prejudice and other sources of bias. Therefore, interviews conducted in this manner tend to be carefully organized and strictly structured, with minimal justification of the study and minimal change and divergence from the protocol. The ideal data collection is an entirely visible research process, which accumulates 'undistorted' data that can be aggregated and marked by detachment and impartiality (Symon & Cassell, 2012). However, Potter and Wetherell (1987) noted that respondents may construct only artificial and restrained responses under such conditions, which is a potential weakness. Profounder understanding that derives from the fullness of context might not be achievable. As a result, meaning and sense making are complicated, and follow-up questions become essential to facilitate understanding. Thus, data become too thin and interpretation uncertain.

This study took Potter and Wetherell's (1987) critique seriously to avoid such potential weakness. Thus I did allow informants to narrate their own stories regardless whether a divergence from the protocol occurred. Interviewing in the form of a somewhat natural conversation, which at times ended up in a dialogue between the informant and the interviewer allowed greater understanding that derived from the richness of the context.

This study combined formal and informal interviews, because I believe that such an approach is more likely to gather richer insights, which is a definite strength. Dingwall (1997) claimed that the closer researchers become to their respondents, the better the possibility of capturing the self of the respondent. The romantic interviewer, who aims to grasp real human interaction, seeks to cultivate interpersonal relations founded on rapport, trust, commitment and warmth between the researcher and respondent, in a way that makes the respondent feel comfortable about talking freely and openly, which builds a further strength, as observed in the interviewing process of my research. Miller and Glasser (1997) supported Dingwall's (1997) assertion in describing the general ambitions of romantic interviews, which according to them is the accomplishment of 'deeper, fuller conceptualizations of those aspects of our subjects' lives we are most interested in understanding' (p.103). Holloway and Jefferson (2000) claimed that information is most likely to be conveyed in romantic interviews. They take this further in stating that interviewers rely on respondents' narrations about their lives as a way to understand them, because 'story-telling stays closer to actual life-events than methods that elicit explanations' (Holloway & Jefferson, 2000:p.32).

Formal interviews were conducted in the form of a dialogue, with the opening question asking to compare German national identity to Korean national identity, and were followed by not a priori sequence of questions. Although all informants were interviewed about the same themes I altered the sequence of questions to achieve the feeling of a somewhat natural conversation opposed to sticking to a question and answer feeling.

Holstein and Gubrium (2003, 1997) and Ellis et al. (1997) noted that ethnographers take seriously the possibility that interviewees may be guided by social appropriateness, anticipating what the researcher wants to hear or cultural norms for desired terms. However, the scholars mentioned above believe that establishing close relationships with respondents, who become participants rather than subjects, can overcome this potential problem. In this study, this was the case due to the time spent during the first and second stage of fieldwork as discussed earlier, therefore the timing of interviews and established relationship between the interviewer and informants contributed towards diminishing desirable answers, guided by social appropriateness. Holstein and Gubrium (1997) described this transformation from respondent to participant caused by the researcher as 'a repository of opinions and reasons or a wellspring of emotions [turning] into a productive source of knowledge' (Holstein & Gubrium, 1997:p.121). Hence, the researcher and the interviewee-transformed interviewee into a participant collaborate in 'co-construction of knowledge' (Holstein & Gubrium, 2003:p.19).

This strength is seen in my study, as my interviewees were transformed into participants. The informants with whom I regularly spoke consisted of my guests, team members, my student and many individuals from the German community e.g. family members of someone working for a German MNC, who I approached in the earlier stated locations, these people were selected to include as wide as possible a range of age and gender. The duration of my formal and informal interviews varied significantly. Some informal interviews went on for hours, in that case it was slightly difficult to document every single detail, however I tried to summarise them as detailed as possible afterwards if; the informant felt uncomfortable with me taking notes at the same time or if such action prevented the flow of information exchanged in our dialogue. The formal, recorded interviews lasted between roughly one hour and just over two hours, with more interviews tending towards the two-hour duration. In general interviews were not interrupted, however occasionally the waiter entered the room to check if everything was ok. Due to the fact that the first couple of interviewees felt uncomfortable being confronted with singing a consent form at the beginning of the interview, I decided to ask at the beginning of the recording for their permission to use and transcribe their responses for academic purposes, after they answered with a clear yes I preceded with the interview. For further details regarding the number of interviews conducted and demographic information see Table I and Table II.

Table I: Formal HanaEins Interviews

Status	Gender	Nationality	Character Group	Industry	App. Age	Informal Follow-up Interview
Owner	Male	German	1	Intl. Trade	55	Yes
Senior Manager	Female	Korean	3	Insurance	39	Yes
Junior Manager	Female	German	2	Engineering	29	Yes
Manager	Female	German	2	Law	53	No
Junior Manager	Female	German	2	Hospitality	27	Yes
Junior Manager	Female	German	1	Automotive	28	No
Manager	Male	German	2	Electronics	40	No
Senior Manager	Male	German	1	Transport	53	No
Manager	Female	German	2	Transport	52	No
Senior Manager	Male	German	1	Electronics	51	No
Senior Manager	Male	German	1	Consulting	48	No
Manager	Male	German	1	Automotive	39	No
Manager	Female	German	2	Hospitality	29	No
Junior Manager	Female	German	1	Pharmacutical	24	No
Junior Manager	Female	German	1	Aviation	30	No
Intern	Female	German	2	Transport	18	Yes
Manager	Male	German	1	Consulting	36	No
Manager	Male	German	1	Intl. Trade	30	No
Senior Manager	Male	German	1	Automotive	52	No
Senior Manager	Female	German	1	Aviation	45	No
Junior Manager	Female	Korean	3	Pharmacutical	28	Yes
Staff	Male	Korean	3	Aviation	33	Yes
Staff	Male	Korean	3	Insurance	34	No
Owner	Female	Korean	3	Hospitality	56	No
Staff	Female	German	2	Education	31	No
Manager	Male	German	2	Media	34	Yes
Staff	Male	Korea	3	Intl. Trade	28	No

Table II: Most significant informal HanaEins Interviews

Status	Gender	Nation-ality	Character Group	Affiliation	App. Age	Informal Follow-up Interview
Intl. manager Spouse	Female	German	2	Stammtisch, German Club	48	No
Intl. manager Spouse	Female	German	2	Stammtisch, German Club, Church	46	No
Senior Manager	Male	German	1	Stammtisch, Chamber of Commerce	45	No
Staff	Female	German	1	German Pub	23	No
Intern	Female	Korean	3	German MNC	19	No
Senior Manager	Male	Korean	3	Guest at German Pub	40	Yes
Teacher	Male	Korean	3	Guest at German Pub	32	No
Intl. manager Spouse	Female	Korean	3	Stammtisch, German Club	38	Yes
Senior Manager	Female	German	1	Chamber of Commerce, German Club, Stammtisch, Church	48	No
Intl. manager Spouse	Female		3	German School, Guest at German Pub	35	Yes
Intl. manager Spouse	Female		3	German School, Guest at German Pub, Church	30	Yes
PR	Female		3	German Embassy, Guest at German Pub	28	Yes
Bureaucract	Female		3	German Embassy, Guest at German Pub	36	No
Staff	Male		3	German Pub	24	No
Diplomat	Female		1	German Embassy	65	No
Staff	Female		3	German School	33	Yes
Senior Manager	Male		3	Goethe Institut student, Guest at German Pub	43	Yes

Status	Gender	Nation-ality	Character Group	Affiliation	App. Age	Informal Follow-up Interview
Manager	Male		3	Goethe Institut student, Guest at German Pub	41	Yes
Senior Manager	Male		1	Guest at German Pub, Stammtisch	33	No
Intl. manager Spouse	Female		3	Church	61	No
Staff	Male		3	German Pub	28	Yes
Student	Female		3	Goethe Institut, Guest at German Pub	34	Yes
Staff	Female		3	German MNC	29	No
Staff	Male		3	German MNC	31	No
Intl. manager Spouse	Female		2	German Club, Guest at German Pub	53	Yes
Senior manager	Male		1	Guest at German Pub, Stammtisch, Chamber of Commerce	55	Yes
Intl. manager Spouse	Male		3	Guest at German Pub	32	Yes
Intern	Male		2	GermanMNC	21	No
Intl. manager Spouse	Female		3	Church	56	No
Manager	Male		1	Guest at German Pub	48	No
Teacher	Female		1	German School, Guest at German Pub, German club	38	No

Body language

Ethnography included the study of body language and people's use of space and their relationship to the researched phenomenon (Birdwhistell, 2010). Body language delivered a view into unconscious thoughts and provided a means for triangulation of verbal data. Further, I was more confident about the accuracy of information provided by a subject if the *HanaEins* member's body language was congruent with his or her words. People's use of space is unobtrusive and it is usually difficult for the subject to mislead the observer deliberately, in contrast to neo-positivist interviews, because this type of research does not require the cooperation of the subject. I collected data in a natural setting and thus tried to avoid the modification of responses. The outsider–insider perspective allowed me to make the familiar strange and to recontextualize the use of *nunchi* as an aspect of performing Korean identity in a multi-ethnic context, and how Koreans and Germans express their identities strategically in business.

Content analysis of related material

The following section discusses content analysis, which is an extensively used qualitative research method (Stemler, 2001). Content analysis in this study took place in the form of interpretive content analysis of vernacular texts and popular literature, such as websites and forums, suggested by *HanaEins* members to gather an overview of German and Korean perceptions of practices related to *nunchi*, identity and the wider meaning of their identity contexts. Rather than being a single method, recent applications of content analysis display three different approaches: conventional, directed or summative. All three are used to interpret meaning from the pre-existing text data; consequently, they follow a naturalistic paradigm. The major differences among the approaches are coding schemes, origins of codes and threats of trustworthiness (Hsieh & Shannon, 2005).

Interpretive methodologies offer conceptual grounds for understanding why research, writing, and reading should be interwoven. Nowadays it is rather usual to think about a double hermeneutic (Giddens, 1984; Jackson, 2006): that researchers interpret actors' interpretations (see also Geertz, 1973), an idea of both phenomenology and hermeneutics. Drawing on scholarly studies, we are to explain a third interpretive moment. Reader-response theory (e.g., Iser, 1989) stresses that textual meaning is delivered not only through the writer's intent or the elements of writing (e.g. metaphor, word choice, rhythm), but it also rests on the previous knowledge, from involvement and positioning in the world, that readers bring to their reading of literature. In this way the interpretative act of reading connects phenomenology to hermeneutics (Yanow, 2009).

However, one main limitation of content analysis is that it is ineffective for testing casual relationships between variables. Researchers and their audiences must resist the temptation to infer such relationships. This is particularly true when researchers forthrightly present the proportion or frequency with which a theme or pattern is observed. This kind of information is appropriate to indicate the magnitude of certain responses; however, it is not appropriate to attach cause to these presentations. A further weakness of content analysis may be that it is limited to examining already recorded information. Although these messages may be oral, written, graphic or videotaped, they must be already recorded in some manner to be analysed.

The most significant advantage of content analysis is that it can be virtually unobtrusive (Webb et al., 1981). Content analysis, although useful when analyzing interview data, may also be used non-reactively: no one needs to be interviewed, no one needs to fill in questionnaires and no one needs to enter a laboratory. Newspaper accounts, public addresses, libraries, archives and similar sources allow researchers to conduct analytic studies. An additional advantage is that it is cost effective. Generally, the materials necessary for conducting content analysis are easily and cheaply accessible. A further advantage is that it provides the opportunity to study processes that occur over long periods or that may reflect trends in society (Babbie, 1998). Qualitative methods literature, occasionally differentiate among several types of triangulation, including several methods of retrieving data. This study made use of observation, participation, interviews and content analysis in the form of documents e.g. diary entries and literature. Reading documents offers ethnographers the chance to find accounts of how researcher handled inconsistent or contradictory findings deriving from triangulation of observation, participation, interviews and content analysis. As Becker (1998:44) contends, simplicity should be 'an empirical finding rather than a theoretical commitment' (see also Law, 2004, on not eradicating the complexity of everyday life).

In this study I engaged in an interpretive reading process of the earlier mentioned texts to analyse discourses relating to *nunchi*, Korean and German identity in order to obtain an understanding of how Germans and Koreans themselves think and represent practices related to *nunchi*, identity and the wider meanings of their identity contexts. My interpretative content analysis of vernacular texts and popular literature does not imply that what I interpreted from them is what the original authors wanted to convey or what their audiences make of it. However, my analysis attempts to gain a wider expertise on how, meanings, values, metaphors, perceptions and experience of *nunchi* and Korean and German identity are understood from a more applied point of view.

Due to the abundance of available sources, my selection has been the popularity of sources as indicated by *HanaEins* members. Thus my selection predominantly focused on popular sources, such as *Das deutsch-koreanische Forum* (http://www.meet-korea.de), the German Club Seoul, (http://deutscherclubseoul.org) and it's newsletter and events such as Kulturcafe (Culture café), *Willkommen in Seoul* (http://www.willkommeninseoul.com), The German School Seoul (http://www.dsseoul.org), the Korean-German Chamber of Commerce and Industry (http://korea.ahk.de) and the Goethe institute (https://www.goethe.de/ins/kr/de/). The analysis predominantly focused on *nunchi*, German and Korean identity representations, the wider context of Koreanness and Germanness and its affect on business as well as descriptions of transnational experiences by *HanaEins* members.

In sum the content analysis, focussed on helping the ethnographer to evaluate the importance of symbols of identity and self-representation, in establishing patterns in themes discussed amongst *HanaEins* members and furthermore contributed towards an understanding of contemporary subjects related to the research

The research process

The following section introduces the process how this research was conducted. Surprises and many unexpected situations were part of this process, which demand a lot of strength and mindful handling. Keeping in mind that I am a researcher yet at the same time work as both an ethnographer and in various job roles I concede that conducting ethnographic research inevitable entails a lot of stress and even anxiety as well as excitement and wonder (Fetterman, 2009; Law, 1994). I dealt with many questions such as, where I will end up and how I will make it work, therefore I have adopted an opportunistic approach from the very beginning, which allowed me to explore and make the most out of given situations, while constantly negotiating what is theoretically desirable and practically feasible (Buchanan, Boddy, & McCalman, 1988).

Nevertheless, I do by no means imply that having a clear research design is not needed, however I would like to advocate future researchers to be open minded to not miss the potential the field might have to offer. "Rather than depending on our tools, we should rely on the way that the process unfolds; rather than thinking of drawing up plans, we should learn to make the most of what is implied by the situation and whatever promise is held out by its evolutions" (Jullien, 2004 pp. 16-17). One specific example was the arrangement of accommodation post relocation to Korea, it was not until after I gathered an overview of the targeted population that I signed a permanent tenancy agreement and left my temporary accommodation, having made such decision helped me to rely on the way the research process unfolded.

The pilot study

In order to study the ways in which *nunchi* and identity are practised within German MNCs in South Korea, I conducted an ethnographic study focusing on *HanaEins*, which consists of several German MNCs and the people who work and manage them as well as the German pub.

The data upon which this book is grounded comprises of a pilot study conducted between September 2012 and September 2013 followed by an extended period of fieldwork, from February 2014 until March 2015 in South Korea, followed by a follow up interview period from July 2015 until November 2015 in Germany. This research is thus the result of 2.5 years cumulative fieldwork not in just one group or place, but in and around a network of identity ties linked to symbols of Korean and German identity, in particular *nunchi*. The pilot study involved formal and informal interviews, a ten-day work placement at a Korean company in the UK and practicing Korean identity specific observation and shadowing techniques.

The following reflective section introduces the pilot research and how it affected my choice of methods used for the fieldwork component of this volume. There seems to be a general agreement amongst scholars that conducting a pilot study is significant to not only test selected interview questions, but also to test if the chosen research methods are appropriate (Bryman & Bell, 2011; Buchanan & Bryman, 2009).

Even though most pilot studies concern themselves with the applicability of interviews and questionnaires, I argue that conducting a pilot study in my research was important to carrying out fieldwork. Whilst carrying out my pilot study the impact on the fieldwork that followed did not become visible immediately, however I was very curious how I would act and feel as an ethnographer at work. It was not a foreseeable pathway that was set out clearly. However I perceived that period, commencing with the pilot study until finally relocating to the field as a journey, which was filled with excitement and uncertainty and it was guided by my internal instincts how practical steps may be taken in applied situations. I describe this as the ethnographic 'mode', which I think started approximately around the time when I started dating a Korean a long time back, that was when I developed the thirst to learn and understand symbols of identity in particular *nunchi*. The pilot study did not just serve to test my research techniques, but also encouraged the attitude, which ethnographic work demands. Furthermore it assisted me in selecting the appropriate methods and facilitated valuable learning cycles before commencing fieldwork in Korea.

Since everyone involved in the pilot study, namely my former Korean partner who I lived with at the time and four more Koreans who we shared the premises with, as well as four couples each consisting of one Korean and one German person living elsewhere, had a perception of what *nunchi* is and how they practise it from their own perspectives. The interpretations drawn may be regarded as representations of the meanings constructed in their realities. However I asked myself how I could enable them to express the discursive meanings, which they consider as relevant. Thus "informal" interviews as defined by Fetterman (1998) were conducted as part of the pilot study. It was not until after when I read the notes taken and discussed what I understood with my partner at that time, that I realized the associated meanings of *nunchi* varied according to their assumptions in their minds and implied national character values. I also realized that interviews depended very much on the given situation, which encouraged me to question my participants more about what they expressed and what they actually wanted to express in asking how and why. It was then when I encountered the limitations that interviewing brought about and got to know the dynamics interpretation offers (Alvesson, 2011). It was not only that I realized that there is a lot of information deliberately being kept away from me but also how they would alter the way they presented information and therefore themselves due to perceiving me as a researcher. Sooner or later I realized that information could only be used to draw conclusions if viewed and made sense of in a specific identity context. That was the moment I decided to conduct ethnographic fieldwork in Korea, however I had very little experience in terms of applying observational and shadowing techniques in the Korean context so I asked my pilot study participants to practice these techniques in an identity specific context with me.

In the subsequent paragraphs I outline how these techniques were practiced to customize them to a Korean identity specific context. In addition to two interviews that were conducted with bilingual German and Korean speakers to check if the translations of questions are correct, some general observation practices taken from Fetterman (1998) were redefined to a Korean identity context with my Korean participants and then practiced. A series of observation practices have been explored at different moments of time and settings such as educational settings, at the office hence at work and in public spaces such as restaurants and coffee shops. This was done in cooperation with several different practice partners, whom one at the time accompanied me to also take notes, which we exchanged and discussed proceeding each session to help me develop the required sensitivity needed for a Korean identity context. These discussions included an exchange of the factors that each of us thought influenced the observation; I was trained how to closely observe details in a "Korean way" without attracting the observed peoples' attention. Additionally we discussed the observed details, which sometimes differed a lot, even though we observed the same situation, which was insightful to understand the details that mattered in viewing it through the Korean lens; where the line might be between judgment and assumption and how we documented our research notes. One of the staggering insights was the language used in note taking, I noticed that my notes were mixed, details observed relating to emotions were documented in German, since it is the language that is closer to my heart, however other aspects were documented in English. Nevertheless, when taking notes in German I could not help processing information in German, which arguably impacted on the applied logic as German entails different linguistic values and draws upon a different perspective in terms of symbols of identity. Thus note taking as a result of observation should be considered as an identity context specific practice.

Subsequently I conducted a ten-day annual leave cover for a friend at a small Korean company located in the UK, which exclusively employed Korean staff, where I was part of the team formally and informally interviewing, participating and observing. Throughout this time period five interviews were conducted with the company's team members while working and after working hours during social gatherings, during which I indirectly and playfully addressed questions encountered, which arose through my observations. This experience allowed me to understand the hands on access negotiation approach, which included building relationships with informants, potential "gatekeepers" and the field site itself, as well as experiencing that the right timing is important for both formal and informal interviewing. Throughout this experience I found out that it is the combination of participation, observation and interviewing that allows me to make sense of unspoken discourses, taboo topics and interactions among actors, which are arguably impossible to capture only using interviewing techniques. It is also to note that the researcher as the main research instrument was more successful gathering data in growing close to his informants in acting like one of them, as opposed to a social scientist, this was aimed for in upholding positive energy and an arguably modest yet still confident self-presentation. One of the major limitations was my limited Korean language skill at the time, which I however rapidly improved in taking Korean lessons at the SOAS language centre in London. The most significant strength was the interest that people involved in my pilot study took, which on one hand motivated me and on the other hand gave me some sense of reassurance that *nunchi* is an under researched semiotic of identity, which needs to be investigated further.

In summary the pilot study was an insightful experience, which broadened my perspectives on the many ways of seeing through the ethnographic approach of being there in addition to the more traditional approach of relying on interviews only. My pilot study will not be directly included in the following empirical chapters of this book, but the material gained certainly had an impact on the ethnographic approach in the field and the resulting ethnographic chapters. While I occasionally cannot help comparing my pilot study's experiences to the latter fieldwork in Korea, I believe that the insights gained from both, contributed to my understanding of methods and to produce insights of how *nunchi* is understood in strategic presentations of self in MNCs.

The Field Research

Keeping in mind the nature of this study's approach and access possibilities, *HanaEins* Seoul was chosen as the field site. *HanaEins* is a cluster of German MNCs, which includes some of the most well known MNCs that currently operate in Korea and includes its actors, who surrender their living and working activities to it. I negotiated access to enter *HanaEins* and its' members in various forms and my role included different work descriptions e.g. intern (personal assistant), bartender, and English teacher. Therefore I became part of *HanaEins* as my role being an employee allowed me to be a researcher at the same time. Czarniawska (2007) points out that in organization research the ethnographer's role implies that, " The researcher assumes the role of a member of the organization or, alternatively, an employee becomes a researcher" (p.13).

The time period spent in the field was 14 months, which were divided up into different stages, which will be outlined in the following sections. Overall I was treated like any other *HanaEins* member, in terms of working hours and workload, however it is to mention that I was expected to work overtime without getting paid for it, due to the management's assumption that I should be very grateful that they have given me this opportunity and the needed working permit, which is very hard to obtain. Being part of the team I was always asked to join *Hweshiks* (company dinners), social gatherings, drinking sessions, karaoke, birthday parties, weddings, and even one business trip. Initially I was very careful in revealing my identity as an ethnographer, and only disclosed such role to potential gatekeepers who would either grant or deny access. I discussed my research topic with them and they knew that *HanaEins* and its members were used as an anonymous case for my research. Furthermore I explained some ethnographic writing rules to them prior to seeking written or recorded consent, following Denzin's (2000) work on writing ethnography, which postulates that even though the reader will be presented with the researcher's learning outcomes, such information is subject to nonmaleficence. In other words, the informants' and MNCs real identities will be protected when the data is presented in using pseudonyms and omitting prominent features that could expose their real identities.

In terms of language and identity context, *HanaEins*, its' members and the MNCs all had an on-going relationship with the German identity context and or Germany itself. All of the MNCs headquarters were in Germany. The prominent languages used within *HanaEins* were German and various dialects of it, English, Korean, Konglish (a mixture of Korean and English), Denglish (a mixture of German and English) and other combinations of the three. I consider myself a German native speaker, who went through the Anglo-Saxon education system since year 10 at high-school, which indicates a good command of English and I am able to engage in conversational Korean, which I acquired during my first year of my PhD programme at the SOAS language centre in London. Additionally, given the location of my hometown I spent a significant amount of time in neighbouring countries during my childhood in which German dialects are spoken and I am therefore able to understand most German dialects and able to adapt to quite a few of them. My adaptability in terms of languages and dialects came in handy in making informants more comfortable as; through linguistic skills I was able to foster trust, which gave me the chance to built up strong relationships in less time, hence getting closer to the subject under investigation.

However a Korean language barrier still existed, which on the contrary offered a somewhat fresh perceptive to the field, while I was still being able to see their everyday activities through their eyes. Having stayed and worked in Korea previously on a short stay assignment meant that I was familiar with Seoul, however it was not too ordinary when I started my fieldwork. Thus from the personal embeddedness perspective (Bell, 1999), within the context of *HanaEins* members in Seoul, I attempted to maintain sensitivity and interdependency while investigating my informants' realities, bearing in mind a certain familiarity.

Getting in, Getting on, Getting out

The following section concerns itself with the arguably three stages of getting in, getting on and getting out (Buchanan et al. 1988). Even though I consider the days spent on my pilot study to be the first step taken, the ethnographic investigation commences with my relocation to South Korea.

The field site of this project was situated in South Korea, especially in Seoul and its surrounding metropolitan area. These locations have been chosen because they are well known for having a large percentage of international German managers and employees (http://www.deutscherclubseoul.org) and I am personally familiar with these places, which made it easier and more efficient to conduct data collection.

The major target group of participants in Korea were domestic and transnational German and Korean MNC managers and employees, especially German expatriates in Seoul and returning overseas Korean expatriates who used to work in Germany and are now back in South Korea. Samples were drawn from *HanaEins* members using a matched samples technique—a method advocated by cross-border research methodologists (Vijver & Leung, 1997) in which 'the samples of cultural groups to be compared are made as similar as possible in their demographic characteristics' (p.30) otherwise, it might be difficult to conclude whether differences in results are due to differences in the interpretations of symbols of identity or other demographic differences. Therefore, international managers and employees working in German MNCs were chosen for this study. In order to find the participants for this study, I used personal contacts in several institutions. The German club in Seoul offered the opportunity to meet, observe domestic and transnational German and Korean managers who are involved in doing business with both countries, it also presented itself as a an opportunity to negotiate access:

> Today the German Club Seoul counts over 140 members. These are
> usually family memberships and therefore the actual member count
> is more than double as high. More and more Germans and German-
> speaking people are coming—mostly because of business reasons—
> to Seoul. In most cases only for a limited time.
>
> (www.deutscherclubseoul.org)

Further institutions in which informants were met and observed in the getting in stage are the *Deutsche Schule* Seoul International (German international school Seoul*), Deutsch-Koreanische Industrie- und Handelskammer (DKIHK)* (German chamber of commerce), *Evangelische Gemeinde deutscher Sprache* in Korea (Lutheran church using German language in Korea) (http://www.seoul.diplo.de).

Attending regular church services, club meetings, speech nights and other events organised by the above listed institutions was a continuing process of negotiating access (Buchanan et al. 1988) and to meet and skillfully establish as well as maintain good relationships with potential gatekeepers, who had the authority to grant or deny access in order to get the chance of participation in a company (Brewer 2000). I was able to understand the bigger picture of my targeted population in observing, meeting but most importantly living amongst them in the same neighborhood. Not revealing my identity, as a researcher was possible at that stage because a visiting studentship at Korea University was obtained before the move, which also allowed me to take an intensive Korean language course during my first months in Seoul. Therefore I assume that my target population did not have any suspicion of me being an ethnographer at work.

Simultaneously, I attempted to retain a sense of scientific detachment, observing while participating in terms of becoming part of *HanaEins* or as Nicolini (2009) phrases it, playing off the interplay between proximity and distance, 'zooming in ' and 'zooming out'. Thus the first part of my study took place over a five-month period, intensive observing of the targeted population and field site. Trust had to be established before intensive research work on the ground was able to begin. The initial contact, the contact person, who helped me to become part of the population, and the nature of first meetings were all very important, but difficult to control. The success of the 'way in' depended on the first impression I made and the time (five months) that I took to establish social contact with decision-makers, who were able to facilitate or block access to the research setting.

Having made use of myself as the basic research instrument as suggested by Moeran (2006), through my social skills, honest self-presentation and genuine interest was sufficient to develop new social relationships that led to mutually beneficial partnerships and opportunities of research. Towards the end of the first stage approximately half way through the last month of it I had identified a list of gatekeepers that I believed had the actual power, curiosity and potential interest in granting further access. I then wrote a list prioritising who I would like to be my main gatekeeper and why he should help me and what I could offer him in return as suggested by Brewer (2000). I then did not leave it to serendipity and approached him in person at one of the attended events to arrange a meeting to talk about a personal matter. I had prepared a one-page document explaining my project and how we could be beneficial to each other, however this negotiation process requested him to be responsible for organising a legal working permit. After ensuring the anonymity of my informants, he agreed to grant full access across the organisation and the rights to interview, observe, and participate as well as taking notes during working hours. Nevertheless we also disclosed that my research is for academic purposes and that the organisation will not influence the data presentation of this work. Nevertheless, him signing the consent document was just the beginning of an on-going negotiation throughout all stages, as my role and the relationship in the field were subject to continuous maintenance, such idea was also support by (Atkinson et al. 2001).

This negotiation process fruitfully resulted in a five-month period of which I spent working as an assistant to the German manager (gatekeeper) and his Korean wife in the company (they also owned the German pub), which I worked at as the bar manager and contact person for international guests, including my future informants. The pub just opened and I was part of the team from the very first day, so it was a guaranteed chance to meet my informants one after another in a social setting, as it was the only German-owned German-run authentic place in all of Seoul.

My intention was to go beyond the limitation of idealised accounts presented to the researcher as an outsider; I also wanted to go beyond the static perspective gained from studying organisational settings only at particular points in time. In my research on *nunchi* in the context of identity and transnationalism, looking at *nunchi* as an aspect of performing Korean identity in a multi-ethnic context, and looking at the ways in which Koreans and Germans express their identities strategically in business, it was important to get an initial overview of the site. An additional advantage gained from having met my informants in the role of being their German speaking bartender and person to turn to after work to digest their day or to take Korean clients, family and colleagues to, was the insight the role as the bartender provided into the border between frontstage and backstage situations. I got to know the difference between meetings that were accessible to researchers and those regarded as secretive.

My boss was very supportive of my fieldwork as well as protecting my identity as a researcher opposed to being a bartender. He made the possibility available to talk to informants freely and at any given time while being on duty. Once an opportunity presented itself where an informant talked a lot my boss usually said, "why don't you sit down have something to eat and talk", which I did most of the time. Whenever German businesspeople visited the venue, which was almost everyday I was ready to extract as much information as possible in a caring way, with the management's support. My boss informed the other employees that it was part of my job description to 'entertain' German guests, in order to prevent suspicion. In order to take notes without attracting my workmates attention my boss permitted me to take notes on my phone. Using a smart phone during working hours is common practise in Korea and therefore did not cause and suspicion. However, the workers on the team and regular informants (guests) were informed after four months and three weeks, once I had sufficient grasp of arising patterns and symbols of the population, to do so without causing misunderstandings.

Another great advantage of conducting research at the German pub was the opportunity to listen to several versions of the same stories. It occurred to me quite frequently that a businessperson's spouse, whom with a good relationship, arguably friendship had been established in the first stage of the ethnographic research through the institutions mentioned early, came in to talk to me while enjoying a cup of coffee and the pub's signature apple cake, which was described as the "most authentic German cake in Seoul" and "reason to visit the pub". These spouses were mainly female with only one exception being male, assuming the influence a wife can have on her husband, this presented itself as an opportunity to me to create lots of minor gatekeepers, who would probably have a higher success rate of persuading their husbands to grant me further access into their worlds in the form of formal interviews, shadowing etc. Indeed, having invested hours and hours of listening and entertaining international managers' spouses, who most of the time portrayed heroic stories narrated by their husbands the night before from completely different angles, was part of the renegotiation process as pointed out by Brewer (2000) and allowed one way of chain sampling (Heckarthon, 1997). Thus this experience was not just invaluable in terms of gaining insights into constructed realities expressed through story telling however it also confirmed the initial hope that maintaining these spouse relationships will have a positive affect on gaining further access when asking their husbands for research opportunities.

The third interval consisted of a four- month period, shadowing and formally interviewing managers and their wives working in and managing German MNCs whom I had observed and informally interviewed on a regular basis during my time, which I spent participating and observing at the German Pub. Some of them admitted that it was only through the established relationship and trust between myself and them and myself and other family members that they were willing to grant me access. One of them renounced, " you have always been there for us, even late at night and lent me your ears so if I can help you I will" another one said, " if you would have asked me six months ago when we met at the Chamber meeting I would have said no, but now that I know you I will take you along." Being regarded not as a student from Korea University anymore, but rather as part of *HanaEins*, gave me recognition within *HanaEins* and between various actors linked to identity and *nunchi*. I asked 27 of my informants, the ones I spoke to (informally interviewed) the most on a regular basis to commit to formal (recorded) interviews and for the chance to shadow them at work. All of them agreed to the interview, only 6 had the chance to let me follow them around within the MNC's premises and 4 more let me accompany them to external meetings outside the premises. Reflexivity is an essential element in ethnographic research. Ethnographers must be able to monitor their personal positions, reactions and comportment as part of the research procedure (Hammersley & Atkinson, 1994). I lived in *Yongsan*, next to *Hanam-dong* and *Gangnam* where most of the 'German life', the German school, embassy, Chamber of commerce, church, the pub and most German MNCs and their employees' homes are located and was therefore able to observe how the population interacted with its surroundings at all times. The ethnographic self will be discussed in a separate section.

Alongside these three periods I interviewed an international German manager, who was sent to Korea for a short assignment of eight months. I met her fortnightly for formal interviews at the same time I was granted access to read her personal diary entries about her time living and working in Korea, once she had completed her eight-month assignment. Throughout the entire time, I spent my days 'off', days on which I was not officially working at the company, interviewing or shadowing people at a significant business complex in *Gangnam*, in which several German MNCs offices are located. I always presented myself in a professional manner, wearing business outfits to blend in. After several visits, a German high-end executive of a German MNC approached me and asked me about my endeavours. Without any hesitation I just assured him that I like sitting in the lobby's café, since it served real *Laugenbrezeln und Cappuccino* (type of baked bread and Italian coffee topped up with milk foam, sprinkled with chocolate powder). It is to note that most Korean cafes do not distinguish between *cappuccino* and *café latte*, and use cinnamon powder instead of chocolate powder. He smiled and we bonded instantly over the shared stance that cappuccino needs to be served with chocolate powder instead of cinnamon. After this encounter he asked me to teach him English twice a week, in doing so I gathered access to mingle around the office for a couple of hours pre and post class, observing the team and asking questions with his consent, following the same rules as agreed upon with my main gatekeeper.

Narrative account presentation

My ethnographic research is presented as a narrative account, with detailed empirical data as the support for my interpretations. I followed accepted ethnographic practices, entailing detailed field notes, with a focus on *nunchi* and identity. I made field notes after each working day and at any other possible time. My field notes were written in the form of diary entries and similar to the pilot study at times in German and at times in English, depending on the documented themes. They did not follow a specific structure, however I tried to document informal interviews, chats, overheard conversations, comments, jokes, remarks about the setting, clothing, mannerism, the atmosphere of situations and other aspects relating to *nunchi* and identity.

Writing field notes regularly was a very useful practice, I read over them whenever I had spare time e.g. on the bus or subway and before falling asleep, in that way I was able to guide future conversations in trying to retrieve more information about themes that I perceived as relevant in my existing field notes. I also included my own feelings in my fieldwork or at times when reading over them again, which personally helped me to improve my methods e.g. if a certain theme made me angry and it was brought up in a later recorded interview I was able to regulate my emotions in order to not disturb my interviewee. A substantial part of my field notes also concern itself with my reflections based upon living in Seoul, with and among *HanaEins* members.

The Ethnographic Self

It is suggested that ethnography as part of the family of qualitative research methods is undeniably strongly influenced by the ethnographer's own as well as national identity, cultural imprints, political values and life experiences (Kamata, 1983; Coffey, 1999; Bell, 1999). As Chapman, Gajewska-De Mattos and Antoniou (in Marschan- Piekkari & Welch 2004) pointed out, "who and what you are as an anthropologist, matters to what you are readily able to discover and …understand" in my study access opportunities and understanding the subject matter have been heavily influenced "by age, by ethnicity and nationality, by sex – by the invisible package that is an individual" (p.292). My research has been affected by arguably all of the above mentioned factors, although I had no trouble understanding English and German the fact that Korean is, however guided by age and gender similar to German, was a limitation, because first of all I am not fluent and second of all I confused the use of honorifics a lot, which has a tremendous impact on how one is perceived.

I realised how crucial this limitation was. As I wrote in one of my field notes:

She totally misunderstood; I never intended to be rude or disrespectful. I wish she could hear her Konglish sometimes. But I never thought she so naïve and does not know that I understood what she said to me – hmmm maybe she wanted me to understand.

Aigo shibla chincha ke sekinen, we na hante bammal jegihesso! (Fuck really you son of a dog, why are you speaking informal Korean to me!).

There were also interesting implications regarding the ethnographic self-being transnational yet possessing German nationality. For myself, being German was a prerequisite to become part of *HanaEins* and in gaining access to the filed site on which this research is based. Being a 26 year old, arguably handsome German man gave me certain chances a woman being 26 and German would not have had.

Identifying as transnational myself, gave me insights into the wider contexts, in terms of language, cultural and political awareness. My age and personal motivations and support from two families who live near and in Seoul gave me the will-power and strength to work long hours in the field. Even though Chapman, Gajewska-De Mattos and Antoniou argue that "you cannot be what you are not" (p.294), I argue that the ethnographic self may be altered to some degree to influence the 'going native' stage. I have taken the advice to grow close to and participate in the native identities, namely Korean and German seriously. Several decisions in terms of self-presentation were made, concerning my appearance and dietary requirements in order to fit in better, such alterations were identified in the pilot study and in the unfolding of the research process. Therefore I discontinued my vegetarian diet, albeit having been a vegetarian for 14 years prior to fieldwork since vegetarianism is a relatively new concept in Korea which is often frowned upon and may lead to exclusion, got specific moles removed, which carried negative meanings in Korean folk religion, started wearing huge spectacles and even applied BB cream, to cater to Korean beauty standards, which regardless of gender carry high importance in Korea.

I wrote in one of my field notes taken during a conversation with an ethnically half Korean half German girl who was born and raised in Germany but recently returned from an internship conducted at a German MNC in *Yongin*, Korea:

> *Omgosh let me tell you, they are so weird, if you don't eat meat they will treat you like some social outcast like there is actually something wrong with you. That's why no one asked me to have lunch with them or join them after work, it's the same with drinking especially soju – and you know me I don't drink, smoke or eat meat. Oh and yeah they have an obsession with small, white faces with preferably no freckles or if only in the right places, sigh. Can you believe that the HR lady told me that I must be bossy just because I have high cheekbones and bla bla they actually believe in all of this. So here is the run down, you better buy a pair of Adidas or New Balance sneakers a North Face jacket, skinny jeans and huge glasses to make your head look even smaller – they love that. Ah and before I forget always shave, and take care of your skin they told Axel he looked dirty because he had a 3 day beard. And last but not least you have to get rid off your beloved old Nokia, cause if you don't have a Samsung or an IPhone with Kakaotalk on it you are perceived backwards and poor and no one can chat to you cause what would they do without Kakao!*

In taking that advice and having changed my ethnographic self to some degree, I managed to avoid learning the hard way of what it means to go native in some aspects. However, I alternated my attire according to predicted situations e.g. contact lenses were worn and BB cream was not applied in formal interviews with German informants as some found my glasses *"ulkig"* (funny) and furthermore noted that "there lives a Korean and a German in me." Therefore, interactions with the filed site and *HanaEins* members are represented and constructed through the ethnographic self's perception, experiences and emotions and how I was perceived.

Thus my own position in the field and as part of *HanaEins* and its' members influenced the creation of this study (Coffey, 1999). Therefore I attempted to continuously uphold the importance of my own, the ethnographic self's reflexive perspective. Hence, I decided to present the empirical chapters of this study as a narrative account with detailed empirical data as the support for my interpretations. Simultaneously, while the ethnographic self has undeniably influenced the insights of this study, the nature of the study, its' methodology and research methods used affected me as well in terms of understanding and my well-being, which might affect the interpretations and conclusions drawn (Coffey, 1999; Lofland & Lofland, 2006). In sum, fieldwork should therefore be recognized as personal and work associated with the ethnographer's own emotions and identity (Bell, 1999; Coffey, 1999; Lofland & Lofland, 2006).

Ethical Considerations

Diener and Crandall (1978) describe research ethics that should be taken into account. According to Diener and Crandall, such considerations should concern themselves with whether there is a risk of participants getting harmed, invasion of privacy and if consent is sought. Additionally, there are other ethical considerations e.g. maintaing mutual trust (Bryman & Bell, 2011).

In conducting my research, I have followed standard ethical practice, as stated by the Association of Social Anthropologists, in terms of considering informants' privacy (ASA, 1999). For confidentiality reasons, some details of the MNCs' locations and operations have been changed. Both the MNC and its employees remain anonymous. When names have been used, they are pseudonyms to protect the real identities. Moreover, additionally to making sure that indispensible research ethics are met, it is to note that not all ethical issues can be met in this research, therefore implicit engagement, regarding ethical choices should be considered (Bell & Wray-Bliss, 2009). Given the nature of the methods used, the research process was subject to consistent change, choices made in terms of ethics had to be reassessed throughout the research process.

The following paragraph discusses the main ethical challenge encountered in this research project. Firstly, although anonymity is considered very important and pseudonyms are given to *HanaEins* members, companies and informants respectively, with attention to detail it might still be possible to identify some of them for people who are familiar with German MNCs and Seoul.

Secondly, even though a consent form was signed by the main gatekeeper and by informants (recorded or signed) before formal interviews were conducted it is close to impossible to obtain overall informed consent when working as a business ethnographer. Thus informal interviews, observational and participative data presented in this book are not regarded as confidential among *HanaEins* members. Major informants, about whom I have written a lot in my field notes and were informally but not necessary formally interviewed, with whom I established good relationships, were informed towards the end of my fieldwork period. Duty of care was taken at all times for the safety of my informants, and once they were informed all of them were given the opportunity to withdraw their contribution. Close to all of them were supportive and even offered to volunteer providing follow up data if need, in fact some of them were worried to "loose me" as a friend after my fieldwork had ended. Therefore an abrupt exist strategy was not taken as some informants, albeit by far not all expressed the wish to stay in touch, thus I did not delete my Kakaotalk account. Much to my surprise I have received regular messages enquiring how I am and how I am getting on back in the UK and if my work has been completed yet. Furthermore, I have been informed by several MNCs in which I carried out fieldwork that *HanaEins* is not the same without me and that I am welcome to come back any time.

In sum, I tried to follow the standard ethical practice as stated by the Association of Social Anthropologists as much as I could; however Bauman's (1993) understanding has also been taken into consideration. Bauman points out that although ethical standards are guided by set codes and rules, getting to know one's own heart and being responsible towards others is a further representation of ethics. I often asked myself the question "would I mind if someone did this to me" to seek ethical answers. Thus, reflexive answers regarding ethical concerns should be considered throughout the research process.

Leaving the field: Tackling analysis and interpretation

Leaving the field has been depicted in many ways encompassing hardships and negative emotions; some scholars even compare it to a break up (Crang and Cook, 2007). The intensity of such depictions underline the depth of how much of themselves ethnographers invest into fieldwork, which becomes apparent throughout the research process but especially when leaving the field site. Moving on to the next step may entail moving, thus packing up and giving away some of one's personal belongings as well as leaving the world and home one has created during the time being in the field (Coffey, 1999). In my case all of these predictions occurred to some degree.

I realised how deeply involved I was in the field and how much it affected me emotionally, as I wrote in my field notes before leaving Korea:

> *My entire life fits in that suitcase, seven diaries, my voice recorder, a couple of USB sticks my mind and heart is full with data and memories and there is no soju left in Seoul kkk … just like that I am leaving in less then 24 hours, it feels surreal – but I would do it again!*

Once I was back in Europe I noticed that many things regarding my own behaviour had changed, I kept bowing to people and handed them banknotes with two hands and my mum repetitively said "eat slowly, no one will steal it from you." During the first weeks back I had to reorganise my life and myself to feel that "I was fine": establishing a regular sleeping pattern again, being able to express myself the way that I was used to without taking into consideration that I have to speak slowly and clearly, using easy vocabulary in order to be understood and no more super spontaneous *Hweshiks* (social and or company gathering). One of the most prevalent insights gathered from moving back on top of that actors acculturate to locations was that symbols of identity such as *nunchi* have an affect on how one perceives others. Such impact became apparent when processing information and when communicating to others as I unconsciously guided my actions and words spoken according to the *nunchi* rules present in the given identity context. After my follow up interview period I moved back on campus to be able to be in close proximity to my supervisor and the library. The distance away from Korea, Germany and *HanaEins* and its members also represents a distance away from the overall fieldwork stage and therefore presented itself as a good opportunity to start the reflexive cycles of analysing and interpreting my fieldwork data. Having left the field for good meant I was able to gain a bird's perspective of what I had experienced.

Analysing and interpreting was a continuous process while conducting fieldwork and ultimately affected the research design and questions asked. Nevertheless, the final analysing and interpretation process was a lot more organised and systematic. The analysis was divided up in two components. Firstly, the analysis of the data gathered in the field, fieldnotes, diary entries, and transcriptions of interviews. The second part was the reading of vernacular and popular texts and literature regarding Korean and German identity to gain a better understanding of the contexts e.g. a summary on Korean folk religion and shamanism was written to understand certain behaviours, which are controlled by such belief systems for example the meanings of facial moles, bone structure and their impact on allocated personalities and HR practises. How the data was analysed and interpreted will be explained in a subsequent section.

Analysis of data gathered in the field

The analysing and interpreting process was an on-going part that continuously occurred during the research process, as pointed out by Humphreys & Watson (2009), which requires practice in order to produce an ethnography (Ybema et al., 2009). Therefore, preliminary analysis of observations, participation and fieldnotes was conducted while still being in the field. Observing *HanaEins* members, writing fieldnotes and reading them was the first stage, which entailed analysing some of the data and also contributed to shape my research. My fieldnotes have been of great help to reflect upon and analyse the ethnographic self and the way in which I constructed and presented the realities present in the field.

Furthermore, fieldnotes have been an invaluable source of input at the time of conducting fieldwork in Korea and rendered an indirect supply of motivation for deeper analysis and interpretation. Indeed, the production of fieldnotes and revising them has been a major stepping-stone to make sense of what I had previously researched and what I experienced in the field. That was the beginning of a consistent engagement in form of interaction between my fieldnotes and the theory chosen for this study. Once the interview transcriptions were completed, the analysis was conducted without any support of electronic software, this approach was chosen after having discussed it with my supervisor.

The following paragraph discusses how the interviews were analysed and interpreted, which did not occur in a chronological order. The first reading cycle included reading all interviews, followed by the second cycle in which broad patterns and themes were identified and colour-coded. This cycle of analysing followed thematic analysis and interpretation. In reading each interview transcript and linking related fieldnotes to them, I established patterns, which evolved from the thematic interpretation (McAuley, 2004; Thompson, Locander, & Pollio, 1990). Themes discussed in this research have been identified, in detecting repetitive story telling in the transcripts, which were also pertinent in my fieldnotes and mirrored in my participation and lived experiences. It was a combination of spoken accounts by informants, their colleagues, spouses and others, together with my observational notes and participative experiences and looking at such data through the light of existing theories of symbolism, self-presentation and emotion work that allowed interpretation of the data. Each theme discussed in the empirical chapters includes accounts of the interview transcripts, fieldnotes and emotions and experiences gathered.

In sum it was similar to a triangulation process, which allows the consideration to explore the various, realities, meanings in telling and retelling similar accounts viewed from different angels, just like in a crystallisation process (Denzin & Lincoln, 2005; Flick, 2002). After that the data was very much alive and messy again, I metaphorically felt myself in the situations again, hearing my informants voices, feelings and bringing back the overall "*kibun*" (state of being or atmosphere). I spent a lot of time working on the single themes and their components, which entailed selecting quotes, allocating fieldnotes and participative experiences. Subsequently, I changed the perspectives from which these were looked at to identify how they correlate and make sense of symbolic meanings. In displacing the single data components and viewing them from different angles, new interpretations and sense making was possible.

Hereafter, I organised my data and kept some of the original German quotes in the text, even though they are followed by a translation, which aims to express the essence of the meaning to the best of my knowledge. The original quote in German or Korean was only kept when I believe that even though it can be translated it will make a difference to native speakers to have it at hand immediately. This approach was chosen because this work offers new insights for scholars as well as practitioners, who might be reluctant to look up the original quotes. The established patterns were then presented in separate chapters. In order to create a logical order and flow of data, reading out aloud as if I came cold at the narrative accounts helped me to put everything in order to present the research in my book. Moreover the analysis process in this volume seeks holistic understanding.

The analysis is not purely based on the ethnographer's interpretation, however the interpretation has to be consistent with the constructed realities of *HanaEins* members and the meaning behind them in relation to the fieldnotes and participation. Such interpretation process, of shifting back and forth resembles a hermeneutic approach of thematic analysis (McAuley, 2004; Thompson et al., 1990). In order to make sense of my participative experiences, interviews and fieldnotes the combination of the three is the key to interpretation, because all three are interconnected.

Most of the time I detected that the essences of quotes taken from the transcripts were traceable in my participative experiences, which was furthermore imprinted by *HanaEins* members' constructed organisational realities.

In sum, that was how the interpretations of the way *HanaEins* members represented themselves were formed, however this does not imply a predestined research process. It is however similar to the formation of Jazz as pointed out by Hatch, 1999 and Humphreys et al., (2003), who indicate that the analysing process for an ethnography might be unlikely to follow a set procedure. All in all the process, analysing and interpreting the fieldnotes, deriving from observation and participation along with the informal and formal interviews, which were transcribed all in combination represent the account of *HanaEins* members in Korea. Furthermore analysis and interpretation process may be regarded as a crystallisation process through narrating the realities of *HanaEins* members.

Detailed description of thematic analysis

The following paragraph delineates the process of the thematic analysis used in detail, and aims at giving the reader as well as future researchers an insight into the single steps taken.

Familiarisation with the data

The first step in thematic analysis permitted the ethnographer to familiarize himself with the gathered data. This step involved reading and re-reading the data, to become immersed and confidentially familiar with its content.

Coding

The second step was establishing an initial list of labels from the data set that had a recurring pattern. Such systematic way of organizing data, to gain meaningful features, which might be relevant to answer the research question, is called coding. It is to note, that this step did not follow a linear process, but more so a cyclical process in which codes in this case, *nunchi* and identity, emerged throughout the research process. Therefore, I imply that shifting back and forth between single steps until I was able to establish final themes was inevitable.

Throughout this step I granted full and identical attention to each data component (field notes, diary entries, transcribed interviews, observations and experiences), because it helped me to discover unnoticed repeated patterns and their relevant data extracts, which were useful for later stages of analysis.

As a result this step set the stage for detailed analysis later by allowing myself to reorganise the data according to the ideas that have been obtained throughout the process.

Searching for themes

This step involved investigating the codes (*nunchi* and identity) and collated data to identify significant broader patterns of meaning. It then involved collating data, which is relevant to each candidate theme (practices and ideology which contain truth telling, single word conversations, *Ordnung* and collectivism vs. individualism), so that I was able to work with the data and furthermore to allow the review of the viability of each candidate theme.

Reviewing themes

The fourth step involved checking the candidate themes against the dataset, to determine that all of them are representative of the data and contribute answering the research question. During this step the themes were refined, which resulted in splitting them into different sections.

Defining and naming themes

The final step before presenting the data involved developing a detailed analysis of each theme to determine the scope and focus of each theme. Additionally it included deciding on informative names for each theme e.g. *Hweshik*, drawer system, the two disjoined layers, the spiral of silence and the positioning process. This takes us to the final step.

Writing up

Ultimately, the last step involved merging together the analytic narrative and data extracts, and contextualising the analysis in relation to existing research.

Level of analysis

The following paragraph briefly indicates the particular level of inquiry employed.

This research follows a group level analysis and examines the realities and experiences of *HanaEins* members and its three character groups (international managers, settled Germans and Chameleons) and the interactions between those and how the single character groups vary in their adaptation of *nunchi* into strategic self-presentations.

Therefore, the group level of analysis employed in this study takes into account the intra- and intergroup dynamics with regards to *nunchi* and identity thus drawing upon anthropology. For example this study sheds light on how the different character groups correspond to the adaptation of *nunchi* into their strategic self-presentations and consequently the level of data presentation operates at the group level of analysis.

Conclusion

Organizational ethnographers work at becoming as knowledgeable about the population they are studying as its members are, while simultaneously holding on to the stranger's perception. Establishing detachment and 'strangeness' allowed me to identify 'new' phenomena more evidently, retaining what is acquainted to members from becoming conventional in their own eyes and sustaining a curious attitude with respect to its reasons and rationales, while fostering an intimate understanding assisted me to gather the import of that which I experienced and observed. Thus I interpreted my own experiences and observations and arranged the interpretations of organizational actors in the light of contextual factors and the theoretical concerns of my expertise (Headland, Pike and Harris, 1990).

This study's ethnographic approach, including formal and informal interviews supplemented with content analysis, formed the research approach for this study's fieldwork. Ethnography provided both a wide viewpoint on the studied population and access to unspoken discourse. It permitted me to grasp phenomena as having real-time elements of inflexibility and flexibility, and optimistic and bad effects on *HanaEins* and its members. It also allowed the assessment of in-house discourses, how they affect distinctive identities and units within *HanaEins* and its members, and how these units relate to external discourse. Ethnography was thus used as the primary research method because it is believed that multiple possible realities are constructed by the study. The research objectives involved in-depth fieldwork of relatively long duration, and the nature of the study necessitated exploration and interpretation using inductive reasoning, and working in close contact with people. Content analysis entailed the gathering and analysing of popular and vernacular texts to supplement participant observation, interviewing and observation. It facilitated the study with the reader-response theory's (e.g., Iser, 1989) affect that textual meaning is also delivered through previous knowledge.

Chapter 4

Habitat and Identity

Introduction

In Korea's leading business community, German transnational businesspeople construct a shared setting appropriate for their international business activities in making use of strategic self-presentation. While this approach may seem to describe exactly the complexion of a business identity, centred on coincidently shared commonalities, deriving particular links to their home country Germany and their new home Korea, a more detailed analysis uncovers that strategic self-presentation is only possible through the vivid exchange with other groups and the acknowledgement of coexisting identities within the transnational German businesspeople community. In pursuance of the exploration of the complexion of *nunchi* in transnational business settings, I shall examine Seoul, the location in which the German transnational businesspeople function and the manner in which they describe the nature of the city through strategic self-presentation.

Feeling like an ant: Seoul the "Mega City" in East Asia

Seoul, the capital of Korea, or as the city government terms it Seoul the Soul of Asia (Seoul Metropolitan government website), in which most of the German transnational businesspeople have been interviewed for this study, is crucial to their self-definition as a transnational group with a shared identity. The manner in which the interviewed population of transnational German businesspeople described Seoul seemed at first as steadily positive, stressing the features that best support the transnational German businesspeople activities. Nonetheless a more detailed examination does not disclose one shared depiction, but a process, describing the complexion of a group, which participates in several commitments with Korean and German entities, made of different identities.

German perceptions of Seoul

The German transnational businesspeople that were interviewed for this study frequently depicted Seoul in ways appropriate with their image as a group possessing a shared privileged identity. A lot of informants as noted above spoke of Seoul as "not Korea, not Asian" rather of an undecided "Russian – American" confused place. Germans looking for "real Koreanness" went to traditionally renovated cities (e.g. *Andong*), the mountain areas, the coastline, small islands down south, outside of Seoul, or to tourist sites elsewhere in Seoul such as I*nsadong* or *Gyeongbokgung* Palace. Korean facets of self-presentation, such as the class tension within Seoul were heavily mentioned.

It seems that the Germans were very much aware of it, as most, predominantly high-end executives, people in positions to hire others, expressed confusion at the surplus of university graduates, who are not compatible with their German competitors due to a lack of obtained skills and a shortage of apprentices, "A German high school graduate exceeds most Korean MA graduates unless they are from a SKY University, what's the point in having universities that won't get you anywhere", (Renate). Besides, they also regularly depicted Seoul in terms of its Korean or "Korean-Confucian" business practices, in contrast to primarily to the East Asian and German one. Their portrayl of Seoul, furthermore, emphasised its conservatism, in a sense of limiting "world-openness "to two areas, *Yongsan-gu* in particular *Itaewon* and *Gangnam-gu* in particular around *Gangnam* station. Most informants established an archetype in which Korea is portrayed as "kleinrariert, stolz, selbstverleibt und zum Teil rassistisch" (narrow-minded, proud, self-obsessed and to some degree racist), but the certain areas in Seoul, which I mentioned above, as experimental and to some degree "world-open".

It is to mention that the name *Itaewon*, when divided into two characters, stands for "The place of foreign people", *Itae* meaning foreign and *won* meaning area. This can be traced back to an old legend deriving from the *Chosn* Dynasty. And even today, *Itaewon* mirrors the most international area of Seoul, being home to everything Koreans classify as "non-Korean" including overt prostitution on "hooker hill" and a noticeable LGBT scene on and around "homo hill", Seoul's only mosque is located at *Itaewon* and the area is well known for its international nightlife including many international restaurant and pubs. Many embassies can also be found within the area of *Itaewon* and it is one of the only areas, in which interracial dating is not heavily frowned upon, which might be due to the presence of the American army base and the area's unique history.

Koreans of all ages enjoy visiting *Itaewon* from time to time as it resembles Seoul's exotic Disneyland for adults at night-time and for underage people during the day, in which Korean identity – "the Korean Way" may be ignored to some degree without being publicly lectured or punished by others. To some Seoul inhabitants including Korean and non-Koreans e.g. Germans, going to *Itaewon* is comparable to "some time out", "a short holiday" or simply "being free for one night".

Gangnam is well known for Seoul's financial district, foreign language institutes and abundant plastic surgery clinics. German MNCs employees particularly remarked on the city's cultural and ethnic homogeneity and commented on the lack of ethnic and cultural diversity with the exception of *Itaewon*. Interestingly, this discourse does take into account that Korea is one of the most ethically homogeneous countries in the world with only very few areas in which cosmopolitanism is displayed. Moreover, it was always remarked upon that the openness to foreigners was highly selective; informants all state that speaking a foreign language in public attracted negative attention. German transnational businesspeople thus present most parts of Seoul as conservative.

Seoul was moreover described as using symbols of nationalism and propaganda e.g. national flags everywhere and banners stating that *Dokdo* Island is Korean. Political aspects as such were for the most part mentioned but not explained, likely because they did not prevent transnational German businesspeople from their daily activities.

Symbols of alcohol consumption also featured predominantly in descriptions of the city: Carla attributes to the popularity of Seoul to get intoxicated "I have never in my entire life seen so many drunky drunk people on any day of the week after working hours, vomiting, staggering, sleeping on the subway or having fallen asleep while waiting for the subway, whilst trying to get home." My informants also focused on luxury department stores such as *Shinsegae*, *Lotte* and *Hyundai* department store or especially among the younger employees, trendy shopping areas such as *Dongdaemun* and *Hongdae* were mentioned.

Nearly all visitors to the MNCs went out for Korean BBQ dinner and or Karaoke, both of which were regarded as things that have to be experienced. Thus, the transnational German businesspeople made use of symbols, which differ to their own to establish a clear distinction between them and Korea's capital, Seoul.

A range of Korean and German considerations induces the transnational German businesspeoples' classification and construction of Seoul. Furthermore, Seoul's transnational German businesspeople are affected by the distant identity context of Germany, even while they live in Korea. The awareness of the differences in class and education system also suggests influence from Germany, while Germans believe in fair opportunities for everybody regardless of background they seem to be at odds with the Korean systems. Finally, even relatively diverse parts of Seoul such as *Gangnam* seem to be conservative, Germans gain the impression that Koreans through their self-presentation view multiculturalism and cosmopolitanism as something that predominately occurs within the transnational and not the Korean setting.

Additionally, Seoul is also defined with reference to what it is not or what it is missing. Underlying the descriptions which German interviewees expressed of Korea's capital city, there appeared to be an embedded contrast to their own. Any big German city, Berlin was mentioned the most as it is the German capital, is smaller in population but bigger in size, older, more visually attractive in their eyes, contains more ethnic mixing, less polluted, and contains more in the way of cultural offerings e.g. thatres, exhibitions etc. and international shopping and dining opportunities.

A further inferred difference was with other groups of Germans in Seoul, such as exchange students and visitors; *Anguk*, was viewed by most transnational German businesspeople as a real piece of Korea, to which to go to when escaping the dazzling city for a bit of peace, for the other group it was a famous tourist sight marking Korean high culture. To put it briefly, Seoul is an area, which can be defined in diverse and complex rapports, according to the specific requirements of the individual or group under investigation. Nevertheless, this process of selection and definition does not merely take place within the transnational German businesspeople community. More readily, it is formed and affected by Korean and German patterns of self-presentation and identity construction, and ultimately in conncetion with other transnational Germans such as academics, diplomats and retirees, who form an extensively related transnational unit, including many entities with diverse identities.

Self-Presentation and Seoul

Given such a setting, it might not be unexpected that self-presentation in the form of symbolism enlists such significance. Seoul regularly emphasizes its position through rituals such as Buddha's birthday, which is huge compared to Christmas despite the significant attention paid to Christmas, which takes on the form of another couples' day comparable to Valentine's day and signs such as hundreds of police officers and soldiers positioned around the city in buses and on the streets. Additionally, there are similarly more distinguished indicators, for instance the architecturally diverse high-rise buildings mixed with neglected after war architecture which makes it possible to identify CBD areas in *Gangnam-gu*. Seoul's nature, especially those characteristics defining it an international city, that being part of Seoul in that matter revolves around symbolism, and consequently self-presentation takes on a big role, as it is through self-representation that actors define their places and therefore define themselves in the setting of Seoul.

The transnational German businesspeople, present themselves as a group through such symbols, e.g. membership in particular organisations such as the German club, sending their kids to the German school, going to the same church, bakery, and attending the same *Stammtisch* (table of regulars at a pub) to exchange thoughts of working and managing across borders and life abroad etc. Through the definition of their shared identity through strategic self-presentation, Seoul's transnational German businesspeople continue to be a separate group, while blending into their Korean surroundings and therefore try as one *HanaEins* member put it, try to make the best of both lifestyles.

Also, similar to Seoul, transnational German businesspeople, are made up of a diverse range of people, professions and corporate settings. Single members appear to shape an homogeneous transnational identity in terms of shared approaches of how they present themselves in business, when considered as a group, however within this unit, differences with regards to duration of sojourn in Seoul, purposes for coming to Seoul, regions of origin, professional career development and so on exist. Such classifying differences differ over the development of an actor's working life. Just like Seoul, transnational German businesspeople encompass a number of different factors in transnational business settings and have distinctive kinds of involvement with Korean and international groups.

German MNCs in Seoul consequently use symbols as resources of self-presentation exclusive of reference to a particular place. German MNCs identify as a group which makes use of its business position, being the powerhouse of Europe and their positioning as somewhat being Korea's brother country as many Korean clients term it due to similar histories of separation and nation rebuilding in terms of the economy. The self-presentation of the MNCs, defined by their actors therefore, distinguishes transnational German businesspeople as a separate group in Seoul; notwithstanding they are part of it, indicating complex interactions amongst entities.

As a result of the fast pace of changes occurring in their settings, transnational German businesspeople are obliged to understand Korean as well as German meanings for prevelant symbols of idenoty quickly. This is an observable process in their daily interactions with their Korean colleagues; a *fob* (fresh off the boat) generally attracts a lot of attention concerning manners, behaviour and dress code. One informant who has worked and lived in Korea for over 16 years pointed out in a humorous way, "women need to learn how to be women all over again and gents have no choice but getting an entire new wardrobe, start drinking like a fish and smoke like a chimney and overall one needs to get used to feeling like an ant cause Koreans are all over you." What he essentially meant was the meaning of space and contact in daily interaction; Koreans tend to get awkwardly close at first e.g. sharing cups, commenting on each other's looks and so forth. Within a time frame of the first six months most transnational German businesspeople adjusted to understand the setting's average more.

Fobs (newly arrived employees) to the MNCs discover how to acclimatise and adjust from their workmates, daily activities, such as taking public transport, where to shop, what to eat, places to go and places to avoid etc. In addition the city's government self-representation like the Korean media and cultural events such as Buddha's birthday, lunar calendar New Year affect newcomers on another level. Ultimately, in the case of high-end executives being relocated from Germany, most of them receive help from a local relocation agency, finding accommodation, setting up bank accounts, getting their driver's license converted and so on. The transantional German businesspeople consequently obtain Korean symbols of self-presentation through various official and casual means, which they vitalise in their strategic self-presentations in the setting of Seoul.

Transnational German businesspeople have to deal with German ways of self-presentation due to their international commitment. This is a standing fact indeed as all Germans, who were part of this study, were raised in a German identity setting and moreover have ongoing relationships with Germany. Short-term international German managers and employees make less frequent return visits than long term transnational Germans, all of my informants had an ongoing association with their country and area of origin. The intensity of interaction differs; informants with families tended to have more contact than singles for example, however solely being employed by a German MNC guarantees an involvement with Germany. A lot of informants read German online newspapers or magazines; some mentioned that they watch German TV on the ZDF or/and ARD App (admitting that they miss watching German TV commercials and that they do not change the channel when commercials come on when they visit Germany). The transnational German businesspeople therefore continuously absorb and uphold knowledge of specific means of self-presentation in the German identity context through continuous engagement with their home country.

Moreover, the flexibility or ability of performative self-presentation makes the resource of managing this diversity of engagement, as actors strategically present themselves within Seoul using symbols of national identity, but perform in the way they assign different meanings to them possible. All Germans seem to use the same symbols when presenting themselves as actors, however some form of flexibility exists as all define Germanness, through *Ordnung*, language, through images of industry and Europe and especially *Weltoffenheit* (cosmopolitanism) and the skill to adapt to outside settings while being abroad. However, the symbols mentioned have different implications of the single entities of transnational German businesspeople within the *HanaEins* unit. Once again, it is the strategic vitalization of a rather performative self-presentation, which differs these subgroups and yet allows exchange between them.

Conclusion

The transnational German businesspeople that work in Seoul present themselves as a cohesive exclusive group with a shared identity in terms of approaching business and private life, dissimilar to other groups, based on the ways they depict and experience Seoul. On the other hand their strategic self-presentation, suggests that diversity within *HanaEins* and external engagement is their significant asset, opposed to homogeneity. Although the transnational German businesspeople in Seoul appear to be in possession of a separate shared identity they are on no account an inflexible unit, even in the though business setting of Seoul as stated by an informant "Ich hab schon viel geshen und erlebt in Asien und auf der Welt aber Korea ist eine ganze andere Nummer" (I have seen and experienced a lot in Asia and the world but Korea is a terrain of its own). I shall now review if this chapter's inferences are reinforced by an investigation of the transnational German and Korean employees in German MNCs in Seoul.

Chapter 5

Seoul's German MNCs: Interpretation of *Nunchi* and Self-Presentation in German MNCs in Korea

Introduction

Despite the fact that the transnational Germans in Seoul seem in their private spheres and their connections with Seoul's business community to be a unified cluster, however on a more detailed inspection seem to construct a diverse unit, related to various dissimilar representations of identity, the same appears to be the case in their working lives. Just as in the special previous consideration of Seoul, although a concise inspection of the constructions and self-presentation of German branches of MNCs in Seoul could imply that the MNCs themselves and their employees are unified formations, a more detailed inspection indicates a greater multifaceted actuality.

Throughout this chapter, I call into question the understanding of *nunchi* in self-presentation in transnational business, in exploring how evidently linked up MNCs' workforce members in actuality incorporate several different approaches to *nunchi* and identity. And furthermore how the understanding of them determines the managerial success of transnational German business practices in Korea.

As previously pointed out in the literature review on identity and *nunchi* most of the work does not branch the two streams of literature the latter one mainly being represented by identity context insiders opposed to business anthropologists, therefore I have begun to consider a more complex perspective, arguing that identity context specific interpretations of *nunchi* relate to particular forms of identity in terms of self-presentation within MNCs.

Thus, an investigation of the manner in which the employees of Seoul's German MNCs present their identities at work and outside of work, interact with all entities and each other may as well demonstrate an all the more complex illustration of *nunchi* and identity in transnational business, and proposes innovative insights into the possibilities the two are viewed in MNCs and organisational performances in transnational business settings.

The Setting in a Nutshell: German MNCs in Seoul viewed by their Members

While non-members entering the Korean branch of a German MNCs may perceive it as a cohesive organisation whose employees all express their national and professional identities in seemingly similar rapports, a consideration of the actions through which they express themselves brings out a range of identity presentations within the identical business setting. In the following passage I will depict the identity presentation of the MNCs which form the setting of this study, and its employees who are employed by them, with a focus to inspect whether there are shared implications of the concept of *nunchi* for our understanding of identities of strategic self-presentation in MNCs.

HanaEins Seoul

HanaEins is a group of German MNCs, which comprises some of the largest German MNCs, which currently operate in Korea and furthermore maintain a good presence of foreign branches in developing and developed economies around the world. The longest serving employee had been part of *HanaEins* for 25 years, working between the two nations, Korea and Germany. The longest serving employee, who continuously worked and lived in Korea, has already been working there for 16 years, the shortest-serving employee, was monitored from day one, the arrival in Korea until her 10-month assignment had been completed. *HanaEins* virtually contains close to all

German employees working for German MNCs in Korea. Most *HanaEins* members tended to be present in the higher ranks, with the exception of younger employees, who tended to be just *Abteilungsleiter* (division manager) and trainees and interns, who were even younger, who mostly reported to a Korean team leader. Overall Germans were found in all levels with a higher concentration for top-end management positions and positions related to such, partly due to their native level of German language skills, which are essential in German MNCs.

During narrations of depicting their workplace setting, *HanaEins* members tend to refer first to its business purposes and secondly to its uniqueness in terms of self-presentation of Germanness and Koreannes. The focus of *HanEins* as an entity lies on drawing a distinct separation of the two strategic self-presentations with a main focus on the German market. Members also often stress the forced need to maintain a movement of social structure between German and Korean employees and a rather natural one amongst *HanaEins* members. Single offices enjoyed fully funded regular activities e.g. *Hweshiks* (company nights out including dinner and drinks and other kinds of entertainment), which will be discussed in detail later on. Some of these are formally promoted and planned, however some of them especially when only selected people are invited occur in a spontaneous manner, but are somewhat mandatory to attend. Informal gatherings and social activities were held regularly amongst Germans and were promoted by word of mouth in German to keep it preferably German. Workplace environments have repeatedly been described as a *Heile Welt* (man made harmonious world). Sometimes employees started their sentences with "auf gut Deutsch ist diese Atmosphaere erwartet und meistens nicht echt" (Quite frankly speaking, this atmosphere is expected and most of the time it is not real). German employees expressed being homesick for a "real" working environment in which they can show their true identities. To their members their working environments despite working for German MNCs in Korea were "ok," however "not as German influenced as they would have liked them to be", in terms of representing a German MNCs in Korea.

The following is a brief description of a standard German MNC's office, which is with minimal variances representative for *HanaEins* members' offices.

All offices were *Großraumbüros* (open-plan offices), which usually had the managers' areas, which were divided into booths with at least one wall being out of glass or a glass door, in a position overlooking the open-plan spaces. These spatial arrangements allowed the managers to gently clarify hierarchy practices, while using soft power measures, in constantly monitoring the open-plan office space. The CEO and CFO had visibly bigger offices with noticeably nicer décor and the facilities to accommodate more people in case of smaller meetings or greeting guests. Both offices, displayed symbols, representing the German-Korean friendship, such as joined German and Korean flags, complementary gifts such as USB sticks or pens, which had Korean as well as English or German writing on them and tea and coffee along with German and Korean snacks were usually on display. The same was the case of the official meeting rooms, which were equipped with state of the art multimedia and presentation equipment, the only difference was that the glass used was opaque, which allowed others to see if there is a meeting but not who is in the meeting. The rest of the open-plan working space was taken up by small working "stations", desks clustered together, according to teams, some divided by desk dividers and some without. It was easy to define, which desks Korean staff occupied and which Germans occupied. Germans tended to personalize their working space, with symbols, representing personality and interests: family pictures displaying spouses or loved ones, the "special" coffee cup which is exclusively available to one member of staff, small plants, calendars in German, stickers with words of motivation on them (in German) and so forth. Korean desks however displayed much less of the occupier's personal interests or personality, despite a family photo here and there, air humidifiers, and slippers, all of the same style (blue or black with parallel white stripes at the front) and cosmetics were more prevalent.

Furthermore, desks occupied by male Koreans were not as tidy as a desk occupied by female Korean staff members; this distinct difference in tidiness was not noticeable among German desk occupiers. Furthermore, there was a small pantry, which was mainly used to get coffee that the MNCs provided free of charge, a water purifier and chiller a fridge and a microwave for communal use. The overall décor of the office tended to be very sophisticated, there were no sharp visual distinctions between high-end executive offices and the open-plan floor, except spatial separation and size and slightly more upmarket furniture in the latter ones. The walls were painted nicely and framed prints of the MNCs' product or services caught my attention. Slogans of encouragement such as "be the change" added character and a sense of belonging to the overall impersonal, thus professional look. Most offices were located in sophisticated serviced office buildings, with an impressive lobby, where security guards and exceptionally beautiful Korean receptionists greeted guests, who were than signed in and picked up by a member of staff.

Additionally it is to mention that each MNC had reserved parking spots either in front of the building or in a heated underground garage, which was connected to the office floor with a lift "I go down the lift at home, enter my pre-heated car, drive into the garage at the office and can totally escape Seoul before the madness starts, " said Klaus, a *HanaEins* member. Allocated parking however was only available to high-end managers, the CEO and the CFO. Car ownership amongst Germans was also very significant in terms of self-presentation, status and hierarchy with their Korean counterparts.

In general the official length of the working day is 8.30 AM till 6 PM but such working hours were flexible in terms of an earlier start and does not include after hours *Hweshik,* which most of the time forms an essential event of the working day and is somewhat mandatory. Most employees tried to practice punctuality, due to Koreans trying to misuse German managers' generosity, finger print systems to check in and check out were instilled in most MNCs. Generally, there was a strong tendency to stay late as most Korean employees said that "no one can leave before the boss has left." Everyone went on a one-hour lunch break, employees tended to eat in language groups e.g. Korean, German and Konglish if challenged by hierarchy. Seldom people left others alone to eat unless someone specifically chose to eat alone. The same informal rules applied to company dinners and informal meetings, which were the "backstage" at the office, areas such as the washroom for the ladies and designated smoking areas for the gents, coffee shops during lunch hours and places serving food and alcohol served as the "backstage" to which clients and visitors only had selective access. Other than that the office a whole was the "front stage".

The German Pub– Home to *HanaEins' Stammtisch*

The pub occupied 3 floors of a magnificent purpose built building in the heart of *Itaewon,* with two commercial floors, which guest are able to access and one floor comprising the kitchen and the office, which is not visible nor accessible to guests. All floors accessible to the public were immaculately decorated with authentic German antiques and furniture even the beer glasses and plates were imported collectables. A regular *HanaEins* member remarked, "Stepping into Hirsch is almost like being back at home" (Hirsch is a common German pub name evoking traditional German country side culture). The commercial areas were the "backstage" of the pub in which *HanaEins* members were observed and informally interviewed while also being on their own "backstage". Areas seen by *HanaEins* members were decorated in a homely German style, with wooden furniture, the two *Nebenzimmer* (VIP rooms) stood out especially due to their Bavarian touch and sophisticated non-cliché beer tent style décor. The official trading hours were noon till midnight during the week and 3am on weekends.

The pub is thus more personal, less formal, posses close to no demarcations between public and private areas and technically provides a more obvious spatial "backstage" for *HanaEins* members.

In merely loose terms, there were far more German employees at the pub than there were Korean employees, who used the facilities of the backstage on a regular basis to be themselves. Korean employees however only managed to really let go and switch to backstage behavior when being out at Korean venues or being completely intoxicated. There seems to be a noticeable gap in worldliness and educational background between *HanaEins* members and their Korean counterparts, who as seen in sum are not as highly educated or influenced by cross-border engagement as the German transnational businesspeople in Seoul. *HanaEins* thus appears more education focused, worldly, adaptable to international settings and aware of ongoing processes in and around them, which they analyse strategically in questioning and searching for the origins of causes. German transnational businesspeople are thus capable of differentiating between front and backstage settings, the use of performative identity and the variation of truth interpretations than their Korean counterparts with regard to working in German MNCs in Seoul.

In terms of national identity, *HanaEins* members also tended to define themselves as German on the, for them obvious backstage, the pub, but as transnational and globally aware businesspeople to their Korean colleagues on the front stage, the MNC. Most of them spoke of a clear distinction between performative and national identity and when to perform national identity in order to vitalize it as a performative tool to express and use *nunchi*.

Most *HanaEins* members emphasized strong discourses of Germanness foregrounding German traits such as long-termism, loyalty and telling the truth (see Binney 1993; Lawrence 1980; Posen 1993) which they claim to fully live on the, for them obvious backstage when dealing with other Germans. This behavior is subject to change, with the awareness of alteration when acting on the international front stage on which Koreans and Germans work and live together.

In sum, then, *HanaEins* appears to have a definite, unified national identity, based on their role as transnational German businesspeople in Seoul. There were, however, significant differences between the for them obvious backstage the pub and the front stage in terms of how they presented themselves with regards to *nunchi* and identity. *HanaEins* thus appears as a transnational group possessing only one identity, but the fact that even a brief inspection reveals performative presentations on front and back stages, strongly suggests that *nunchi* plays a significant role in the self-presentation of a transnational business group.

I shall now consider the nature of *HanaEins* members, working for German MNCs in Seoul, and whether Korean and German representations of identity in terms of *nunchi* are opposed to each other, or something more complex.

Chapter 6

One cast, three different character groups: The make-up of the *HanaEins* ensemble

Though predictable knowledge would advocate that *HanaEins* Seoul should either exist of a unified cluster, a transnational business community dominating the setting, or two national identities, the actuality was rather dissimilar. With regard to national identity, three character groups could be roughly distinguished within *HanaEins* Seoul, which were discerned by the use of *nunchi* and identity in language, truth interpretation, hierarchy, management style and body language, including self-presentation and dress code. Thus, the groupings, which are to follow below, may be best described as defining themselves through differences. In other words, *HanaEins* members working for German MNCs in Seoul categorically mentioined the *HanaEins* formation, especially the MNCs being divided between "German" and "Korean" identities, and acted in ways, which assumed the existence of further subdivisions of this. However, these groups are a theatrically abridged sorting scheme used for the suitability of analysis in the examnination of this study. Nevertheless, for the initative of this chapter I am about to split up all informants according to these groups. The locution "character groups" will be used to refer to these categories hereafter.

Character One: German International Managers

The first character group was the *German international managers*, which may be divided into two additional subcategories: long term international managers, and newcomers. The long term international managers had been given the chance by their German MNC's Head Quarters to take on a top management role abroad, usually between three and five years. All international managers were educated at university level; most of them were in their early forties and older, despite not all, and already had families, had spent a significant amount of time at the MNC's Head Office or a another major office in Germany and had previous international working/living experiences. Most of the international managers applied to take on the chance of living and working in Korea, mainly to further their career paths in the foreseeable future and if they had children to enjoy the company's expat package, which includes tuition fees for a private school "Unsere Kinder wollen nicht mehr auf eine öffentliche Schule zu Hause, das heißt meine Frau und ich müssen durchhalten bis sie mit dem Abi fertig sind" (Our children don't want to go to a public school at home anymore, which means my wife and I have to hang in there until they've finished their A levels).

Newcomers, likewise, were either from the German MNC's Headquarters or from a different branch in Germany and were sent to Korea as a compulsory component of a trainee program or short term international assignment and ended up in Korea due to being rejected from their first choice, usually being an English speaking country or China. Close to all were still in trainee programs with the MNCs or young professionals, mainly single and were part of *HanaEins* for between three to ten months, and were subject to higher exposure to Korean recruits due to their low ranking in hierarchy hence power. The international managers of *HanaEins* consequently appear to be a unified character group, but are relatively small compared to other character groups due to their function and cost.

With regard to identity and *nunchi,* the international managers leaned more on the German rather than Korean presentations of self on both the front and backstage. However, most of them did make an effort to accommodate Korean interpretations of *nunchi* in identity on the, for them obvious front stage – e.g. bowing, dress code, way of speech and management practices such as formal and informal meetings. Most of the amendments made in the expression of embracing *nunchi* as part of their identity, were performative as in the example given above, or to do with unwritten laws and regulations which they were unable to break.

Even though close to all international managers were pleased to incorporate certain Korean practices into their way of managing, they tended to focus more on getting the "job" done than more Korean-focused employees, and occasionally complained about Koreans not understanding the line between friendship, colleagues, work and privacy: " My friends are my friends and my colleagues are my colleagues and I need my friends and family to complain to about work and I don't want to spend endless hours with my colleagues, drinking and singing karaoke while I could be spending quality time with my family and real friends," announced one international manager. The German international managers therefore created a separate identity group due to their power and privileges within *HanaEins*, which was dissimilar from short-term international managers with less power and privileges.

Case Study: Rainer

Rainer is in his early fifties, and had always been working for a German MNC nationally and internationally. Before having accepted the offer to return to Korea after several years in Malaysia, he was appointed to be the CEO of the Korean branch. Up to day he had spent eight years, building and leading the Korean branch, he was asked to return to Seoul, due to his extensive experience in managing Koreans and working in Korea. Due to the MNC's HR departments difficulties of finding a suitable candidate an even bigger remuneration package brought him and his family back to Seoul even though initial hesitation of leaving Malaysia existed. *HanaEins* members generally described him as " aufrichtig, fair, deutsch und Koreanisch-diplomatisch wenn es sein muss" (sincere, fair, German and Korean-diplomatic if needed). Rainer has a wife and a son. His wife worked for the DSS (Deutsche Schule Seoul) and his son left Korea as soon as he had completed his A levels. The family visited Germany approximately once a year, and initially stayed in Korea for the son to finish high-school, they have intentions of leaving Korea in the foreseeable future.

Character Group Two: Settled Germans

The second character group was the *settled Germans*. This particular group was moderately distinct with reference to demographics such as background, age and length of time spend in Seoul and as part of *HanaEins*, but all were residing in Korea for other purposes than purely business. Most of them either followed their spouse or got married to Koreans or were returning adoptees in search of their roots or children of former Korean migrant workers (mainly miners and nurses), who's families remained in Germany. They tended to be more performative in terms of *nunchi* and identity and seemed to be better at acting more Korean in using symbols of Korean identity when expected. This might be that the demarcation of their front and backstage awareness somewhat melted more together in comparison to other *HanaEins* character groups.

In regards to *nunchi* and identity, the settled Germans represent an invaluable resource for character group number one and character group number three, Koreans working for German MNCs, as their natural adoption and application of *nunchi* in their identities served as an example for both groups to observe and learn the vitalization of *nunchi*. Nonetheless they could be easily distinguished from other *HanaEins* character groups by their smooth transitioning of using *nunchi* as part of their identities: while for the most part, they tended to perform *nunchi* naturally, they feel the urge to embrace "hard core" Germanness, which implies the plain and unaltered presentation of symbols of German identity, from time to time when no Koreans were around as well as the regular need to complain and criticize Korea and Korean identity from a somewhat insider perspective to other settled Germans. The settled Germans, albeit being foreigners in the Korean identity context, almost perfectly absorbed performative *nunchi* into their identities, mainly in line with the third character group, the German speaking Koreans also referd to as Chameleons.

Case study: Andrea

Andrea came to Korea from Germany four years ago to be with her Korean fiancé, they got married, which got broadcasted on German national television in a show called "*Die Auswanderer*", since then she finished her Master of Physics at Korea University and worked in various jobs in which her German language skills as well as her ability to work with a purely Korean team, due to her *nunchi* skills were the main essentials. She is an invaluable *HanaEins* member working for a MNC in her field while being one of the major mentors, in terms of explaining and demonstrating the incorporation of *nunchi* into everyday as well as working life. She prefers to speak Bavarian to standard German and also feels comfortable communicating in colloquial Korean and fluent English. She quite often makes jokes about Korean characteristics, such as pretentiousness, xenophobia, drunkenness, narrow-mindedness including bluntness and the lack of speaking a second language well even though they have studied it for numerous years. She also brings up a lot Korean idealism, optimism, and romanticism in comparison to Germans. When speaking about Germans and Germany she always stresses that she misses being truthful and colleagues who can handle the truth since she claims Germans to be capable of rational and analytical thinking. She seldom criticizes either of the nations without explaining the reasons for doing so. She is planning on having children soon and recently bought a house together with her husband in Korea.

Character Group Three: German speaking Koreans (referred to as Chameleons)

The third character group, the *Chameleons*, consisted of non-German, Korean *HanaEins* members who expressed a convincing association with Germany and close ties to German identity, and who speak German well enough for it to be their working language. The Chameleons formed a character group which presented itself with considerable variation, including Koreans who grew up in Germany, Koreans with German partners, who previously generally studied in Germany and Koreans who studied Germanic studies at a Seoul SKY university (Seoul National University, Korea Univeristy and Yonsei Univeristy) and spent some time on exchange in Germany. Most of them had joined *HanaEins* due to their German language skills and dislike for Korean companies, most of them stress the appreciation for more freedom and emphasize the opportunity to show their talents better within the *HanaEins* circles. Many of them joined their particular German MNC after having returned from abroad as their first job and have stayed with the same company ever since, even though they would get paid better working for local Korean MNC, however most character three group members claim that the given freedom and working style outweighs the potential pay rises with Korean employers and have no intentions of changing employers. Most, though not all, tended to have university degrees from international universities or a Korean SKY university, if they did not posses a degree their German language skills outweighed the value of an equivalent degree. They tended to socialize with the settled Germans, the international German managers and people with international backgrounds, given the fact that most of them spoke English as well and enjoyed talking about their experiences gained overseas.

In regards to *nunchi* and identity, the German speaking Koreans were on the face of it largely similar to the settled Germans, in that they tended to practice a natural performance of *nunchi* in their private and public identities according to the given circumstances. However, there was a clear distinction in terms of performance and identity, whereas the settled Germans tended to express their frustration only amongst themselves, the German speaking Koreans tended to be openly critical of Korean identity performances and were proud of their ability to quickly understand and adapt to German identity performances, in expressing positive feelings about Germanness. While this group shares a number of similarities with the settled Germans, the German speaking Koreans only tended to strongly emphasise and bring up their connections with Germany, when a for them beneficially opportunity presented itself.

Case Study: EJ

EJ was born in Seoul and moved to Germany at the age of seven, when her father was sent to Frankfurt to set up a branch of a Korean *chaebol*. She joined primary school in second grade and stayed until the end of high school, right after her father was sent to the US to fulfill the same duty, where she went to university. After the completion of her degree she had to go back to Korea and took a job with a German MNC, for which she has been working ever since. She is currently working in a managing position and describes herself as more international than Korean, hence her frequent jokes about not having found a partner in Korea "Ich bin einfach zu stark für einen Koreanischen Mann, Männer hier mögen schwache Frauen und ich bin in Deutschland groß geworden, ich habe eben auch eine Meinung" (I am just too strong for Korean men, Korean men like submissive women and I grew up in Germany, I do have an opinion as well). She has never been married and has no children.

Table III: Summary of character groups and positions within HanaEins

	Identity	German Identity	Korean Identity	Use of *Nunchi*
German International managers	German	Strong	Weak	Medium
Settled Germans	German	Strong	Medium	Strong
Chameleons	Korean	Medium	Strong	Medium

The character groups' views on *Nunchi*

The German international managers portrayed *nunchi* in terms recalling a specific sense of being transnational and able to distinguish between Germanness and Koreanness. They highlighted its role in transnational settings in this case working in German MNCs in Seoul, comparing its forms and applicability with those of other branches around the globe, especially East Asia and Germany. All international managers spoke of a set of intercultural management skills, by which they seemed to refer to loosely formulaic "Asian" vs. "Western" attributes, discussed in literature on national identities. Yet, while outlining their daily working lives further, they tended to concentrate on explicit Korean behaviors, which did not make sense to them and were not in line with what they have previously read in "Asian" vs. "Western" literature. Close to all of them also portrayed their work place as being in tension between Koreanness and Germanness, the longer staying international managers adding to this the complexity of *nunchi* with which they perceived *nunchi* for the most part. One of the international managers renowned that ignoring *nunchi* may be fatal: "Koreans give up easily, they will just quit even if they do not have a new job lined up – hmm sometimes they join up in groups and quit at the same time if one does not manage them in the way they want to be managed." Even though Korean employees work for a German MNC in Korea, they hardly care about understanding or obeying their German superior but expect them to show *nunchi*.

Without reservation close to all international managers additionally stressed the German identity symbol of *Weltoffenheit* in comparison to the Korean approach of classyifing themselves as the "other" in terms of Korea *vs.* the world. Most international managers noted the way in which Koreans start their sentences: " *Hangug esonen …. Hangug saramdari…. Woori nara eso ….,* " (in Korea…Korean people…Where we are from) in order to reject any ideas or approaches from others who do not originate from Korea or are not ethnically Korean. They also note that everything needs to be *Koreannised* in order to find acceptance amongst Koreans such as serving Korean side dishes with any meal, especially *kimchi* or other pickles. Furthermore they describe the acceptance of ignorance and overt nationalism in everything the Korean does as *nunchi* e.g. one international manager said, "Koreans love to fish for compliments in telling you, doesn't it taste delicious, isn't it great, Korea is the best, Koreans are the smartest etc. and in the same sentence they bluntly diminish and hurt your feelings in saying things like bread is just bread, it's all the same and German beer tastes like soup but Korean beer is the best and so on, but they expect you to praise everything they claim to be right and not to show any emotion or defend their hurtful and untrue statements about the rest of the world." The German international managers, hence depicted *nunchi* as the acceptance of the Korean identity and clearly stated emotion rules in their statements and behavior at work and in daily life, without overtly criticizing, commenting or approaching the Korean counterparts about what they trigger with their very direct identity performances.

The settled Germans depicted *nunchi* in similar ways to the German international managers, but with significant differences in how they perceive and practice it themselves. As somewhat Korean identity insiders they add meaning and interpretation to the observed and experienced directness, bluntness, and nationalism including racism Koreans show in their self-presentations. The settled Germans go beyond purely accepting and avoiding criticism in their definition of *nunchi* and add that most Koreans are a product of their society, which according to them is an artificial construction of the government, hence the top ten *Chaebol* families, given the massive influence conglomerates have in politics in Korea. "Why do you think most, actually close to all professors who work at Korean universities obtained their PhD's abroad? …. Right because being different, thinking outside the box being innovative isn't acceptable in Korean society; here they are raised to be the same and live each period of their lives as prearranged, if one doesn't obey one will be excluded and alone forever," said Christoph, a settled informant. Another settled German adds, "There is no such thing as investigative journalism; the media outlets are strictly controlled by *Chaebol* families and Korea is a huge TV nation, whatever they are fed from above they are willing to accept and believe."

The main difference of the interpretation of *nunchi* between settled Germans and German international managers is that the settled Germans understand why Koreans behave the way they do and they adhere to it. This makes the settled Germans' identity highly performative as they apply *nunchi* in the same way the Koreans do with the clear distinction of being emotionally and sociologically aware why they perform in an expected way or as the international managers put it accept the Korean identity and clearly stated emotion rules. They also spoke of *nunchi* as something extremely limiting, depending on age, gender, area of residence, income, one parents' wealth and social status overall. Breaking the set *nunchi* rules is regarded as being rebellious, inappropriate and excludes one from the "*woori*", the us, the collective group, which ranges from micro to macro contexts. Andrea comments:

> Der größte Unterschied zwischen den Deutschen und den Koreanern ist das den Koreanern alles strengst vorgegeben ist durch ihr soziales *nunchi* Verhalten von oben herab. Da kann mein Mann z.B. aus circa 8 verschiedenen Haarschnitten und 5 verschiedenen Brillenstile aussuchen und muss mindestens ab und zu mal Golf spielen aufgrund seines Berufs. Bei den Deutschen ist da viel mehr Freiheit, bei offener Kritik und Wiedersetzung schließen die Koreaner einen einfach komplett aus (The main difference between the Germans and the Koreans is, that for Koreans everything is strictly assigned due to their top down social *nunchi* behavior. For instance, my husband is able to choose from approximately 8 different hairstyles and 5 different spectacle styles and definitely has to go and play golf sometimes due to his profession. The Germans embrace a lot more freedom, however if one overtly voices critique or resistance, Koreans just expel one completely).

The settled Germans thus defined *nunchi* as a strategic performance of the self on the front stage with the main difference of knowing why and how they achieve the desired Korean outcome. *Nunchi* is therefore seen as a performative tool due to the settled Germans' ability to monitor and regulate it.

The Chameleons, much like the international managers, also drew attention to their sense of being transnational and able to distinguish between Germanness and Koreanness. All spoke of intercultural awareness, by which they seemed to refer to loosely formulaic German attributes, such as punctuality, directness in terms of truth telling and discipline, however some also referred to more complex concepts such as *Ordnung* and the ability to think logically and the drive to plan long term vs. short term hence sustainability. Listing differences was their key to define *nunchi*, all of them were familiar with the term but hesitant to define it at first. All of them admitted that the concept of *nunchi* is something innate that Koreans do not think about but act upon. They took this further in defining *nunchi* as "the Korean Way", and describe it as a collection of masks, which the single actors put on according to the given circumstances in order to maintain harmony and personal advantages. Defining *nunchi* as a way of fitting in and contributing to the "*Woori*", they perceive it as performative when they think about it but as natural when they apply *nunchi*.

EJ noted, " Die Deutschen sehen, was sie in den Medien sehen und denken, Korea hat *Samasung, LG, Hyundai*, Technologie und … gibt so viele große Buildings. Und dann denken sie, da ist einfach sehr modern, aber wenn sie hierherkommen, wenn sie wirklich die Leute kennenlernen, die Leute sind eigentlich nicht modern. Sie sind sehr konservativ. Und meistens wissen nicht, wie sie mit Ausländer tun müssen und … wie ich gesagt habe, Koreaner sind harmoniesüchtig. Deswegen werden sie Ja, ja, ja in vorne sagen, aber trotzdem etwas anderes tun und die meisten Ausländer denken, das ist nicht richtig, das ist falsch. Koreaner werden das verstehen, wenn jemand so Ja, ja, ja vorne sagt und etwas anderes tut, werden sie schon verstehen, aber für viele Leute die in Europa aufgewachesn sind, sie glauben Ehrlichkeit ist das Wichtigste. Aber wenn sie Koreaner sehen, Koreaner sind nicht richtig ehrlich, sie sagen etwas, aber tun etwas Anderes. Deswegen denken, sie sind nicht ehrlich" (The Germans see what the see in the media, Korea has *Samsung, LG, Hyundai*, technology and … there are so many tall buildings. And then they think it is very modern, but when they come here, when they really get to know the people, they people are actually not modern. They are very conservative. And most of the time, they do not know how to act torwards foreigners and ... as I said, Koreans are addicted to harmony. That is why they say yes, yes,yes to your face but still do something else, and most foreigners think that is not right, that is wrong. Koreans will understand if someone says yes, yes, yes to their face but does something else, they will actually understand, but for many people who grew up in Europe, honesty ist he most important thing. But when they meet Koreans, Koreans are not really honest, they say one thing, but do something different. That is why Germans think Koreans are not honest).

In sum, the Chameleons broadly define *nunchi* as "the Korean Way" which at a second glance includes all masks which control all front and backstage performances at work and in the private sphere. The Chameleons are however proud of understanding "the German mind" and can therefore work in both identity settings.

Analysis

Consequently, it appears that all character groups, which make up *HanaEins* define *nunchi* in somewhat related approaches. Nevertheless, the interpretations of *nunchi* contrast from character group to character group, also depending on time spent in Korea, hierarchy (power) and language skills. For example, all three-character groups, brought up the coexistence of national identities and did this using *nunchi* and its components to create differences in use and interpretation to underline Germanness or Koreanness. Notwithstanding this, whether *nunchi* was depicted as consisting of different elements, balanced or incompatible varied from character group to character group, comparatively with its single members' possession of power and hierarchy status. Whereas all *HanaEins* members conceded the significance of *nunchi* as a differentiating phenomenon of daily work activities in MNCs, the active awareness of *nunchi* varied depending on whether the informant was close to or distant from embracing strategic Korean identity. Truth-telling and the interpretation of what constitutes truth was a key part of *nunchi,* but whilst the international managers had difficulties understanding such inclusion of *nunchi,* character group two and three portrayed various facets of truth telling as part of *nunchi*. The definition of truth telling varied considerably. As above-mentioned, ultimately, a clear correlation between hierarchy and power influences perceptions on *nunchi* strongly, from character group to character group. On the other hand, *HanaEins* members who tend towards a more Korean approach of incorporating *nunchi* into their identities, define *nunchi* in similar terms, but with different interpretations, advocating not the same outcome of *nunchi*, but varied interpretations of symbols of identity and forms of self-presentation.

Answers to the variances in interpretation appear to depend entirely on the knowledge, experience, and exposure, which each character group has to *nunchi*, and on their strategic incorporation of *nunchi* into their business activities relative to such knowledge. When I conducted my recorded interviews, I was mindful that my interviewees gave answers with reference to their own reputation of being transnational, in order to strategically assure their reputation within *HanaEins* overall. Besides, newcomers, especially international managers' self-presentations and the understanding, incorporation of *nunchi* altered progressively all along the study, as they grew closer to the subject matter and learnt the performative yet strategic part that *nunchi* assumes to be a prerequisite. Therefore, the definition of *nunchi* does not only vary from character group to character group, but in line with the character group's position and future outlook within *HanaEins* overall, inferring that the use of *nunchi* has a resilient part of strategy to it.

Conclusively, we should bear in mind that these strategies are established and applied through and with other character groups within *HanaEins*. Members who describe German identity as more truthful, worldly and down to earth than Korean identity, are for example adopting symbols of truth telling, language and hierarchy used by settled Germans and Chameleons to define and practice *nunchi*.

Additionally, it is also noteworthy that all three character groups, despite their time spent in Korea, immensely shared the same opinion that although similar concepts of *nunchi* exist they are by far not the same e.g. when the Chameleons compare "the Korean Way" to the concept of *Ordnung* they try to harmonize elements of emotional intelligence, which are rationally and logically traceable with identity specific feeling rules hence *nunchi*. Therefore, the German international managers, settled Germans and Chameleons are not functioning completely individually, however all three act as educational props and in response to one another within and outside of *HanaEins* character groups, thus their distinctions in interpretations.

In short, then, amongst *HanaEins* members still, one may differentiate three major, visibly distinct character groups that all describe their experience and vitalization of *nunchi* in their workplace settings in related ways, but individualize these through altered interpretations of self-presentation. The range of interpretation, moreover, is contingent with the fact that each character group defines its experiences and utilizes *nunchi* differently and strategically and therefore strategically presents itself to other character groups and the Korean counterpart. Therefore, *nunchi* takes on a perfromative act of self-presentation, and incorporates a number of diverse symbols of identity, which may or may not be expressed similarly within *HanaEins'* symbols of identity, suggesting again that *nunchi* in MNCs' business and everyday activities is manifested in strategic performances of symbolism.

Chapter 7

Unusual or just different:
Managerial Change through the Adoption of *Nunchi*

During the course of the study, *HanaEins* gained some new members, the so-called "newcomers", from all three-character groups. Their new membership allowed me to learn about and define *nunchi*, in comparing the experiences of the old and new *HanaEins* members. The event of new members joining, especially at high end management levels, was not only disturbing to existing structures at particular MNCs, but immediately triggered friction between recently joined *HanaEins* members and their Korean subordinates at the office, which were not pleased to accept changes in management style imposed by *HanaEins* members, but forced them to a certain degree to learn and incorporate *nunchi* into their management style. An investigation of how different *HanaEins* character groups responded to their Korean subordinates' expectations, reveals not only the differences in the Western concept of emotional intelligence, but also how their definitions of *nunchi* relate to their particular strategies for strategic actions. By considering carefully how the different *HanaEins* character groups handled the learning process of *nunchi*, we can see *nunchi's* relevance to international business studies, the ways in which *nunchi* relates to the Western concept of emotional intelligence and the role *nunchi* plays in MNCs in Korea.

Background to the Integration of *Nunchi*

While an outsider newly joining a Korean branch of a German MNC in Seoul might assume a somewhat international approach to conducting daily business operations, including how to hold meetings and exchange of thoughts, a closer examination reveals a diversity of self-presentations in such activities e.g. meetings, occurring in the setting. In this section I will set the stage for the next chapeter's examination of the self-presentation of *nunchi* and identity of the different *HanaEins* character groups and their Korean counterparts.

"Als ich in meinem ersten Meeting saß, das ich selbst organisierte, dachte ich ich saß im falschen Film und wusste icht nicht mehr wo Vorne und Hinten war und ich glaube die Koreaner auch nicht." (The main result of the very first meeting that I organized and attended was that everyone, both myself and all the Koreans, felt heavily confused and left wondering what's wrong with us", said Andreas, a well-established *HanaEins* member.

Koreans are extremely patriotic and astonishingly homogeneous in terms of behavior and the way they carry themselves on the front stage. It becomes operant that Koreans show a strong sentiment accepting "the Korean Way" which forms all Korean symbols of identity, hence all visible and invisible aspects of their lives e.g. the way they dress and the way they think or express their opinions.

Koreans say and think they work a lot. They have little time for their families and leisure activities, however they do not express any longing of missing such things. Andrea reports, in all my years in Korea, "I have never heard a Korean say, I'd like to spend more time with my wife and children, because I spend too much time at work!" In fact, it is more the case, that Koreans "live" at work (in der Arbeit leben), which results in a lot of time spent at "work", which in *HanaEins* members perspectives is not spend effectively. A newcomer sighs, "Also ich meine, sie sind viel anwesend, aber du kennst es selber: Filme schauen, schlafen, viel Privates etc. gehört alles zur Arbeitszeit dazu." (Well I reckon, they are great in terms of attendance, but as you know, watching films, sleeping and private matters etc. are all part of their working hours). *HanaEins* members on the other hand get up at 6.30 am, take a shower, go to work and are ready to start working at 8 am on the dot. They take an hour lunch break and at 5 pm they are usually done with their daily duties and ready to go home, exceptions occur under special circumstances, which demand to stay behind. However it is to mention that *HanaEins* members work extremely goal oriented and usually manage to go home on time, due to their strategic way of organizing their time and prioritizing their tasks.

Their Korean colleagues however, gradually arrive at work with being up to 25min delayed, which for them seems to be impertinent. Upon arrival female colleagues first of all change their shoes from high heels into slippers and then collectively vanish, their first informal, non-scheduled meeting takes place in the ladies bathroom, while putting make up on. The following quote supports the above observation, "Meine Abteilung kommt ins Büro und wechselt die Schuhe. Und zwar nicht wie ich von 'Laufschuhe' in 'Pumps'. Nein, man wechselt von 'Straßenschuhen' in 'Hausschlappen', mit denen man dann den ganzen Tag durchs Büro schlappt. Konsequenterweise geht man dann auch mit Zahnbürste und Zahnpasta in der Hand nach dem Mittagessen zum Zähneputzen. In mir löst diese Kombination eine Art 'Campingplatz' Gefühl aus" (My team arrives at the office and changes their shoes. But not the way I do from joggers into heels. No they change from proper shoes into slippers, in which they walk around the office all day long. Consequently they all take their toothbrush and toothpaste and brush their teeth after lunch. This combination evokes a kind of 'camp site' feeling in me.) The male Korean colleagues, similarly, are to be found smoking in small groups, usually consisting of working units in front the office building, which is their first non-scheduled meeting for the day. Post arrival, upstairs most male Koreans also change their black leather shoes for the previously mentioned blue or black slippers, which have white stripes on them. These informal meetings occur on a daily basis in the early mornings and throughout the day, *HanaEins* members are not asked to join, furthermore are these meetings held in Korean and it is not obvious that they are actual meetings.

This leads on to official meetings, mentioned above, organized by the *HanaEins* member. Everyone gathers silently around a table in a meeting room staring at the newcomer (high-end manager). The newcomer briefly introduces the topic, which is to be discussed, once he is ready to start a round table discussion, he discovers that he is left in silence staring at blank faces. His Korean subordinates only react and answer, when he approaches "orders" them to speak up. In response he receives a brief synopsis, agreeing of what he said in the introduction. Everyone leaves confused and unsatisfied. Right after 5 pm, a Korean colleague most of the time mentions " Hey, Arbeitskollegen, lasst uns noch Bierchen trinken, auf einen Absacker" (Hey, everyone, let's go for drinks). The general *HanaEins* newcomer's reaction is "seriously, I wanted to go home." Germans rarely go for drinks with their entire team, except on special occasions, such as birthdays, Christmas parties and New Year gatherings and farewells. A settled German remarks, " Ich gehe in die Arbeit um Geld zu verdienen, aber da lebe ich nicht. Also es ist nicht mein Lebensmittelpunkt. Und die Koreaner haben eher ihren Lebensmittelpunkt in der Arbeit und, ja sind wenig zu Hause, die leben in der Arbeit, da sind ihre Freunde, da sind ihre sozialen Kontakte." (I go to work to make money, but I don't live there. Work is not the centre of my life. The Koreans tend to have the centre of their life at work and are rarely at home, they live at work, that's where their friends and social ties are). Some *HanaEins* members seriously started to question whether the average Korean would be happy living a German lifestyle. They renounce that it would probably be terrible for the Korean to go back home at 5 pm and stay on his/her own. Most Koreans claim to either sleep or meet their friends for drinks in their spare time, which leads us to a major theme, drinking and company dinners, so called *Hweshik*.

The *Hweshik* Ritual

The fact that colleagues turn into friends and that working matters are heavily intertwined with personal matters makes it inevitable that most Koreans find it hard to separate personal and business related comments and criticism. "Everything you say or do is taken personally by the Koreans, there is no separation between criticizing someone's work or someone's personality", if one criticizes one aspect of someone the Korean will take it as a complete rejection of the entity as a whole. "Weil man so viel *nunchi* braucht, deswegen braucht man *Hweshik*, damit man versteht was der andere kommunizieren möchte" (Because one needs so much *nunchi*, *Hweshik* is needed to understand what others are trying to communicate.) Some also classify *Hweshik* as essential "teambuilding", which is necessary to understand and regulate the daily operations in a company in Korea. The root of *Hweshik* is the Confucian rule that a younger person must follow and do what an older person says, this verifies and justifies the still existing untouchable "Korean mind", their seniority and hierarchy system, which can be detected in all areas of private and public life including work settings.

Based on this longstanding Korean identity component the Korean is conditioned to be extremely modest as implied by EJ, "at least you have to pretend to be modest" and obedient towards authoritative people, which in most cases are purely defined through age. This results in a strong notion of being "addicted to harmony", virtually all informants report that harmony needs to be assured at all times, even if one has to lie, be quite or deliberately do something wrong just because he was ordered to do so by a senior person. The only people who are allowed to express direct criticism are people, who are older or have a "professional expertise" due to Confucian tradition, such as one's parents, teachers or professors. It is striking to *HanaEins* members to experience that, even if an older person is wrong and everyone else knows about it people can not directly warn him because it is against their Korean identity or as they term it "the Korean Way, the Korean Mind". EJ, adds, " Confucius never covered such topic because age is unchallengeable, one just has to wait until the older person learns, through *nunchi* that he made a mistake. Yes, one just has to be patient and wait."

Many *HanaEins* members face these kinds of situations, when they are not in the natural position to lead a team, meaning, they are not the oldest, preferably male and married. "Weil sie in einer Deutschen Firma arbeiten, muss der ältere Mann oder die ältere Person zuhören, was der Junge sagt, aber trotzdem wird er denken: "Ich bin älter." Und was dann passiert ist, die älteren Leute, sie sagen dir ins Gesicht: "Ja, ja, ja." Aber machen danach was Anderes. Also they say one thing but they won't do it" (Because they work for a German company, the older man or older person must listen, to what the younger person says, but he will still think: "I am older." And the next thing that happens is, that the older people agree to your face: "Yes, yes, yes." But they will still do it differently. They say one thing but they won't do it).

HanaEins memebers define this as the "*Abnickenprocess*", which describes the nodding of the head with a confirmative "*eng, eng, eng*", or "*mmm, mmm,* mmm" sound, which is equivalent to a "yes, yes, yes." This process represents a strategic Korean identity performance of *nunchi* to instil and assure harmony, "Koreaner sind, sehr Harmonie süchtig, Es muss Harmonie hergestellt werden!" (Koreans are very much addicted to harmony. Harmony must be created)! A second variation of the "*Abnickenprocess*" exists as well, which on the contrary includes a negative connotation, indicating a performative lie to instil harmony. This variation similarly contains the confirmative sounds, followed by an abrupt, almost mechanic turning of the head into a 45-degree side position, accompanied by a surprising "*chhhhh*" sound (This sound is created in slightly opening the mouth, while simultaneously inhaling oxygen vividly, while pressing ones tongue against ones front teeth). Whatever information follows this sound is a performative lie in order to instil harmony and the preservation of ones *Chaemyon* (face).

Strategic *nunchi* serves as a tool in Korea to "be in the better position" and to fit in, contribute to the harmonious, yet expected interaction, which is predestined by hierarchy and "the Korean Way". That's why the almost daily-expected call for *Hweshik* is inevitable to function in and work for a MNC in Korea. It offers all *HanaEins* members and their Korean counterparts a platform to build *jung* (special bond similar to friendship), as explained in the literature review, and to get to know others and exchange information more freely, as compared to formal meetings, as mentioned above. "Man muss ein Bisschen beaobachten, wie die Leute, ihre Gesichter verändern, oder wie sie sich bewegen und manchmal sagen sie einfach Dinge und geben Hints " (One has to observe, how people change their facial expressions or how they move and sometimes they give hints.) In order to get to know people, create a laissez-faire environment or as the pre-existing literature terms it, make the opportunity available that employees are able to express themselves to their leaders, *Hweshik* is needed. *Hweshik* is portrayed and experienced as a returning ritual filled with symbols of identity, which follow strict procedures and rules, however it also offers the chance to express true feelings to a certain extend, the heart of *Hweshik* is strategic alcohol consumption.

Preceding the almost predictable suggestion to go for drinks at approximately five o'clock the arguably most important part of the day is about to begin, the interplay of performative identity, underlined by a strong *nunchi* sentiment. "The drinking part, is very very important…business is generally done while drinking," remarks a *HanaEins* member (note: in the original quote the word *saufen* was used which is a vulgar term for binge drinking). It is highly possible that business partners or clients do not even swing by the office and are met directly at the first *Hweshik* venue.

The second option is an internal company *Hweshik*, which is only attended by the MNC's employees. *Hweshik* consists of three, sometimes four, rounds. This rule applies across industries and socioeconomic backgrounds in private and business settings and one cannot go home before the person with the most power above one has not left. Dining out is relatively cheap in Korea compared to Germany. The first round consists of food, usually Korean BBQ or chicken accompanied with beer or *soju* (Korean style vodka). After the first round, which takes approximately one to two hours, all attendees change location to a second place called *sulchip* (literally: drinking house), where a lot of alcohol is served along with *anchu* (snacks on the table to share, generally consumed with a lot of *soju* and beer, e.g. Korean stew, a platter of deep fried snacks or dried fish.)

The third round has two options to it, which depends on how Korean the setting is and on who is paying. If the most powerful, hence most senior Korean wants to show off and all attendees are male he will take everyone to a 'naughty' *Norebang* (karaoke place), if he does not have to impress anyone or does not feel the need to commit a 'collective sin', which serves the purpose of team-building, "we have all done it, we all lie for each other," the fostering of the *"Woori"*, everyone will be taken to a regular *Norebang*, where no prostitutional services are offered, forced upon the subordinates through peer pressure. Beer consumption or *Somek* (a mixture of *soju* and beer) is standard while being at the *Norebang,* however only small snacks are provided. "Ja, und dann, wenn dann noch welche (lachend) können, dann geht es weiter wieder zum Trinken," (Well, and after that, if some are not wasted enough (laughs) everyone has to continue drinking) remarks Andrea pitifully. After all, if it happens to be an all male round, the last stop is a *jimjilbang* (sauna, bathhouse), "Alle gemeinsam" (everyone together) go there. The sauna itself does not serve the purpose of sweating; it simply serves the purpose of cheap and collective accommodation, "Also ich meine, ich habe es nicht verstanden, warum schläft man nicht daheim? Mein Mann schläft drei Häuser weiter in der Sauna, trotz dem das er nur zehn Minute nach Hause hätte, dann schälft er lieber mit seinen Kollegen (lacht) in der Sauna am Fußboden, weil iregendwie die Gemeinschaft da toll ist" (Well, I mean, I never understood, why he won't sleep at home? My husband stays three houses down the road, even though it's only ten minutes to get back home, but he prefers to sleep on the floor at the sauna, together with his colleagues (laughs), because apparently the collective feeling is great."

My own participation as well as the Chameleons' revealed that a freer flow of inner feelings and opinions is possible under the heavy influence of alcohol during *Hweshik* rituals. "Also es ist sehr interessant hier in Korea, wenn man hier in Korea viel Alkohol getrunken hat und ein bisschen frech wird, ist das schon okay...Was manchmal passiert ist, sie haben Streit, wenn sie so betrunken sind, obwohl der andere Chef ist. Und trotzdem werden sie sagen: "Ach, der war betrunken. Es ist okay. Geht schon" (It is very interesting here in Korea, if one had a lot of alcohol and starts challenging and criticising seniors, it's generally acceptable. Sometimes it happens that they start arguing, when they are really drunk, even though one of them is the boss. And still they will say: "Well, he was drunk, it's alright, never mind"). The semiotic of alcohol consumption during *Hweshik* rituals manifests itself as part of performative *nunchi* in Korean identity, however the quantity of alcohol and regularity of *Hweshik* are not to be underestimated. "Aber man muss richtig viel Alkohol trinken, richtig betrunken sein. Wenn man nur eine Flasche trinkt und so frech wird, kann der Chef das nicht leiden" (But one really has to drink a lot of alcohol, and be really drunk. If one only drank one bottle and starts being out of line, the boss won't like it).

The following is an illustration of a newcomer's first Hweshik ritual and the discovery of nunchi symbols in identity.

The first time I had to go for *Hweshik*, what they called company dinner, with my Korean coworkers was mainly about alcohol consumption and was completely different to what I expected. Everyone had a beer in his hands, when we toasted I was the only one that tried to look people in the eyes while clinking our glasses, the rest starred elsewhere, into their glass, the ceiling to the floor and I sort of started to wonder. I thought to myself, well yeah it might have happened accidently that they missed eye contact. But suddenly, when everyone was about to drink, something surprising happened! Everyone turned away. Away from the most senior person and I ended up being the only one staring directly at our boss, while he drank his beverage. That sort of got me thinking, hmm! One probably can not drink one's beer on the same eye level and has to hide it due to the most senior person's authority, even though it is more than obvious that everyone is drinking. In that kind of situation, hierarchy and authority gets visualized, because second thoughts revealed that one always has to turn away from the person next to one, into the younger person's direction to clarify and acknowledge the power distribution within the group.

Two hands or one hand? An observation of the hands indicates who is older. A general rule of thumb is that the one, who holds his glass with one hand and who pores with one hand, is probably the most senior hence most respected person. That is *nunchi* that people develop over time in paying close attention to details. Most criteria for example, the use of hands and turning away while drinking, serve the purpose of clarifying, verifying, instilling and visualizing hierarchy. Doing so is the most important duty in Korea, whenever one goes somewhere new in Korea or meets new people the re-establishing of the hierarchy becomes essential. Who is older, who has a higher position, who has finished his educational path already, who is working, who is still a student? The first indicator is the bow, when greeting others, the deeper the bow the more respect is granted. Some might already know each other, that is why the next step is observing how people drink and turn. Paying attention to symbols of identity continues until one is able to figure out one's own position within the group. After having observed everybody's bowing and drinking behaviour it is time to listen carefully and detect, which honorifics are used with whom to further clarify every individuals position within the group. Who uses "*yo*" at the end of the verb, which is the polite form and who uses "*imnida*" or " *siseo,*" which are even politer honorifics and who just uses "*banmal,*" which is colloquial language. The newcomer notes, "That's what *nunchi* actually is and what one has to develop, that when joining a group in Korea, any group, that one is able to position himself and knows the relationships in terms of hierarchy and power between entities present and is able to alter one's own behaviour to the expected one, according to the situation."

Two disjoined layers

Nunchi is seen as a strategic semiotic in Korean identity especially in business and situations in which one needs to accomplish or achieve something. Koreans are conditioned to hide their inner emotions and opinions, "die haben so einen Schutzmantel" (they have a coat which protects them). Koreans have two layers, the outer layer and the inner layer. Both layers are disjoined from each other, which means that they "können nach außen was ganz anderes darstellen, als was sie innen fühlen" (are able to portray something completely different on the outside, compared to what they feel on the inside). This becomes apparent in symbols of *nunchi* in identity such as the *Hweshik* as a ritual, following "the Korean Way" and strategic lying to either secure harmony or an opportunistic advantage.

The most common lie, which was experienced the most, is the hypocrisy of giving and receiving compliments to create a nicer, friendlier atmosphere. "Man kann bzw. muss also gewissermasen Dinge von sich geben, die man nicht wircklich meint, oder nicht so empfindet" (One can or must to a certain extent say things, which one does not really mean or feel.) That's how the outer and inner layer are formed and understood. *HanaEins* members conditionally manage to adjust, however not as dramatically as Koreans practice it, "Koreaner machen das, homogen über die ganze gesselschaftliche Schicht verteilt," (Koreans do so homogenously and equally in all social classes of society.) German and Koreans strategically perform lies for the sake of *nunchi*, however it seems that Koreans are not able to distinguish between the factual truth and the performative alteration of the truth. As Andreas indicated, "Die Übergänge sind fließend. Also er empfindet faktische Wahrheit … die faktische Wahrheit spielt nicht so die große Rolle, da hält er sich nicht so dran wie der Deutsche. Der Deutsche liebt Fakten, Zahlen, belastbare Fakten. Der Koreaner sieht die zwar auch, aber ist immer bereit, sie abzuwandeln. Um halt einfach ein Gefühl des gegenseitigen Wohlfühlens zu schaffen" (The transitions are smooth, the Korean knows what factual truth is … the factual truth however is not really important to the Korean, the Korean does not stick to the factual truth like the German does. The German loves numbers and figures and substantial facts. Even though the Korean is aware of the factual truth, he is always willing to modify it, to achieve a feeling of mutual comfort).

The engrained symbols of identity, which are executed through *nunchi* performances, dominate all actions of how the Korean behaves and thinks. Even though an awareness of the factual truth exists, the performative *nunchi* action legitimizes the alteration of the truth and acts as a replacement of what is factually right. "Also sie lügen sich dann irgendwie selber was vor. Sie, verdrehen die Wahrheit und glauben das selber dann. Also ich glaube, sie wissen, dass es nicht wahr ist, aber weil es einfach oft genug jemand sagt, wird es dann zur Wahrheit " (Well, they somehow lie to themselves. They prevaricate the truth and believe in it themselves. Well I think they know that it isn't true, but because someone has said it often enough it becomes the truth), added Andrea. This strategic *nunchi* performance, whether it was performed naturally or followed a pure act of identity presentation results in a harmonious front stage setting. The backstage setting however is neglected. "Also es geht halt hauptsächlich um die Harmonie. Die Fassade. Also es muss vordergründig harmonisch sein. Wie es Hinten ausschaut, ist total egal" (Well, the main purpose is primarily harmony. The façade. It must primarily be harmonious. What it looks like behind the scenes doesn't matter at all), said EJ. The Chameleons stress the importance of *nunchi* performances in everyday behaviour and how the factual truth, the meaning of what is right and wrong gets replaced with what feels right or what is socially expected to be right. Additionally EJ noted, "In Korea, die Meisten denken nicht an richtig, sondern was geht sozial, in Korea kann es sein wenn es nicht richtig ist, aber alle so machen, obwohl es nicht richtig ist, wird es trotzdem akzeptiert. Aber in Deutschland muss man es einfach richtig machen, das ist einer der größten anderen Dinge von Korea und Deutschland" (Most people in Korea don't think about what's right, but what is socially acceptable. In Korea it may be possible that, although something isn't right, but everyone does it that way it will be accepted. That's one of the biggest differences between Korea and Germany).

The following illustration of a HanaEins member's farewell Hweshik, serves as an example to exemplify the above mentioned strategic nunchi performances in Korean identity._

The first round took place at a restaurant, to have dinner. The boss (female) was approximately 1.5 hours late, however after her arrival she spared any kind of small talk and immediately initiated drinking games. "In Korea trinkt man nicht aus Genuss, man trinkt "aggressiv" mit dem alleinigen Ziel in kurzer Zeit sturzbedrunken zu sein" (In Korea, one does not drink to enjoy, people drink "aggressively" with the one and only purpose to get hammered within no time), noted Sylvia. Beer and *soju* were served. *Soju* is a spirit, which insufferably just tastes like alcohol. One is never allowed to refill one's own glass, however one pours *soju* into one's neighbour's glass, who then does the same for you. It's pretty much an endless handing around of the bottle. While drinking one has to turn away from the hierarchically higher person and covers the *soju* glass with the entire hand so that the elders are not able to observe the subordinates' alcohol consumption, even though they provided it. "In my opinion one shouldn't worry so much about being observed while drinking, but more so about one's behaviour after having consumed so much alcohol. But that's the German pragmatic approach", adds Syliva. One is regarded especially "strong", if one can drink *somek* (an 0,2ml glass of beer with a decent shot of *soju*). Her boss eagerly mixed one *somek* after another and summoned her repetitively to drink it all in one go, "Sylvia! One shot." Shortly after she ordered her to prepare a *somek* as well and give it to the person that she "favours" the most in Korea. The colleague next to her immediately announced, "Sylvia, that's most definitely Jade (her boss,) isn't it." She promptly got it and her colleagues helped her out as much as they possibly could. Furthermore one of them unobtrusively handed her a small bottle of "magic potion" (*Condition*, a Korean drink which prevents hangovers), with the hint, "drink that and you will be able to handle the alcohol better." Her boss upbraided her right after dinner in front of everyone for not having come out drinking more often during her time in Korea and awarded her to be an "amazing drinker".

The second round was at a *Norebang* to sing karaoke. Our group consisted of approximately twenty people, who all had to squeeze into a roughly 12-15 square metre karaoke room. A colleague commented Sylvi's comment that the room is tiny, "Yeah, we are all going to get really close."

The first bars of "My way" started and Sylvia began to sing, "and now the end is here, and so I face the final curtain … and than it must have been the *soju*, I went nuts: while singing these lyrics – yeah that's it, that's exactly how it was, my time in Korea, that's how I feel, the lyrics of the song are straight from the heart". There was no way of return and with all her energy she released her emotion into the microphone. "I've loved, I laughed and cried, I've had my fill, my share of losing. And now, as tears subside, I find it all so amusing." Her colleagues were absolutely shocked but applauded a lot. When she was asked to join everyone for the third round she kindly declined and said, "It's late and the show is over for me." The following morning she returned to Germany.

The Spiral of Silence

The vertical structure, hence the hierarchy system is untouchable in the Korean identity context and strictly followed through till the very end. This is a major difference, compared to the German system, even though a hierarchy exists, Germans "würden ganz bis zum Ende nicht auf diese hierarchische Art und Weise miteinander arbeiten" (wouldn't follow through working in this hierarchical way till the very end), remarked an international manager. This leads to misunderstandings. These are mainly misunderstandings in reciprocal expectations. The intensifying process of feedback illustrates these misunderstandings. One does not receive an expected feedback, hence reacts in the wrong way, which leads to an intensifying process of the initial feedback, this process is misunderstood and kicks off a downward "spiral of silence". The actual problem manifests itself in the unintentionally caused intensifying processes, because these processes are not talked about or openly discussed, a way of simple and clear intervention is non-existent. German identity performances would allow questioning and clarifying misunderstood feedback patterns, however due to strong existence of *nunchi* within Korean identity such questioning and clarifying is not possible.

I term this phenomenon "the spiral of silence", which describes the notion of keeping quiet to feel on the save side or to evoke the feeling of not causing any more misunderstandings. However, the above-mentioned intensifying processes continue in silence and are very difficult to detect and solve. Korean identity performances assume an on-going exchange of *nunchi* in all situations. German identity presentations in business are however relevant to a specific case and relevant to specific problem solving. *HanaEins* members, escpecially the international managers and settled Germans, tend to narrow or break the issue down and like to keep it that way, in order to find tailor made solutions, based on logic and rational self-presentation. The Korean approach on the other hand is rather emotional opposed to being logical and rational; when the German says, "Moment, es ging doch nicht um dich als Mensch, es ging um die Sache" (Hang on, it's not about you personally, it's about a specific matter), the Korean does not know how to separate the two, him as a person and whatever he does or says respectively.

It then becomes a matter of how symbols are prioritized within German and Korean identity. The question is, do I feel insulted first and than motivated, or do I feel motivated first and than to some degree offended? German symbols of order (*Ordnung*) and logical thinking, assume a clear separation of the person as such and this specific semiotic suggests, "ah, er hat mir einen kleinen Klapps gegeben, aber irgendwie hat er mir weiter geholfen" (ah, he taught me a lesson, but he sort of helped me out). The Korean semiotic of *nunchi* on the contrary views the same scenario as, "oh, er hat mich hauptsächlich beleidigt und, na gut, er hat mir ein Bisschen sachlich weitergeholfen" (oh, he mainly insulted me, and well he was a little helpful). This superimposition, which occurs due to the different interpretations of German and Korean identity symbols, implies that the factual truth, regardless of the person is kept separately in German identity performances and that emotions are kept aside as long as it is clear, that "wir um eine Sache streiten, ist die Sache ganz klar im Fokus" (we argue over an on-going matter, the focus is clearly on the matter) and not on the person.

The Korean approach results in extreme mood swings, which in that form are unknown to *HanaEins* members, especially to character groups one and two. Their solution is to arrogantly ignore the other person completely, "Sie lösen es gar nicht. Und sind dann eher bockig oder eingeschnappt. Sprechen nicht mehr miteinander. Aber auch Koreaner untereinander. Die sind dann einfach so: Man spricht einfach nicht mehr miteinander," (They do not solve it. They are rather stubborn and huffy. They stop talking to each other. Even Koreans amongst Koreans. They are just like that: they just stop talking all together to each other), until someone who is higher up in the hierarchy steps in and orders everybody to go for compulsory *Hweshik*. "Und dann muss man auch mal zusammen einen saufen gehen, dass man wieder spricht miteinander" (And then, everybody must go and get drunk, in order to talk to each other again), noted Klaus. The importance and power of *Hweshik* rituals is seen in the above quote, which indicates that *Hweshik*, serves as the solution to "the spiral of silence." A *HanaEins* member reports, "wenn man dann genug getrunken hat…dann sagt der Chef: Nun ist aber gut. Das waren vielleicht auch Missverständnisse" (Once everyone had a fair portion to drink…the boss might say: Alright, it may also have been misunderstandings).

Initial contact: Identity and *Nunchi*

Koreans eagerly (*krampfhaft*) try to establish commonalities, regardless of being amongst purely Koreans or *HanaEins* members. Within the Korean identity context that is the first step of what I term the "positioning process", which is a must do in Koreas hierarchically society. The process is structured and visible to *HanaEins* members, it always commences with an explicit depiction of the initial stage of not knowing someone and the according behaviour followed by the first contact.

"Natürlich rumpelt man sich im Bus und sonst überall an und man nimmt keine Rücksicht auf einander, man spuckt sich vor die Füße, ist völlig in *Ordnung*, unbenommen…aber nur weil man nichts miteinander zu tun hat" (of course everyone bumps into each other on the bus and everywhere else and people are not considerate at all, they even spit in front of each others' feet, there is nothing wrong with that, they are not well behaved at all… but just because they have no existing relationship), remarks an international manager. The very moment one gets in touch with each other dynamics change and the first step of the "positioning process" takes place. "In dem Moment wo man sich trifft und etwas miteinander zu tun bekommt ist es für Koreaner unwahscheinlich wichtig zu wissen, in welcher Beziehung man zueinander steht und was aus dieser Beziehung zueinander entstehen könnte" (the moment two parties meet and an exchange takes place, it becomes incredibly important for the Korean to know in which position one stands to one another and which potentials such relationship might have), said Andreas.

As a result the second step takes place, which entails asking many questions, which for the German in this case *HanaEins* members are extremely personal and direct, this questioning time takes place, so that the Korean is able to sound out what may come of a potential relationship. *HanaEins* members classify step number two as, "eine sehr intelligente From des Abtastens … das Ziel der Koreaner ist es nur festzustellen, welche Beziehung man haben könnte miteinander" (an intelligent way of scanning the other person…the Korean's aim is just to figure out what kind of relationship might be possible), noted Rainer.

The next step, step number three is the performative act of "overcoming taboos" within German identity. As part of this step *HanaEins* members performatively forgive their Korean counterpart for being rude and impolite. *HanaEins* members perceive touching upon absolute German taboos as being disrespectful, uneducated and *"abgekatert"* (collusive), therefore step number three takes on the form of an act, in which they present themselves as adaptable on the front stage. Symbols of absolute taboos in German identity are, asking personal questions on initial meetings as well as judging a book by its cover. Close to all *HanaEins* members remark that they would never immediately ask about someone's parents, children, marital status, age and someone's political and socioeconomic position.

HanaEins members express having difficulties with step number three as it is against their nature however they proclaim that it is manageable in vitalizing performative *nunchi,* "Stellung empfinden wir glaube ich als sehr schwierig, weil ich möchte dich als Mensch kennenlernen. Also wir empfinden den Mensch stellungsfremd… für den Koreaner ist Stellung ein sehr wichtiges erstes Orientierungsmerkmal" (we perceive, categorizing people as very difficult, because I want to get to know you as a human being. We view people for who they are not for what they are….but for Koreans the positioning process is a very important measure to gain orientation). Classic examples are strategic explorations of finding out how long a *HanaEins* member has been in Korea, hence how long he will stay and what the reason for his stay is. The Koreans immediate behaviour is very much dependent on how much he could gain from investing in a relationship, "Because if he will leave next week, I don't have to take so much care of him. That's obvious isn't it! But if he will stay for another five years, it might be that we will benefit from each other," remarked one of my Korean colleagues.

Within the German identity context it is assumed that the above-mentioned human aspect is always the centre of attention when meeting new people. "Das hat glaube ich ganz viel mit unseren Traditionen zu tun…wir vergessen oft, das wir ganz tief, ganz tiefe Mechanismen christlicher Natur haben und diese christliche Natur heist immer dem Menschen begegenen, ohne seine Stellung kennenzulernen. Jesus Christus ist immer zu den Zöllnern und Prostituierten gegangen…Das heist Stellung speilt keine Rolle oder wir sollten sie vermieden" (I think it has a lot to do with our traditions…we often forget that deep down we have strong mechanisms of Christian nature, and this Christian nature implies meeting people without judging or categorizing them. Jesus Christ visited customs officers and prostitutes, which means the positing process does not matter or we should avoid it), noted an international manager.

This implies that participating in and accepting the "positioning process" becomes a performative self-presentation of strategic *nunchi* for *HanaEins* members, as the semiotic of the "positioning process" is clearly not part of Germanness to such extent. However clear taboos do exist within Koreanness as well. Anything that is not conforming to "the Korean Way" is viewed as non-existent in Korea and absolutely taboo, single mums and sexual diversity are the most prominent topics amongst many. "Vor allem im sexual-moralischen Sinne gibt es natürlich genug Tabubereiche. Also wenn es dann irgendwie auf Homosexualität kommt oder solche Sachen, dann ist natürlich schnell mal die Laterne aus. Oder wenn es auf Alleinerziehende kommt, oder so was, dann wird es schwierig…weil sie einfach nicht ins Raster passen" (There are many taboos, especially in the sexuality discourse. If the topic touches upon homosexuality or single mums people get pushed over the edge easily… because they just do not fit into the given way of how one should be), explained a settled German.

The "Drawer System" and the "Positioning Process"

Initial contact, the "positioning process" and what I term the "drawer system" are highly related and occur more or less as a domino effect. The *HanaEins* member is important to his or her Korean counterpart, based on the *HanaEins* member's knowhow, knowledge, skills, a good product, the company or simply if the *HanaEins* member is well to do. If the *HanaEins* members fulfil one or several of these criteria, the Korean counterpart's *nunchi* level will automatically rise. *HanaEins* members bluntly define the Korean to have a conditioned opportunistic nature, which manifests itself in strategic *nunchi* performances.

This widespread almost homogeneous behaviour is standard practice in Korea and easily noticed, bearing the "two layers" in mind. Exchanging business cards right after having greeted someone during the initial contact triggers the Korean to put one into a "drawer" (*Schublade*), according to which title the business card carries. It is assumed that one's title and age go hand in hand with the Korean seniority system. Within minutes a new hierarchy is established and once one has been put into a drawer it is close to impossible to revoke such decision. "Aber für Koreaner extreme wichtig um mal abzuchecken, die Visitenkarte lege ich da hin und die Visitenkarte lege ich da hin" (But for the Koreans it is extremely important to find out of which importance someone's business card might be to him or her), said a Chameleon.

Two options exist, one either receives the "you could be useful for me drawer" if the Korean views you as someone who can get him further, which means he has hidden expectations and tries to win one over through his strategic self-presentation or secondly, if one depends on the Korean, one turns into his "Werkzeug" (tool). "Koreaner zu Deutschen ist halt insofern oportunistisch, wenn er von dir irgendetwas erwartet, ja einen Vorteil hat, ne… Und dann ist er sehr devot, stellenweise, und sehr opportunistisch. Überfreundlich, hyperfreundlich, bis hin zur Schleimerei oder zur Unterwürfigkeit" (Koreans act opportunistically towards Germans, if they expect something, if they have an advantage…partly he is very devote and very opportunistic. Over the top friendly, hyper friendly even bootlicking and tends to subservience), noted a settled German.

The second scenario, demarcates a rather harsh facet of how *nunchi* in performative identity occurs, however it is very much the living reality of younger *HanaEins* members, who are not married yet and have weak ties with Korea. "Du bist der Bittesteller, oder du willst was von ihm, dann wird es stellenweise recht grenzwertig, weil dann die Kriterien der Mitmenschlichkeit und des sozialen Umgehens, wie wir das in Deutschland kennen nicht mehr zutreffen. Du wirst dann behandelt wie ein Nobody, passt in deren Rankings nicht rein. Und nachdem du in keine Schublade passt, bist du gewissermasen auch ein Nobody… du bist halt ein Werkzeug für ihn… dann spürst du so eine Art herablassendes Verhalten, und du gehörst nicht dazu… es grenzt an Rassismus…da du nicht zu den Koreanern gehörst und nicht in das System gehörst, die sind schon aufgrund ihrer nationalen Einstellung, glaube ich haben sie auch sehr viele rassistische Ansätze" (Things get quite sketchy if you are the one asking the Korean for something, because in such case social rules and any sense of benevolence like we are used to in Germany don't apply. They treat you like you are nobody because you do not fit into their ranking. And since you do not fit in the draw system you are kind of nobody…you are just a tool for them…you will feel that they treat you contemptuously… and you do not belong to them…it is close to racism… because you do not belong to the Koreans and do not fit into their system, their national attitude contains a lot of racist tendencies), outlined a settled German. It is to mention that all Koreans and the Chameleons state a clear-cut definition of what it means to be Korean.

This definition differs significantly from the altered contemporary understanding of what constitutes Germanness. "Koreaner bist du nur durch Geburt, dass man sich mit seinen Landsleuten, mit seiner Rasse identifiziert, Koreaner kann man nur durch dieses Blutsverhältnis sein" (You are only Korean by birth, you have to identify yourself through being like other Koreans and belonging to the Korean race, you can only be Korean through these blood ties), noted a Chameleon.

In sum the adoption of *nunchi* into the self-presentations of German and Korean identity are different due to a disparity in meaning allocated to symbols of identity during rituals and self-presentation. I shall now consider the single character groups' responses to the adaptation of *nunchi*.

Responses of the character groups

The three character groups, considerably, all responded to the integration of *nunchi* in their strategic self-presentations, which revealed their distinct positions based on their national identity and one another.

The German international managers, to start with, portrayed themselves as truly international and good at adjusting, despite it was them who had the most difficulties integrating *nunchi* into their strategic self-presentations. Close to all of them described Korean identity, in terms of working with Koreans, as an experience that can not be compared to standard international business, since to them Koreans are "extremely backwards" in regards to international business. They believe that Koreans had and still have, very little exposure nor interest in understanding and operating in transnational settings and deny a coexistence of different meanings attached to symbols of identity, "for them it's either "the Korean Way" or no way", (by which they meant the German symbols of identity), noted an international manager. Some, generally newcomers in executive positions, also spoke of tension caused by the fact that even though their Korean colleagues work for a German MNC, they are disrespectful towards German symbols of identity. They noted that both parties should try to adjust to some degree, however for them it was possible to analytically understand "the Korean Way". The German international managers thus described themselves as, "der Klügere gibt nach" (the smarter one gives in) the smarter ones, being able to understand Korean symbols of *nunchi* and to perform strategically in line with such on the front stage.

The German international managers, also, described the adoption of *nunchi* into their strategic identity performances in business very much in terms of being a one-way street. Andreas remarked that the major problem was that in Korea, "most Koreans have never been outside Korea...for them it's their way or no way, they seriously believe and express arrogantly that they are the best, due to their ignorance they don't have a clue about the outside world." He renowned that in his experience *HanaEins* members, will try to make an effort to understand the Korean symbols of *nunchi* in self-presentation, but are upset if such gestures are not returned, and despite embracing certain rituals, international managers are upset when they are deliberately lied to or not taken seriously because of age and marital status. He rationalized, that the Koreans expect a universal monointerpretation of *nunchi*, because of their legendarily on-going war situation, seclusion from the rest of the world, hence pseudo democratic government, which practises hidden censorship for everything entering and leaving Korea.

Moreover, the international managers tended to speak of the differences of symbols in Korean and German identity and focused on the major differences in values and how knowledge is obtained and conveyed in German identity opposed to Korean identity settings. For example, the time spent at work, being more efficient through prioritising duties, "We work smart not hard... the Koreans start around 9am and rarely manage to go home before 22.00pm. They don't manage to get more done than in other countries they just complicate everything and that's why things take so much longer", noted an international manager. Hence, the international German managers, not only described themselves as being the smarter ones, understanding the differences in Korean and German self-presentations but also adapted Korean *nunchi* symbols strategically to manage and maximise the success of the German MNCs in Korea, which they work for.

The settled Germans also defined themselves in relation to the adoptation of *nunchi* into their strategic self-presentations as smart, but in a different way to the international managers, presenting themselves as both *HanaEins* members and locally involved rather than outside observers. Several explained their role at work as that of "the middle man" between Koreans and the German international mangers, in terms of language and symbols of identity; the settled Germans often expressed frustration with their Korean colleagues, due to their lack of speaking Korean in an easy and slow manner to non-native Korean speakers, "one either speaks Korean fluently or not at all and they get so upset and are unforgiving if non native Korean speakers mix up the honorific forms. On the other hand they expect us to understand their poor and horrible English and we have to keep smiling all the time", remarks a settled German.

The same applies to symbols of identity; one of the most outstanding examples is the differences during the initial contact and symbols of respect. The settled Germans were heavily disturbed that Koreans expected everyone else to understand them when they showed no interest at all in understanding others; "He greeted myself and my son and completely ignored my wife, he didn't even shake her hand nor did he give her flowers and during dinner he had the audacity to answer his phone all the time without excusing himself", exclaimed a *HanaEins* member. The *HanaEins* members overall under the leadership of the settled Germans initiated a *Stammtisch* (table of regulars) to exchange and listen to shared experiences in order to make sense of their own and others reactions to the adoption of *nunchi* into their self-presentations. Generally, settled Germans also expressed to feel that their national origins diminished their involvement in the setting and that their Korean counterpart assumed them to have troubles of understanding and practising *nunchi*.

The settled Germans therefore expressed their perceptions of the adaptation of *nunchi* using the same terms as the international managers, but with different interpretations of their approach in accordance with their different role within *HanaEins* overall. They outlined the situation not so much in terms of *HanaEins* members being the absolute smarter ones, as in terms of Korean identity being the more inflexible one in terms of self-presentation and emphasised that therefore *nunchi* can be performed strategically without the Koreans noticing it, in vitalising their knowledge about the setting. Opposed to all *HanaEins* members presenting the same adoption of *nunchi* into their strategic self-presentations then, there are differences between the character groups; the settled Germans suggest that *nunchi* performances are more natural to them due to their involvement in the setting.

Furthermore, the Chameleons much, like the settled Germans, portrayed themselves as "a middle man" between Koreans and character groups one and two, but similar in their case their interpretations were somewhat altered. Like the settled Germans, they voiced frustration with what they termed the Korean counterpart's inflexible identity presentations; they were actually more judgemental than character group one and two. The Chameleons had a strong interest to mingle with both the settled Germans and the international German managers, which allowed them to be part of *HanaEins'* extracurricular activities and grow close to, maintain and understand German identity symbols. They overtly criticised Koreans in front of other character groups for not taking an interest in understanding hence respecting German identity; it is to note that by this they did not only refer to self-presentation at work but to Germanness in a broader context. Through strategic, overt criticism of inflexible Korean self-presentation and praising character group one and two for their efforts of adopting *nunchi*, they acknowledged their own association with German identity notwithstanding them being theoretically closer to Korean identity than German identity.

Nevertheless they strategically voiced such criticism or praise to position themselves in the best possible light in front of character group one and two. It occurred that they revealed their real agenda to put themselves in a better position, when they spoke to for them obvious Koreans due to their ethnic appearance who actually happened to be German international mnagers or settled Germans how *"nunchi opda"* (*nunchi*-less) character one and two members are. At the same time they criticised Koreans for being inflexible in front of character group one and two members to secure their advantages of belonging to *HanaEins* overall.

On the other hand, the Chameleons defined the adoption of *nunchi* in similar ways to the other two character groups, but with an approach on the matter, which highlighted their personal advantage rather than embracing genuine symbols of German identity. Ultimately, the Chameleons similar to the two other groups describe themselves as smart. Nonetheless in this case they do this in splitting the concept of *nunchi* from German identity completely and assume that *HanaEins* members as well as Koreans believe that they belong to only one group, when the reality is that only their strategic front stage presentation belongs to *HanaEins* overall.

Close to all informants presented the situation in terms of "German" and "Korean" identity settings, but as the imposition of one upon the other rather than as *nunchi* between them, as an illustration this account from an interview with Alex:

> "So I decided to give small Christmas presents to our staff and since
> we are a German MNC, I wanted it to be something German e.g.
> ginger bread or hand painted Christmas ornaments. I consulted one
> of my German speaking Korean staff members and he said " That's a
> great idea I love that so much it reminds me of my time in Germany,

but oh no don't do that they won't appreciate it at all that's not a good gift for them you should give them something Koreans consider as a real gift such as a gift box of "Spam" (tinned meat) or a gift set of "Dettol" (disinfectant.)" Minutes later I walked down the corridor and heard him talk to a Korean (non German speaking) colleague: "this stupid German wanted to give us cookies or useless decorations, he has no idea about Korea, we don't want to eat their *madopso* (tasteless) food, *kechosso* (give it to the dog)."

In sum, thus, the Chameleons defined the adoption of *nunchi* and their position to it in comparable ways to other groups but their interpretations of the relationship between *nunchi* and German identity is quite different to that of the others, representing German identity as not capable of understanding Korean *nunchi* performances.

Analysis Reflecting the Views

HanaEins overall, which seems to be cohesive from an outside perspective, then, actually contains at least three distinct subgroups, each with a somewhat altered perpective in terms of identity and the adoption of *nunchi*. Notably these follow national interpretations of symbols of identity and their meaning in strategic self-presentation.

The international managers spoke in terms of general distinctions between national identities and the necessity to get on with Korean identity being a "one way street" to which one has to learn to adhere to in order to be successful. The settled Germans focused instead on the inflexibility in Korean identity and the lack of worldly attitudes. The Chameleons on the other hand focused on the singularity of symbols of identity such as *nunchi* and reassure the still existing blood discourses of identity in Korea. While one might, generally speaking, claim that all the problems originate from the matter that two national identities were forced to work in closer contact in the German MNCs, fundamentally each of the character groups has a somewhat special style to the adoption of *nunchi* into their self-presentations.

The consequences of this was the appearance of an indirect competition between character groups - as each group unintentionally wanted to be the most knowledgeable one and most "transnational" one. However, the settled Germans always managed to mediate between groups without showing off, they were able to integrate newcomers well and gently contributed towards teaching symbols of Korean identity without patronising other *HanaEins* members.

The differences in interpretation also mirror different strategic plans within the adoptation of *nunchi* into identity. Whilst there is a shared notion of *nunchi* symbols e.g. how to receive and give business cards, for instance, *HanaEins* members with the intention to stay in Korea for quite some time tended to integrate *nunchi* better than those who were only on short term assignments (a few months, less than a year). Even though these different plans could not be said to unsettle the adoptation of *nunchi* they did lead to different motivations. The international managers integrated *nunchi* with the aim to develop a "*nunchi* switch", in order to be good transnational businesspeople, who made their adoptation highly performative in their strategic self-presentations. The settled Germans integrated *nunchi* permanently to make life and work easier, their strategic self-presentation of *nunchi* in identity thus seemed a lot more natural compared to the international German managers. The Chameleons expressed their *nunchi* through strategic self-presentations of German and Korean symbols of identity, whenever they wanted to secure an advantage for themselves, this approach follows a natural performance of Korean identity, *nunchi* is thus automatically integrated.

Moreover, all of these approaches of adopting *nunchi* do not arise in isolation, but with reference to each character group's motivations. The occurrence of other interpretations impacts the process of defining *nunchi*. *HanaEins* members demonstrate their commitment to different groups by refusing or tolerating the meaning of a specific character group's interpretations. A settled German might, for example, tell a Korean colleague the non-factual (slightly altered) truth, which he would never tell to a international German manager since to them that would be lying, however when talking to an ethnographer he designates it as embracing *nunchi*. Ultimately, informants were moreover mindful of the flexibility of the definition of *nunchi*. Close to all interviewees brought up that the different national attitudes of Koreans and Germans, Koreans being overly positive, "wearing rose-coloured glasses" all the time and Germans being too serious, "asking too many questions" became an implied symbol of the need to incorporate *nunchi* in transnational business between Koreans and Germans. Informants thus are aware of *HanaEins* groups' definitions and Korean symbols of *nunchi*, and present themselves strategically with concern to these. Thus, *HanaEins* overall does not act as a bounded identity, but relates on the single character groups and to their Korean counterpart.

This strategic performance, furthermore, is expected in the case of practicing *nunchi* (see Stoewell 2003). For the adoptations to be delivered, *HanaEins* members must be able to shift from one set of symbols, and therefore identity, to another. This is accomplished by defining the views of the adaptation, and this in turn takes place through the different interpretations and exchange between character groups, as they have to learn a new way of self-presentation. Assuming that adoptation is a considerable part in international management, playing with symbols of identity is an unavoidable part of transnational business life, because the different character groups within *HanaEins* adjust their self-presentation according to the situation, so that mutual goals are achieved.

Additionally, the fact that *nunchi* is a complex and multi-faceted concept implies that new definitions may be added to the existing ones and may be accepted by various actors. Therefore, the variety of interpretations is not only intrinsic in transnational management settings, but also needed for *HanaEins* members and their Korean counterpart to operate in the constantly changing sphere of international business.

The difficulties in integrating *nunchi* in German identity originated from the unrecognised fact that there were at least three different character groups within *HanaEins*, each with a different position relative to Korean identity and other groups and their different purpose with regard to adopting *nunchi* into their strategic self-presentations. Additionally, the fact that the range of *nunchi* interpretations occurred within *HanaEins*, implies that the concept of *nunchi* its facets and relation to identity are under-researched in international business studies. I shall now consider how "the Korean Way" affected the recontextualisation process of symbols.

Theoretical approach to "the Korean Way" and identity

Introduction

There have been debates over "the Korean Way" and its significance in business. Predominantly Western scholars such as Hofstede (1991) and Trompenaars (1994) classified Korea to be as one of the most collectivist countries in the world. On the other hand however, East Asian scholars such as Hasegawa, Watanabe, and Kusayanagi take a different stance (in Chang and Chang, 1994) and depict Korea and its corporate practices as highly competitive and individualistic. While most Korean scholars implicitly agree that "the Korean Way" in business has formed, based on traditional Confucian collectivism, I disagree on its detailed nature.

HanaEins members working for German multinational corporations in Seoul often postulate Korean employees' collective focus; most of them are exasperated therefore, by egocentric, self- centred and instrumental forms of self-presentation, Cho and Yoon support such claims in their analysis of Korean corporate culture (2001). This section's aim is to provide the reader with a bigger picture to demystify the reader's including scholars' confusions of "the Korean Way's" orientation. To understand the paradoxical topographies of "the Korean Way", the origins of its core existence will be outlined and deployed in breaking it down to symbols of Korean identity.

Origin of "the Korean Way"

Numerous potencies have been advocated in the literature in association with the formation of "the Korean Way", particularly that of the *chaebols* (Chang and Chang, 1994; Chung and Lee, 1989; Shin, 1992; Song, 1990; Steers et al. 1989; Ungson et al., 1997). After careful reviewing of the literature, three main dynamics have surfaced in which the single symbols of "the Korean Way" are found. I have named each section according to its characteristics, firstly, 'Confucian policy' (unwritten law deriving from Confucian thought); secondly 'military mind-set' (created by the regime of *Park Jung-Hee* since 1961) and thirdly 'authotarianism' (dictatorship-like governance of *chaebol* owners). All three rubrics form the heart of "the Korean Way" in business and the private sphere.

Confucian Policy

The most significant constituents of "the Korean Way's" Confucian policy are emotional harmony, hierarchy, discrimination against out-groups, networking and high context orientation (Alston, 1989; Cha, 1994a, 1994b; Chang and Chang, 1994; Gudykunst et al., 1987; Hall, 1976; Hur and Hur, 1988; Triandis, 1995).

Alston (1989) notes that the meaning of harmony varies among East Asian countries, in Korea however *inwah* (Korean harmony) stresses the emotional aspect of relationships and relationship building. Another notion defining harmony is *kibun*, which refers to a state of being, a mood, and atmosphere of people and them, surrounding them. Maintaining harmony may refer to not hurting someone's *kibun*, especially that of people superior in hierarchy or people who are very close to one. Furthermore harmony serves the purpose of respecting other people's *kibun* and therefore permits them to 'save face' in front of others (Hur and Hur, 1988). The hierarchy system embraced in Korea is purely based on Confucian thought. Validated by this strict norm, close to all relationships in business and the private sphere are demarcated through social prestige; entailing, age, gender and position in society. The Korean language embodies that in terms of its honorific forms used. Politeness is strictly outlined in exchanges between entities of different statuses. Koreans often feel self-conscious at first meetings, because one's own rank in a new hierarchy needs to be established as soon as possible. Harmonious relationship building stresses pre-eminence and focuses on obedience to those of higher positions in hierarchy (Cho and Yoon, 2001).

Moving on to out-group discrimination, Triandis (1995) emphasises that collectivism does not mean merely prioritising group interest over individual concern. Triandis defines it as the differentiation between in-groups and out-groups. Koreans have a resilient affinity to differentiate themselves from others. For Koreans, those to whom one has not been introduced, with whom one has had no earlier dealings and with whom one anticipates no future collaborations, are considered a threat, a possible rival rather than common outsiders (Hur and Hur, 1988). Gudykunst et al. (1987), note that Koreans only show collectivist manners to in-group members; and individualistic as well as egoistic behaviours to out-group entities. Koreans generally feel apprehensive and have troubles collaborating with out-group members, taking into account that they try to smoothly harmonise and customise communication with in-group members.

Chang and Chang (1994) foreground that Koreans rely on building personal networks, which are embedded in blood relations and commonalities such as shared hometowns and experiences while growing up as well as academic achievements. Chang and Chang found, that Koreans trust their own family members the most followed by school friends and people from the same region, however their study showed that Koreans do not trust Koreans unknown to them effortlessly and the trust for foreigners ranks the lowest among all.

Additionally Hall (1976) remarks that Koreans have difficulties in clearly articulating their opinions due to "the Korean Way's" implicit rule to build more contextual information. Hall notes that Koreans are accustomed to context communication, rather than content communication, which can be linked back to the five components of "the Korean Way" to maintain harmony, hierarchy, networking and to foster discrimination against out group members.

Military mind-set

Another vital source shaping "the Korean Way" is the military mind-set inherited and transmitted from political circumstances exclusively belonging to Korea. Post World War Two, the Korean peninsula was split into two and triggered a brutal war. Given the circumstances, survival has become a key issue and shaped the basic principle for its institutions. Commencing in 1961 until 1993, disputes between the North and South have enabled the military to take over, which has, in turn, influenced and controlled almost every aspect of public and private life (Cho and Yoon, 2001). Initially, the military mind-set is understood in terms of the development driven policies of the military regime. The *Park Jung-Hee* regime has gained power through a successful coup and forcefully promoted industrialization and economic growth. Grand development targets, mainly in terms of meeting economic growth have been set by the regime leaders since 1962. The ruthless implementation of the military regime's policies infiltrated every aspect of private and public life and profoundly influenced "the Korean Way" (Cho and Yoon 2001).

"The Korean Way" has been paired with the 'military way' and 'can-do spirit' familiar from Korean cliché (Kearney, 1991; Kim, 1990). The military regime took advantage and exploited the tensions between the North South division to execute its power. Former army generals and veterans exercised substantial authority at all levels of society at least until the 1980s, arguably longer, before handing over to their offspring. Furthermore this mentality gets promoted and ingrained into "the Korean Way" through the exposure of men to the military philosophy, military service is mandatory for all men in Korea. The experience of life in military bases contributes severely to practises and mechanisms on how organizations should be set up and run. "It influences behaviour even in later life, predisposing men to emphasise hierarchical command, a result-oriented 'can-do spirit', and aggressive competition" (Cho and Yoon, 2001 p.75).

Authoritarianism

The Korean economy is dependent on conglomerates, *chaebols*. Their economic and social power to influence "the Korean Way" is so enormous that the Korean economy is often identified through them. Among many features depicting Korean *chaebols*, the most significant to "the Korean Way" might be the power and execution of such through dictatorship-style management of their owners. According to studies on *chaebols*, their owners have been permitted to arbitrarily shape not only organizational rules of paternalistic character but also the country's business strategy (Chang, 1988; Steers et al., 1989; Shin, 1992; Ungson et al., 1997; Yoo and Lee, 1987). *Chaebols'* finances are controlled by their owners themselves or their family members, such as his or her brothers, sons and daughters, who all hold fundamental positions within the *chaebol* (Ungson et al. 1997). *Chaebol* owners follow a strict authoritarian and paternalistic management style, in which close to all decision-making processes, even non-crucial ones are centralised by the Chief Executive Officers. They build on conservative Confucian thought, which is practised within the nuclear family, and promoted then among employees. Therefore they are naturally unquestionable figures; their power is thus representative as well as influential. Founders such as *Jung-Young* of *Hyundai*, *Lee Byung-Chul* of *Samsung*, and *Kim Woo-Jung* of *Daewoo* are feared personalities and partially accountable for the nature of the contemporary "Korean way."

Numerous studies examined how much determination Korean companies put into enforcing "the Korean Way" and how employees feel about such ideological enforcements. Large corporations tend to supply more funds to enforce "the Korean Way" through indoctrination and symbolization (Cho, 1995; Park and Lee, 1996) Sharp differences in attitudes between medium size businesses and *chaebols* and other companies were found. Employees of MNCs and *chaebols* have much more favourable attitudes than those of small companies (see Park and Lee, 1996).

Essential features of "the Korean Way"

"The Korean Way's" most noticeable feature results from in-group-out-group discrimination. In contemporary society, in which group memberships are too overlying to form visible in-group frontiers, corporations postulate these in relation to competitors (Kramer, 1991; Rabbie and Horowitz, 1988; Tajfel and Turner, 1979). The fact that most employees spend most of their daily time at work strengthens the significance of in-group-out-group borders. Once the second become evident and dominant, employees and organizations manage to use one set of rules for members of the in-group and an alternative for members of the out-group. The dynamism of "the Korean Way" is multidimensional. The three dimensions that describe it are in-group harmony, optimistic progressivism and the hierarchy system. Their amalgamation creates internal dynamics for the in-group alongside the dynamics between in-group and out-group. In-group harmony is very important and forms the root of "the Korean Way's" dynamism. For the sake of in-group harmony employees are expected to make sacrifices such as just fitting in for the sake of unity (Chung and Lee 1989).

An additional important feature of "the Korean Way" in business is 'optimistic progressivism'. Cho (1995) notes that progressivism and optimism are as significant as traditional collectivism for most Korean companies. It furthermore creates an atmosphere of strong competition with out-group members. 'Work hard' is one of the most common sayings embraced to ratify the progressivism it often causes employees to 'hurry up', which results in process-neglecting approaches (Cho and Yoon 2001).

"The Korean Way", demands employees to obey and appreciate hierarchical order and top down leadership within company. This principle is built on the Confucian rule that controls human relationships according to the Five Codes: between ruler and subject; father and son; husband and wife; older brother and younger brother; and friends. Except between friends relationships are unequal and differences in especially age, sex, role or status are emphasised (Chen and Chun, 1994; Condon, 1977). Chen and Chung (1994) remark, that hierarchy is strongly vitalised in organizational practices. The emphasise on particularistic relationships predestines behavioural patterns, this predictability carries a set of specific rules and patterns for communication, to assist employees to avoid disconcerting situations and serious trouble (Hwang, 1988). In addition hierarchy contributes to an elusive boundary amongst personal and public relationships, which therefore animates a solid desire for personal bonds for business transactions (Yum, 1988).

In summary, these basic features of "the Korean Way" are visible in organisational practises, validated through Confucianism to make in-group members reciprocally interdependent. This contributes to a prominent in-group boundary and evokes strong competition with other groups. All in all, the three dimensions of "the Korean Way's" dynamism, boost strategic self-presentation seen through strong inter-group boundaries and competition. I shall now consider the nature of "the Korean Way", which is captured in the military and family metaphor.

Picturing "the Korean Way": Military and Family

The essence of the above-discussed literature may be traced back to two metaphorical roots, naming, military and family. "The Korean Way" follows a set of believes in which organizations operate in similar terms compared to the army and the Confucian principle of the family. Cho and Yoon argue that this a natural consequence of the "Korean way's" influences by the Korean construct of the family and experiences and relevance of military life. Family life is the most important form in which Koreans absorb the Confucian norms, underlying "the Korean Way." Such norms "generate notions of proper behaviour among unequals and in running organizations. Moreover, Korea is a male-dominated society. All men have to serve the nation in the military for at least a couple of years. Their exposure to military life reverberates over their whole careers", (Cho and Yoon 2001, p. 79). Thus vitalizing "the Korean Way's" constructs of family and military behaviour, strengthens and reinforce in group harmony, hierarchy and optimistic progressivism. In short, "the Korean Way" manifests the military-like organization style, underlying Confucian values of family, to control a solid and inflexible way of self-presentation at work and in the private sphere.

Functions of "the Korean Way" in business practises

Empirical research has shown that decision-making in Korea as well as in Korean work places follows a strict authoritarian manner (Chung and Lee, 1989; Lee and Suh, 1998). In addition research results have shown, that the authority to make decisions goes way beyond its licit latitude in Korea, "the Korean Way" however suggests that decision making is based on emotion work rather than logical and rational reasoning. Findings demonstrate, that "the Korean Way" allows managers to have greater authority than responsibility for people in higher-ranking positions, although subordinates have more responsibility than their decision-making seniors. As a result, this encourages employees with lower positions not to work independently and not to make decisions on their own or to greatly delay them if they have to (Cho and Yoon, 2001).

On the other hand, "the Korean Way" maintains a centralised approach to management practices with a clear and unquestionable formal structure. Organizations in Korea are vertically designed, which makes their organizational hierarchy obvious and recognisable. It is to note however, that this sharp reporting outlet enables favouritism, encouraged through informal networking. In order to build up such personal bonds and networks, *Hweshiks* after work facilitate such opportunities, which in turn reimport strong levels of informality and emotionality into the existing formal structure of "the Korean Way".

HRM practices

Human resource management is one of the most identity bound management practises (see Rowley, 1998), because it concerns itself with non-tangible and not-easily-treatable resources. "The Korean Way" has influenced HRM practices in Korea mainly in terms of harmony and the concept of family. In selection and recruiting, companies in Korea assume applicants to be able to embrace "the Korean Way's" traits, such as blending in naturally. Therefore, it is the norm to find that employees follow "the Korean Way" undoubtedly and prefer the notion of 'pure bloodism' in the company (Cho and Yoon, 2001).

Park and Ahn (1998) found that seniority is the major factor determining pay rises and promotions, which derive from "the Korean Way's" incorporation of the two metaphor principles, family and military, discussed earlier on. Their study shows that seniority comes first and is more important than performance, which is seen in employees' remuneration packages. "Some 57 per cent of surveyed companies rated seniority as the most important criterion for a manager's salary in Korea. This contrasts with German companies, in which only 17,4 per cent considered seniority as an important factor for a manager's salary increase" (Park and Ahn in Cho and Yoon, 2001, p. 84).

Furthermore, Steers et al. (1989) stress severe competition inside Korean company's concept of family. Joining MNCs in Korea are extremely competitive and only graduates from prestigious universities are considered. In addition, gaining power and respect within Korean companies is only available to inner circle group members, which aggravates competition among employees to reach their set goals.

Conclusion

In this Chapter, I have given an integrative view on "the Korean Way" in business, its main characteristics, origins and functions in corporate practises. The bigger picture presented in this chapter to make sense of and understand this study's empirical findings, should be taken with caution, because identities undergo constant change, so does "the Korean Way." Admitting this latent hindrance, I provided a broad mechanism underlying Korean identity and business practices: "the Korean Way." "The Korean Way" depicts how corporate practices have developed into leading topographies and encouraged certain types of organizational practises.

In sum, "the Korean Way" is a product of tempestuous social dynamisms in a developing nation, resulting from on-going political and economic tensions and

infused traditional notions of Confucianism.

Chapter 8

Nunchi from within:

The recontextualisation of "the Korean Way"

The connection between *nunchi* and "the Korean Way" is not entirely as the literature might indicate. Moreover, in the case of *HanaEins* members we may observe how *they* define the single symbols of "the Korean Way" in terms of the same attributes, but differentiate themselves within the group as a whole through having different interpretations and valuations of these. Nevertheless, although *HanaEins* members were eager to undertake the notion of "the Korean Way", they neglected to realise the need for recontextualising them according to character groups opposed to as a whole entity, choosing to explain it instead of detachments between Korean and German national identities, produced difficulties with the integration of *nunchi* into identity performances.

Case Study: Peony

Peony is a project manager for one of the world's most famous German breweries. She is in her early thirties and was born in Germany, however she was raised in Korea. She joined *HanaEins* as an intern while she was still at university, and has continued to work for the same MNC ever since. Although her job involves acting as liaison between the Korean and German office she has only spent 18 months living and working in Germany. She is bilingual and is very proud that people cannot hear any accent in either language she speaks. She is dating a German man and dreaming of a life in Stuttgart.

HanaEins, recontextualising symbols of "the Korean Way"

HanaEins' primary approach seemed to be an effort to understanding and adjusting to the Korean setting in the perspective of the different character groups and their Korean counterparts. As Peony phrased it, "Understanding "the Korean Way" is essential when doing business in Korea." Therefore, many informants experienced what the literature defines as the recontextualisation of symbols from on identity setting into another. A well known *HanaEins* member, Rainer, endorsed its application to "the Korean Way", in other words, that *HanaEins* members would also have to become locally consolidated in order to be successful within the Korean market. *HanaEins* members accordingly, due to their ambitions to be perceived as "truly transnational", applied the recontextualised symbols of their own activities. On the other hand, the character groups were said to be intensely concerned with their specific stance on incorporating *nunchi* into their identities when recontextualising "the Korean Way". Peony also touched on the fact that different character groups competed with each other in making sense of "the Korean Way". *HanaEins* overall was identified to take a general, and character groups a specific perspective on the recontextualisation of "the Korean Way" according to their personal motives. A German international manager described the importance of recontextualising symbols of "the Korean Way" in simple terms to just assure smooth business operations rather than due to it being helpful of integrating into broader operations of society and everyday life in Korea, which once again stresses the performative aspect.

Andrea said, that different motivations of recontextualisation were what distinguished the single character groups from *HanaEins* as a whole.

The recontextualisation process of "the Korean Way" is however described amongst *HanaEins* members as several processes, pinned up by different motivations, according to the single character group. The recontextualisation process was described in terms of finding analogue symbols of German identity to make sense of lived experiences in Korea. Most *HanaEins* members felt the need to "logically understand actions and explain them to each other and the Koreans" on the grounds that close to all *HanaEins* members believed Koreans to be so isolated from the rest of the world, due to their history and national identity that they thought that "a different way might exist has not crossed their mind yet." *HanaEins* members furthermore felt that they were expected to replace their way of thinking with ways compatible to "the Korean Way".

An influential *HanaEins* member mentioned that the aim of recontextualisation and in particular the widespread contribution from especially character groups one and two increased their *nunchi* skills significantly, in recontextualising the for them irrational symbols of Korean identity. On the other hand, however, there was no overt reversed recontextualising process, which was initiated by their Korean counterpart. Most Koreans did not acknowledge the coexistence of Korean symbols in German identity and only performatively acted upon symbols of Germanness when forced to.

For instance, a Korean line manager entered a German international manager's office while the international manager's wife; his son and myself were present. The line manager greeted all of use and shook our hands, however he completely ignored the wife. He did not shake her hand nor did he even bother to say hello. "Even though it is common knowledge and we were prepared in our management training course that women are of less value in Korea it hurt me so much that I massively told him off and also lectured him on how to treat women regardless of one's nationality", renounced the character group one member. From that day onwards, this particular line manager used to "jump of his seat and walk over to the door whenever my wife came to visit, which was obviously a complete act he put on."

The recontextualising process was thus discussed as an inevitable process for *HanaEins* members to make sense of their own and their colleagues' behaviour as most German MNCs in Seoul are overpowered by Korean identity performances due to the larger percentage of the workforce being Korean.

Thus, *HanaEins* members' struggles to become accustomed to the different meaning of self-presentation practices, triggered by the recontextualisation process were discussed within *HanaEins* in terms of the different character groups, dominated by the single groups' motivations of recontextualising "the Korean Way." Peony, after explaining that the idea she recieved of the response of the recontextualisation process was that *HanaEins* as a unit felt that their Korean counterpart was imposing its "Korean way" on everyone, she added that all character groups described this as acting "typical Korean, it's their way or no way."

For instance, most Koreans just carry on speaking Korean even though they are able to speak English and know some people around them at the office cannot speak Korean. However, if everyone around them speaks German and they cannot speak German they will lecture one to speak English or Korean. Likewise, if a non native Korean speaker makes mistakes, however is still able to get his or her point across they start pretending that they cannot understand or get angry at one for using the wrong honorific forms. "My German colleagues always try to understand and make Koreans feel comfortable when they speak English or German, they actually give them credit for trying, and it makes me feel so embarrassed when Koreans patronise Germans for making little mistakes when they speak Korean," remarked Peony. *HanaEins* thus described the recontextualisation process as a somewhat one-way street since, except when forced upon them, their Korean colleagues avoided the reversed recontextualising process despite working for a German MNC. Peony even takes this further in stating that Koreans reject analogue symbols of "the Korean Way" in German national identity. Virtually all *HanaEins* members, additionally, raised the symbol of cosmopolitanism, in the sense of *Weltoffenheit,* which in their perspective includes various realities, "it might be different but that doesn't make it wrong", remarked an international manager. Peony defined the "Korean wannabe cosmopolitan" compared to the German "make up your own mind cosmopolitan."

She describes the "Korean wannabe cosmopolitan" with the German saying, "What the farmer doesn't know he won't eat." Most Korean households have a sofa but they actually don't sit on it, they rather gather around a small traditional Korean fold up table, whilst sitting on the floor. However, on the front stage you have to have a sofa, in order to be cosmopolitan and they sit on it when anyone who is not close to them comes around. Similar things occur at the office, close to all Koreans choose an English name to be cosmopolitan, but no one ever uses it which becomes especially apparent when you try to e-mail someone in the office, in that case they do not use their "cosmopolitan name" and they are not known by their English names amongst other Koreans, which makes it redundant to have except serving the "wannabe cosmopolitan" front stage purpose.

Using Brannen's (2004) model of recontextualisation, I identified four main symbols of how identity performances convey meaning and affect *HanaEins* members' successful transfer of firm assets in terms of strategic self-presentation. Throughout this process these assets of self-presentation take on new meanings for *HanaEins* members.

Applying the analytic model to the case of *HanaEins*

Recontextualising entire national identities and their way of thinking such as "the Korean Way" is virtually impossible, however rationalizing exactly which strategic organisational practices of identity performances to transfer is useful. Therefore, I identified "the Korean Way's" core competencies and focus on transferring these aspects fully, as suggested by (Brannen et al., 1999.) Such practises are defined as "strategic organizational practices," which reflect the core competencies of an entity (Kostova, 1999.) The transfer of these key practices is of high importance to *HanaEins* members, because the creation of knowledge through recontextualisation becomes *HanaEins* primary advantage to strategically present itself in Korea (Bartlett & Ghoshal, 1997; Kogut, 1991). Acting upon such knowledge provides *HanaEins* with a distinct source of competitive advantage that differentiates them from their Korean counterpart.

I use this logic to focus my analysis of the *HanaEins* case of adopting *nunchi* into their strategic self-presentations, hence comprehending "the Korean Way." The analysis of the study's fieldwork has identified what *HanaEins* members classify "the Korean Way's" core competencies and strategic organizational practices of its strategic *nunchi* performances into management practices in the German MNCs in Seoul. This division among practices and ideology is particularly useful for semiotic theory building, since these show some of the levels, from conceptual to narrative and discursive (Brannen, 2004). I have therefore divided my analysis of the recontextualisation of "the Korean Way" among practices and ideology, prevalent in daily self-presentations in business activities. For practices, I focus on two of the most pervasive themes, rooted in "the Korean Way" – truth telling – and single word conversations, since some of the main differences in identity performances, *nunchi* and management practises are seen in those. For ideology, I focus on two aspects of the German societal and corporate formula for global success, *Ordnung* and collectivism, which at the same time allows diversiy. I focus on sematic shifts across identities and borders, in *HanaEins* members' narrative and strategic self-presentation use to show how *nunchi* as a linchpin of "the Korean Way" and in Korean identity is perceived in each context.

Table IV summarizes how each of these core competences is recontextualised when transferred from "the Korean Way" into German identity presentations: as displaced signifiers, each takes on new signification in German identity presentations.

The interpretations of the ethnographic data collected, explain the semantic evolution of these core competences with the semiotic framework described by Brannen (2004)

Table IV   Recontextualisation of strategic self-presentations in "the Korean Way" as HanaEins' group assets

It is to note that the meaning of the terms practices and ideology follow Brannen's (2004) interpretations.

Signifier	"The Korean Way"	German Identity
Practises		
• Truth telling	Performative truth alteration	Factual truth telling
• Single word conversations	Single words express entire states of being (high *nunchi* required)	Explicit, logical explanations for state of being (medium *nunchi* required)

Ideology		
• *Ordnung* • •	Emotional, unquestionable Confucian order	Logical order based on facts and education
• Collectivism vs. Individualism	High collectivism and low individualism on the front stage -> low collectivism and high individualism on the backstage	Low collectivism and high individualism on the front stage -> high collectivism, which allows the diversity for high individualism on the backstage

HanaEins members' key strategic organizational practice of strategic self-presentations of "the Korean Way" has been summed up by Peony as the capability to create a "*Heile Welt* – harmonious office" atmosphere. This intangible asset depends on *HanaEins* members' ability to provide a non- argumentative, hyper-happy, non-confrontational and most importantly harmonious environment, which comes from a strong and somewhat totalitarian management competence. While this competence appears not to be the Germans first choice in management style, *HanaEins* members are able to deliver this formula by employing a two-part system of strictly separating reality from imagination and true performances of self-presentation from expected performances of self-presentation.

Throughout my fieldwork I gave this phenomenon the sobriquet of the "*Runterschlucken-lifestyle*" (Swallow your pride – lifestyle). I further attribute *HanaEins* member' success in pulling off the "*Heile Welt* – harmonious office" to a series of semiotic contrasts – hard working/ long hours of attendance, kindness/cheating, superficiality in terms of looks/ no manners, no worldliness/ being race selective, selfishness/ emphasising collectivism etc.

This stance is consistent with that of Jean Baudrillard a philosopher, who deconstructs the opposition between the "reality" and "imaginary" of places and refers to man- made environments that do not resemble the "reality" of the place as "hyper-real," referring to the place's multiple layers of narrative and discursive simulations that create its false reality (Baudrillard, 1983, 1988). In terms of identity in the context of Korea and Germany at large, *HanaEins* embodies "hyper-real" presentations of self, something that its Korean counterpart can only wish for regarding "the Korean Way" outside the "harmonious office." The *chameleons'* attempts at reproducing this human resource *nunchi* competence have produced different results in terms of "the Korean Way's" recontextualisation.

In the case of the settled Germans and the Chameleons, *HanaEins* members had no trouble reproducing its core competence in strategically delivering performative lies (verbal and non-verbal) and having the patience and willingness to put up with single word conversations, which require a *Hweshik* ritual and follow strict *nunchi* rules. Indeed, careful attention to someone's or a groups' *kibun*, when able to benefit from them fits smoothly into presentations of self in Korea.

After all, performative strategic lying is so engrained in "the Korean Way" that colleagues let their husbands "die" instead of telling people the truth that they got divorced or business partners fake entire friendships with another family to eventually find out their colleague's business strategy.

In fact, performative lying is so highly evolved in Korean identity that Koreans have developed a special tone when speaking to others (at the office and to people who are not close to them), to show humble submission and respect when it is actually just a "hyper-real" tool to achieve the "imaginary" as part of the longed for "reality." This and other performnative lying techniques such as the "two disjoined layers" are part of the adoptation of *nunchi* into strategic self-presentation process which the settled Germans and the Chameleons undergo very quickly due to their personal as well as economic motivations. Character group one, the international German managers have not been as easy in reproducing "the "Korean Way's" core competence in terms of practices. In the international German managers' perception, where facts, the factual truth and the ability to express ones personal opinion without being afraid of someone's reaction as well as making an effort to speak in clearly structured full sentences are highly valued, the "Korean way's" implicit rules dictating such constraints of when and how to lie, or cover up someonelse's lie, going along with a fake story and taking the time to listen to single word conversations that are not particularly detailed are perceived as invasive to their own identity performances.

For example many of these one-word conversations include terms such as *Himdoro* (no energy. stressful, difficult), *Himnae* (Cheer up, chin up) *A ja A ja* (fighting), *Ja Jing Na* (annoying), *Jemi-ida* (fun, interesting) *Jemi-obda* (no fun, not interesting), *Hembukae* (happy, content). One is able to hear these words frequently in public and within work settings and especially during *Hweshik* rituals. The same word gets repeated endless times while taking shots of *soju* in the meanwhile. The other person is supposed to support the person in using *nunchi* and not asking questions about what is burdening the other person. This is very time intensive and requires a lot of alcohol.

Due to their only motivation being economic success and solely staying in Korea for that reason, their willingness to lie or dilute their way of speaking is relatively low, an international German manager said, "changing who I am for the worse even though Koreans might like me more" does not come as a second nature to the international managers like in the case of the settled Germans and the Chameleons. This lack of semantic fit between *HanaEins* character group one members and their unwillingness to adjust to some practices of "the Korean Way" is so pronounced it has evolved in a number of negative Korean press coverage (e.g. in the case of a large German car manufacturer), finally resulting in *HanaEins* unofficially and indirectly changing their recruitment policy when hiring Korean employees in return to trying to be forced to thoroughly accepting "the Korean Way." The unofficially but newly formed *HanaEins* recruitment policy first and foremost stresses that all new Korean employees must have graduated from a university abroad preferably one in a German or English speaking country. International graduates are more likely to have the "appropriate skills"; international German managers are looking for, such as expressing their true ideas and opinions more freely in decent English or German. The requirements are no less stringent for the lying component. Finger print machines have been introduced to monitor employees' presence, doctor notes are required for sick leave and internet restrictions have been implemented to stop employees from consistently lying about their activites in the work settings.

HanaEins defends this wholesome German approach as "Trust is good, control is better" as an integral part of the roles the MNCs actors (employees) must play in order to help set the stage for a somewhat more "harmonious office" in which everyone has to "swallow his/her fair bit of pride."

HanaEins through the resistance of the international German managers to fully accept "the Korean Way" has also been successful at getting all actors (employees) at the MNCs to participate in the renegotiated practises. The difficulties international managers encountered in recontextualising "the Korean Way" have contributed to making German MNCs in Seoul more innovative, truthful, more free, transparent and creative as the same rules more or less apply to everyone and employees feel the freedom of expression and creativity through the newly established clear set of rules.

The evaluation of my ethnographic fieldwork and data gathered has indicated that Korean employees although several had the chance to work for a Korean competitor and earn higher salaries, chose to stay with their German employer, since after getting used to the newly established clear set of rules period they felt that their freedom gained exceeds the money they could make. Overall employees stated that once they learnt to understand the logic behind the new skill set compared to the "emotional" side of "the Korean Way" it made their professional lives a lot easier.

Ideologies

As with all signification systems, the symbolic ideologies of the original "Korean way" work only within the greater context of *HanaEins'* relationship with the Korean society. Only by maintaining the contextual distinction between the "imaginary" (harmonious office) and the "reality" (Korea) is *HanaEins* able to reproduce the core competences of "the Korean Way" (Baudrillard, 1983). From social symbols, ideological complexes are defined as follows by Hodge and Kress (1988):

[Ideological complexes are] a functionally related set of contradictory versions of the world, coercively imposed by one social group on another on behlaf of its own distinctive interest or subversively offered by another social group in attempts at resistance in its own interests (1988, p.3).

Indeed, one of the more critical social concerns regarding working across borders and identities is that it brings people from all over the world including their ideologies and paradigms together, which then become subject to revision and renegotiation, however "the Korean Way" does not allow such interplay to take place. Peony has made a strong case for "the Korean Way" to be the modernist medium of control shaping Koreans into "products of society." She describes the "Korean way's" narrative prowess as follows:

"The Korean Way" is comprised of all forms of popular premodern stories, homogenizes them to camouflage and mask their authentic authorship and packages the stories and their themes to control and shape the way Koreans think. "the Korean Way" describes false notions such as single bloodedness and having invented have of the universe as well as lying about their history to conform to the ideally wished for Korea."

Thus, "the Korean Way" is used as a narrative trope in Korea to control and shape citizens as products of an imagined society, in which central messages in stories conveyed are changed to serve the image of the "imaginary." For example, the authentic version of "the Korean Way" ends with the protagonist obeying the "pre-punched model of life" faced with the tormenting choice to accept or terminate one's life through suicide, hence South Korea has one of the highest rates of depression and suicide amongst all OECD nations. This is a resolution quite unlike "the Korean Way's" version portrayed in the literature, where, according to Confucian thought everyone finds his or her place in the society.

In addition to the plethora of "the Korean Way's" romanticised stories of being, analysis of my data provided accounts full with examples of actualities, marginalised in the literature on Korean identity performances and *nunchi.*

By carefully crafting the "pre-punched model of life" the narratives of "the Korean Way" pretend to be collective on the front stage, but overall are extremely rivalling. "Korean national identity and all its mechanisms are extremely rivalling", states Peony.

Believing in "the Korean Way" enables the nation to maintain the pretence of the "imaginary" theme of living in a collective and harmonious society when the reality is somewhat different. " I don't know any society that sacrificed that much, but at the same time produced so many victims, who are completely left alone ... I just don't understand how a nation is able to sacrifice so much and leave all these people behind, " noted a *HanaEins* member. Everyone has to undergo this "pre-punched model of life". Everything in life is regulated according to age, gender and background. In the case of Peony for example she knew exactly from early on at what age she has to go to university until when it is acceptable as well as expected for her to get married and when to fall pregnant and when she will be an *Ajumma* middle aged married Korean woman, who's hair is permed and fulfils *Ajumma* duties. (For a deeper understanding of the *Ajumma* see Bernard Rowan, 1999). Virtually all stages of a Korean life are "pre-punched", including the way one has to dress, wear his or her hair, speak (honorific forms) and the respect one receives in society, assuming one followed "the Korean Way's" expectations.

> *"Everyone who fails to follow or disagrees with the expected conformity of "the Korean Way" gets excluded left behind and even punished. Especially single mums, disabled people, homosexuals, aborted babies; they even get buried on "special" cemeteries just for aborted babies. The abortion rate is so high it's terrible. And I am not talking about the subject of abortion, but about the reasons behind them, which are all rooted in the prudence of "the Korean Way", not fitting into the pre-punched life model. Society punishes everyone who doesn't live conform in this country which lacks acceptance of alternative life models … Why can't I have a baby first, then go to University and then get married? Why do I have to study first, then get married and then deliver a child? I have never gotten to know any country like Korea, which invests so much into development but leaves so many victims behind, who are completely excluded and left alone",* noted an international German manager.

The original signified meanings of "the Korean Way's" collectivism and national identity simulacra begin to break down in the view of *HanaEins* members, because the symbols of strategic self-presentations are decontextualized, by *HanaEins* members whose definitions of logic and collectivism are different from that of the Korean counterpart. Some scholars have argued this discursive notion as simply two national cultures standing in disposition to each other, as they claim German national identity to be on the highly individual end as opposed to collective. Rather, in contrast to these views, my fieldwork proves the opposite. All character groups of *HanaEins* depict their own as well as the German national character to be very collective in comparison to their Korean counterpart. They claim "inclusion" to be the centre of German identity and "exclusion" the main motive in Korean identity.

> "The German society is extremely collective. The German society tends extremely towards a collective feeling of happiness. Which means we include as many people as possible. That means we have

a strong sentiment of responsibility towards our society. This can factually be proven when looking at figures of people who hold honorary positions, volunteering and students who decide to do a "Freies soziales Jahr" (gap year as a carer), which is unpaid after leaving school. Figures show that almost 40per cent of all Germans hold such unpaid positions … we always try to value and include as many people as possible", said Christoph an international German manager.

I argue that although "the Korean Way" is absolutely not logical for *HanaEins* members, the symbols of self-presentation in Korean identity are recontextualised and function as tools to *HanaEins* members, serving to advance a particularly unique ideological discourse regarding *HanaEins'* relationship with its Korean counterpart. "The Korean Way's" form of ideological hegemony or "pre-punched model of life" operates by continually reinforcing the separation between Koreans and *HanaEins* members by keeping up the idea of the "imaginary".

There are many examples of how *HanaEins* members negotiate strategic symbols of identity in self-presentations to accommodate "the Korean Way" into their daily routines in order to manage smoothly across borders and identities. For instance, most of the *HanaEins* members' responses to the artificial creation of the "imaginary"; Koreans claiming "ancient traditions reaching back to 2333 BC mythology … completely ignoring Korea's modern history of having been a developing country and to some degree still being one" being absolutely true, end in "harmonious" silence or the "*Abnickenprozess*", as indicated by a settled German.

The adaptation of such symbols into strategic self-presentations of *HanaEins* members create a harmonious interchange between *HanaEins* members and there Korean counterpart, additionally, such adaptation provides ample room to deal with "the Korean Way's" inflexibility of a single existing truth, which enforces *nunchi* behaviour on the front stage.

On one occasion during an important business meeting, which was conducted in form of a *Hweshik* ritual and served to close a deal between a German MNC's representative (international manager), who was accompanied by two employees (a settled German and a Chameleon) and his Korean client, who was accompanied by two Korean employees, the adaptation of the above led to business success. During the second round of *Hweshik*, beer *soju* and *Budae jjigae* (literally "troop stew"), which is a spicy Korean stew were served and the negotiations took place. The evening went well and everyone was happy as it is supposed to be during the second round of *Hweshik*, however once of a sudden the senior Korean representative after having downed a 0.2 glass of *Cass* (Korean beer) exclaimed loudly, "*Eng*, Korean food is the best food all over not like Germany, Germany beer taste like soup *eng* but in the Korea we have the best." The setteled German present, rapidly answered, "Oh my boss and his wife love Korean food, it's so delicious", followed by listing a collection of Korean dishes they knew. All three *HanaEins* members were at ease and continued to contribute to seal the deal in performing the *Hweshik*. The following day at the office, after the contract had been singed the German international manager thanked the two others for having "saved" the meeting in leading him through the *nunchi* rules that make up "the Korean Way". The international German manager admitted that all he really wanted to do was pointing out the factual truth and origins of *Budae jjigae* and Korean cuisine being monotone, "I really wanted to tell them that Budae jjigae is scrap food as it was invented by *Ajummas* who went through American trash cans next to the army bases and just boiled whatever they could find in one of their super ass spicy soups to kill the germs cause they were simply starving." However in avoiding stating the factual truth and strategically agreeing to the "imaginary" on the front stage, performative *nunchi* as part of "the Korean Way" rendered business success.

This is an example of *HanaEins'* identity symbols being appropriated to advance an idiosyncratic *nunchi* dynamic particular to *HanaEins* members operating in the context of "the Korean Way".

Making use of "the Korean Way's" exclusion strategy is another example to illustrate the adaptation of the "Korean way's" symbols. *HanaEins* character group one and two embrace the collective lying and exclusion strategy when arranging social get togethers. The German international managers and settled Germans deliberately do not invite the Chameleons and their Korean colleagues to social events that are conducted in a German manner in order to uphold the "imaginary" and to sustain the credibility of their performative front stage presentations. Such social events serve the purpose of a "reality-check" to collectively complain about the "imaginary" and confirm that the adoption of *nunchi* symbols seen in "the Korean Way" are strictly performative and not natural or permanent.

Other examples of profiting from the adoption of symbols of the core competences of "the Korean Way" are seen in the way *HanaEins* members play with "the Korean Way's" inflexibility. International German managers often receive a "but this is Korea" as a standard explanation which does not make any sense since it fails to answer the queries in a to *HanaEins* character group one members' logical way. Therefore "the Korean Way's" inflexibility got turned into an HR asset. In the beginning the international German managers tried to understand, however since they felt like being pushed over by their Korean employees they became just as inflexible in terms of time management rules, efficiency and transferring responsibility.

> Klaus remarks, *"in the beginning I granted a lot of overtime because they were never able to finish their workload in the assigned time – then I realised it's because they don't work efficiently, I told them straight, you get paid from eight till six and I expect you to get your work done and if you do not know how to approach something don't hesitate to ask, oh and everyone has to leave the office by seven, if you are not done with your stuff by seven it's your responsibility to finish it at home."*

Andreas supports this and told his staff, " I don't care if you work in a Korean way or whatever but at the end of the day it has to be done without any excuses." Forcing their employees to take responsibility and standing up for their work made use of the symbol of inflexibility and rendered good results over time. Peony described the typical Korean manager as a "cheer leader" a leader that does nothing else but cheer on his or her staff all day to push them to do their work and makes them work over time. Knowing that they have to stay behind and cannot leave before the manager has left makes them waste a lot of time. The recontextualised semiotic of inflexibility made them work efficiently as they learnt to prioritise tasks according to urgency and not according to the seniority level of the person who assigned the work.

In all of these examples of adopting recontextualised symbols of "the Korean Way" into strategic self-presentations as an asset *nunchi* is carefully managed by *HanaEins* members.

In sum, in the case of the settled Germans and Chameleons, there was sematic fit with "the Korean Way's" symbols of self-presentations and recontextualisation evolved in natural ways due to their motivations not purely being business oriented. The international German managers however took advice from especially the

settled Germans and purely implemented recontextualisation as strategic front stage performances. This suggests that recontextualisation needs to take place as interplay between the character groups of *HanaEins*.

Conclusion

In this chapter I have examined an important organizational phenomenon, the role of core competences in "the Korean Way" in the recontextualisation process of adopting *nunchi* into strategic self-presentations. Furthermore I have used Brannen's (2004) process model demonstrating the effects of the social semiotic context on "the Korean Way" and strategic fit. In previous studies researchers have looked at broad cultural differences, managing across boarders and transferring organizational practices through expatriation. This study contributes to each of these by showing how "the Korean Way" as an important identity dimension affects the success of *HanaEins* members. Whether it is practices or ideologies in strategic self-presentations, recontextualisation affects each of these. Implications of these contributions include different approaches in recognising and managing the recontextualisation process of "the Korean Way" for different character groups, understanding that different character groups in one identity context do not have the same motivations, hence recontextualisation slightly differs.

As the analysis of the recontextualisation process of "the Korean Way" for the single character groups shows, shifts in semantic fit, of the four core competencies, played significant roles in adopting *nunchi* into strategic self-presentations. In the case of the settled Germans and the Chameleons the recontextualisations were received rather positively as opposed to the international German managers whose motivations differed significantly.

The notion of semantic fit presented in this chapter suggests that while initial recontextualisation might be anticipated with deeper contextual knowledge of the target national identity, semantic fit must be monitored and managed in its original place, because of the dynamic aspect of semiosis.

This is because as *HanaEins* members implement recontextualisation of "the Korean Way" into strategic self-presentations, they continue to undergo recontextualisation. Therefore, it is in the best interest of *HanaEins* to anticipate recontextualisation, recognise them as they occur, and manage them to assure competitive advantage in the case of the settled Germans and the Chameleons or as an opportunity for organisational learning and strategic realignment for the German international managers.

This study's conceptual model of recontextualising symbols of identity offers several contributions to theory.

First it delineates the process of how the recontextualisation of "the Korean Way" changes in identity specific settings over time in order to be successful instead of serving as a fixed formula of how to do business in Korea. Second, it stresses the holistic affect which semiosis has, comprising the initial, on-going and reflexive cycles which trigger recontextualisation. Third, recontextualisation of "the Korean Way" provides an explanation for how and when symbols of identity might be seen as an asset and, thus, be better utilized as a strategic way of self-presentation to secure organizational advantages. Fourth, it foregrounds that "soft" symbols of identities, such as *nunchi* are more vulnerable to recontextualisation. This is an especially significant contribution, since the trend in working and managing across borders and identities, tends to transfer a somewhat transnational organizational system, which "the Korean Way" explicitly *nunchi* is not yet part of, but soon might will be.

Finally, the conceptual model of recontextualisation contributes to method by providing an analytical framework for applying symbols in identity analysis to organizational ethnography and the wider sphere of business anthropology.

HanaEins members are the living proof that even if one assumes to work in one identity setting, symbols of identity evolve and MNCs that fail to realign their firm assets through recontextualisation lose out. Therefore managing and monitoring semantic fit are necessary when a group such as *HanaEins* changes its work environment to a Korean identity context. This is especially true and important for groups such as *HanaEins* who ought to achieve long-term continuous success in a different identity setting.

In terms of practitioners practises the difficulty is finding a balance between blindly trying to apply previously acquired "intercultural business" knowledge and unquestioningly accepting the rules of the new identity setting.

The successful integration of *nunchi* as part of "the Korean Way" in strategic self-presentations can rarely be set on forecasts rather than actual results, since it involves "making the familiar strange" – a process demystifying the complexities of every day life (Burgelman, 1991). Being aware of recontextualisation, its occurrence and how it occurs enables *HanaEins* members to realise the full potential of strategically adopting *nunchi* as part of "the Korean Way" into their presentations of self in MNCs in Seoul.

Chapter 9

Nunchi revisited: The presentation of *nunchi* and emotion work in management

Introduction

In these terms, bearing in mind the German transnational businesspeople of Seoul, *HanaEins* members' activities and uses of *nunchi* in strategic self-presentations, thus supports my initial hypothesis that *nunchi* and identity are more complex and multi-faceted concepts in transnational business, than most of the previous work on the subject advocates; and furthermore, that the variations within it are determined partially by self-presentation of the single character groups and *HanaEins* as a whole.

Taking this into account, I infer that the actors involved do not form a solitary *nunchi* recipe, connected to the Korean national identity, however that they play a part in an evolving recontextualisation process, integrating more Korean and German identity symbols in a complex, ever changing setting of management styles.

To begin with, in this chapter, I re-introduce Goffman's theory of the "presentation of self ", how we manipulate our clothing, hair, accessories, setting and so forth in order to present a specific kind of self when encountering others. I will take this analysis one step further in applying Hochschild's (1979) argument that emotional cues, which includes a large percentage of what defines *nunchi*, may be among the most important in human interaction in business.

Nunchi: the language of Korea

In pursuance of reviewing the complexion of managing real *nunchi* feelings in transnational business, I shall first go back to the ideas of Arlie Hochschild, and her depiction of the "emotion work" concept at the workplace due to the fact that it may offer a more suitable approach of how we control *nunchi* as part of our strategic self-presentation management (Hochschild 1979, 1983).

According to Hoschschild (1979), there are numerous ways in which emotion work is conducted. The first one is cognitive: The actor tries to change the way in which he or she thinks or perceives a certain phenomenon in order to alter the way the actor feels about it. The second approach involves kinetics. In adjusting physical movement, actors may direct their emotions into a designated direction. Thirdly, managing emotions includes the use of expressive gestures, e.g. bowing to greet people. However the most significant way in which we manage our emotions is through deep acting. Hochschild's concept draws on the work of Konstantin Stanislavski to create the distinction between deep and surface acting.

Deep acting requires the actor to transform into a character to a degree that the act is not an act anymore; the actor reacts exactly like the character would. In surface acting, the actor only pretends to be a certain character. The act always gets performed, keeping the audience in mind, their participation and perceptions. Deep acting on the other hand, assumes that the actor becomes the character for the entire duration of the act to such an excess that the audience takes on a secondary role. In Hochschild's model, most of what Goffman argues, appears to be surface acting.

Goffman's front stage is divided into three main features: the setting, appearance, and manner. The first two are tools that most *HanaEins* members can put on and use in a short amount of time. Such tools do not require deep acting of *nunchi*; because such are only part of the front stage and never reach below the surface of the front stage.

However, manner refers to the way we behave and strategically present ourselves; hence manner touches upon presentations that may well live below the surface. These qualities are more imbedded than setting and appearance, however Goffman fails to analyse in detail how manners are prepared or evoked for the strategic self-presentation. Hochschild's model provides the centre of the idea behind deep acting. In deep acting a mood or emotional reaction is self-induced and the emotion gathered, provides the basis to express a strategic *nunchi* response in "acting" or managing ones impression management.

There are two principal ways of how one invokes *nunchi* through emotions. Firstly, exhortation, which involves the actor in making direct efforts in inducing or preventing a feeling. For instance, when Carmen first joined *HanaEins* as a division manager of a well-known German aviation MNC her female Korean colleagues expressed that she is not up to date with the latest fashion trends and make-up skills, in her second week the girls got her a voucher for a plastic surgery clinic to get Botox as a birthday present. Carmen hated the idea of plastic surgery and the terrible directness expressed by her female Korean colleagues, but she knew that she had to be appreciative; so she exhorted herself and provoked her emotions by saying "It's the thought that counts and for them that would have probably been the best present ever."

This idea of Hochschild's presents us with an enlightening new backstage – this backstage is inside the actor rather then in a setting. But, because we are coming at the emotion directly, exhortation does not mirror true deep acting. In applying exhortation emotions gets promptly manipulated by the actor. In expressing *nunchi* through exhortation, the actor might feel that it is fake or even feel guilty for not feeling as expected or having performed a strategic lie.

"I really wanted to tell them that I hated the idea and that it is one of the first things Germans get taught when they buy a gift for someone they don't know very well – you don't buy them soap or anything related cause they might get the feeling that you think that he or she stinks, so I just went along with it and acted like I liked it when I actually detested it ", said Carmen.

The second way of managing emotions uses our imagination and targets emotions felt directly. This is the feeling of going back "to that which gives power to a sight, a sound or a smell" (Hochschild, 1983, p.40). In other words, through speedy recontextualisation we present clear cues to our self, cues which are emotionally recontextualised using our imagination. These cues then elicit emotions in form of *nunchi* reactions in the same way daily life in one owns identity context does. This implies that, rather than trying to directly manipulate our *nunchi* presentations through exhortation, thus producing an action *HanaEins* members fool themselves into reacting to an emotionally recontextualised motivation.

This imaginative approach uses recontextualised emotional memories. *HanaEins* members evoke or call to mind the memory of an incident where the character group members felt the emotion they are supposed to feel according to the previously examined symbols of "the Korean Way" related to Korean identity. Since all *HanaEins* members are professionals, each of them has an accumulation of emotional experiences to fall back upon. Long-term *HanaEins* members especially the settled Germans, report that after approximately two years those emotional experiences get triggered inadvertently. There are certain symbols that take us back to a past memory and help deliver the right *nunchi* presentations in the present.

A good example is when a *HanaEins* member was absolutely not capable of getting "Korean style angry", meaning shouting in an authoritarian style with a drill voice like in the army, to humiliate the highest ranking Korean employee at the MNC by calling him by his last name followed by the suffix –ssi (which was used during the Japanese colonial regime) to humiliate him in front of the entire office to regain respect.

> *"I went in to my office and plugged my head phones in, listened to ACDC which brought back the memories of my army days back in Germany when I was only 20 – my locker wasn't tidied up in the way it was supposed to be and my superior humiliated me in front of everyone like there was no tomorrow. The moment I walked through my office door in to the open plan office, I was transported back to my army time. I felt the blood boiling in my veins, while standing at the very front, in front of the entire office feeling the anger I felt back then – and I did what I had to do and when Mr Park said "but this is Korea every manager tries to put some money in to his own pocket" I completely lost it and did the most humiliating thing possible in Korea I swiftly touched him on his head followed by brushing over his face (which is the most humiliating action a superior can do to a subordinate mainly in the army or at exclusive Korean Hweshiks in that instant I fired him."*

It all came back to Christoph as an emotional recontextualised memory and he was there in his twenties again. Most *HanaEins* members had experiences like that. In deep acting we deliberately bring those memories back, in very specific ways to convey the most accurate *nunchi* performance needed. We use our specific memories; good or bad, to motivate our *nunchi* performances with recontextualised emotions, to legitimately feel those emotions in order to strategically present a specific kind of self. In addition actors enforce their recontextualised emotional memories to deliver a somewhat stronger and trust worthier *nunchi* performance in convincing themselves that the emotions experienced are true at the moment of delivering the *nunchi* performance.

For example, a settled German, who was very well integrated into her team at a leading German automotive MNC and enjoyed great respect from her male and female Korean colleagues in and outside her workplace was not willing to risk jeopardising her insider status in disclosing her partner being of the same sex. She avoided speaking about her private life as much as possible, however her Korean colleagues kept asking in a very direct and persistent manner, "you are so pretty Angela, you should really get married soon, it's not a good idea for you to be alone, why don't you make a boyfriend – you know you really should do it." She classified her colleagues as "typical Koreans" who will say or do anything to uphold the delusional perfection of the "hyper-real" front stage image of the imaginary to live in accordance with "the Korean Way's" "pre-punched" model of life.

"To find people who really live their lives is hard to find in Korea most people just exist, that's it, but they don't really understand the difference of living and existing so I did what everyone else does in this place – I gave them what fits into their world, " said Angela. She held her weekly meeting on a Friday at one of the close by coffee shops when one of her Korean employees slipped in, "it's the weekend, are you going on any dates Angela?" Angela described her feeling in that situation as detached and slightly annoyed, however she also understood her employees' point of few, because "that's all they know and are able to ever imagine and accept – "the Korean Way" of life", so she took a deep breath leaned back and quietly renounced, *"it was five years ago, just before I moved to Korea when my husband and one year old son died in a terrible car accident, so I just moved away from everything because I don't want to be reminded of my loss"*, while conveying her *nunchi* performance she called up an emotion memory of when she lost her granddad and even managed to spare some tears. From that day onwards she was never asked again about her love life and her team members viewed her as an even stronger and bolder woman hence respected her as team the leader.

Another indirect method, which is used by *HanaEins* members to manage *nunchi* through deep acting, is the use of personal props. In the case of *HanaEins* members, such props include colleagues of different character groups, family members and physical items, which display status, national identity and professionalism. Goffman demarcates physical settings as important features of managing the self in every day life, using them as a tool to communicate to others who we are or as whom we want to be perceived as. Hochschild's model takes this notion further in adding that physical places may influence *nunchi* management in affecting the way we feel in certain places. Some obvious examples of settings used by *HanaEins* members, that are used to strategically manage *nunchi* and people's *Kibun* are *Sul Chip* for *Hweshik* rituals, Karaoke rooms, golf courts and saunas. Less obvious places are, the smoking area in front of the office building, the ladies bathroom, the office in general, the German pub, or Western style restaurants, each place elicits a *nunchi* response in us and indicates a *nunchi* feeling which indicates and directs *HanaEins* members of where to avoid certain topics or behaviour. Thus *HanaEins* members strategically use specific places and their annotated *nunchi* vibes to express themselves verbally and non-verbally in favour of the *nunchi* vibe to maximise the given situation and its setting's potential. *HanaEins* members intentionally use props to act upon symbols of Korean identity, which evoke *nunchi* strategically to achieve business success. *HanaEins* members gave us the example of the settled German, "saving the deal during a *Hweshik* ritual" as discussed in the previous chapter, when the settled German quickly picked up on what his boss (a German international manager) was about to say and applies *nunchi* through being his prop, in manifesting how delicious Korean food is. His subordinate's *nunchi* performance, then, could act as a check on his *nunchi* management if he ever felt going for the factual truth in such setting again.

Nunchi Rules

I argue in line with Hochschild that emotions as well as *nunchi* are a kind of pre-script to action. This implies a clear connection between how we perceive *nunchi* and how we act. This *nunchi*-action connection became visible in the concept of deep acting, allowing the actor to manipulate the way he or she feels in order to produce a trustworthy *nunchi* response. However there is more involved than just the sense of authenticity. *HanaEins* members' self-presentations must be aligned with the norms and expectations that are found in every setting of the "Korean way." Each setting, each definition of the situation, requires different kinds of strategic self-presentations and thus *nunchi* management. Hochschild calls these scripts for emotions *feeling rules*:

" Feeling rules are what guide emotion work by establishing the sense of entitlement or obligation that governs emotional exchange" (p. 56). I argue that *nunchi* and *nunchi* rules are highly related, to feeling rules, which derive of the concept of emotion work guiding the strategic self-presentations of *HanaEins* members and their use of *nunchi* in MNCs. These *nunchi* rules imply what to express, how to express, when to express, where to express and how long to express *nunchi* through strategic self-presentation.

    HanaEins members' narratives do not provide a listing of *nunchi* rules that different situations may require, instead the patterns formed through the analysis of the empirical data let me formulate a strategy that helps to detect when and how *nunchi* rules occur. How are *HanaEins* members aware of when a *nunchi* rule is operating in a given circumstance? The strategy developed implies that, if *HanaEins* members evaluate their emotions, then a *nunchi* rule takes place. Some *nunchi* rules are easier to recognise and therefore easier to strategically perform as others because they are actually formalised to some degree.

    For example, *HanaEins* members are aware of the abundant directness in questions asked by Koreans, which touch on absolute taboo topics in German identity during initial meetings and will not take offence. *HanaEins* members know that it is 'normal' to ask categorising questions in order to apply the "draw system" effect. These norms are driven by national identity and vary through different national characters and ages. But most *nunchi* rules are not formalised. German identity assumes that emotions occur naturally. In fact, Germanness emphasises the importance of nature, the occurrences that feel most natural are the ones *HanaEins* members respond to without evaluation. A combination of 'gut feeling and logic' is how *HanaEins* members gauge the authenticity of their emotions; this itself is a *nunchi* rule. However the desire to view emotion as natural tends to make *HanaEins* members not see or pay attention to the times when they evaluate the way they feel. Therefore anytime *HanaEins* members ask themselves "what am I feeling?", "what am I supposed to feel?" or "why am I experiencing this feeling?" They are experiencing a *nunchi* rule.

    Asking these kind of questions indicates that *HanaEins* members stand beside their emotions, rather than directly experiencing them and evaluating them from a particular and objective point of view. Hochschild's model claims that both the desire and ability to evaluate and understand our emotions derive from societal feeling rules, which in the case of HanaEins take on the form of *nunchi*. *HanaEins* members are encouraged by the rules and the rules give them the opportunity to stand besides the emotional experience to evaluate it.

Another way to detect that a *nunchi* rule is present is being reminded by the rule reminders other actors give to *HanaEins* members. Rule reminders generally take place in two variations. The first variation is when we are asked to talk about our feelings. Requesting or offering accounts is an important part of interaction. Accounts are legitimate stories that are given why someone behaved in an unexpected manner. I would like to recall the incident when Sylvia was asked by her boss to mix a *somec* for the person, who she likes the most in Korea during her farewell *Hweshik* ritual; her colleague immediately announced, "That's Jade (her boss) isn't it Sylvia." Even tough Jade was one of the people that Sylvia liked the least; she mixed a *somec* for her. Reminders of *nunchi* rules act as requests for an account of unexpected or inappropriate emotions encountered. For example when Sylvia fulfilled her 10 months assignment in Korea she was extremely happy to have completed it and was happy to go home instead of sad that she had to leave. So her Korean colleagues asked her, "Why are you so happy when you are leaving us and Korea?" In asking for such an account they were unwittingly pointing out a *nunchi* rule to Sylvia.

Sometimes the reactions *HanaEins* members encounter for not meeting a *nunchi* rule are more direct. These reactions sometimes take the form of punishment: "It's better if you find a new job" (EJ) or "You can't possible go home the boss wants to go to *Hweshik*, and it was your decision to work in Korea" (Hannah). Other times these actions indicate directions: "Isn't Korean food the best, it's so delicious?" or "I really like our new team leader, and I know you do too!"

These *nunchi* reminders, whether requests for accounts or the actions of other actors all reinforce the existence of *nunchi* rules. I also argue that *nunchi* rules are differentially distributed according to age and power. Especially in a traditional Confusion society such as Korea *nunchi* rules are of higher importance to people finding their place in lower ranks of the hierarchy system. However some of the most prevalent differences in *nunchi* rules in German MNCs in Korea have to do with gender. The *nunchi* rules surrounding masculinity are much different from those for femininity. A man may become angry and start humiliating others in shaming subordinates with his voice and at times even subtle physical punishment such as brushing over someone's face and hitting them on the head. A female employee could never do that to a male employee however, women are socialised to endure their emotions within work settings and express their feelings elsewhere.

Gender and *nunchi*

Due to their subordinate position in Confucianism and therefore in Korean society overall, women have a particular relationship to *nunchi* in the form of emotion work. Firstly, most women in Korea are still dependant upon men for financial support; *nunchi* becomes a commodity that is exchanged in various professional and private relationships. *HanaEins* members reported that female members are more likely to be asked to control their negative feelings, such as anger and aggression through *nunchi* management. Furthermore a lot of strict *nunchi* rules apply to female strategic self-presentation in MNCs in Korea.

> *"They expect us to always be cute and sweet and speak with this caring slightly higher voice, we are not allowed to be rough at any time and can't even make vulgar jokes or laugh loudly – what gets me the most is everyone knows that women smoke but instead of standing with the men in front of the building we have to gather behind the building where no one can see us and some of these girls even squad or hide in the alleyways, at the end of the day a woman is just like a man"*, remarked Carla.

In today's Korea, aggression in men is seen as masculine and somewhat positive behaviour, "I have never seen so many men of all ages and kinds, what I mean is like business man in suits even putting up a fight on the street, especially when they had *soju*, like in Korea", noted Luzi; but in women it is seen as unacceptable and damaging.

Conclusion

The main concern with the vitalisation and adoptation of *nunchi* is that it becomes an essential tool for all actors in Korea in work realted settings and the private sphere. This study offers a way of seeing and understanding *nunchi* as part of the presentation of self. *Nunchi* is not simply an emotional reaction that is privately experienced by an individual actor; it evolves in the situation of the encounter, and thus *nunchi* reveals something about the strategic self-presentation of the actor and results in righteously imputed expectations. *HanaEins* members describe the way *nunchi* is managed as an involvement of deep acting, in which they exhort themselves, induce *nunchi* through imagining emotional memory and the use of personal props. Consequently, deep acting is prompted by and takes place within the *nunchi* rules of the situation. *Nunchi* rules are features, which lead *nunchi* performances as emotion work and identity performances in expected national identity specific direction. *HanaEins* members know that *nunchi* rules are occurring, when they are asked to give an account of emotions, or question their own emotions or when one is punished by someone else. Finally, *nunchi* rules are differently distributed by power and hierarchy status and by gender, I shall now move on to this study's conclusion.

Chapter 10

Conclusion:

Defining *Nunchi* across Borders and Identities

Introduction

Throughout the past ten chapters, I have explored a range of prospects in which *nunchi* is adopted strategically by *HanaEins* members, transnational businesspeople in German MNCs living and working in and around the metropolitan area of Seoul, South Korea. The outcomes of this undeniably restricted insight into the world of *HanaEins* members advocates that *nunchi* in transnational business necessitates complex relations between symbols of identity and strategic self-presentation expressed through the recontextualisation of *nunchi* performances at the workplace and the private sphere. More notably, the results of this research have implications for both academic and industry specific implications for business anthropologists and international management studies as well as for transnational businesspeople, working in transnational settings. In this concluding chapter, I will repeat my conclusions drawn and review the theoretical contributions and limitations of this study, as well as outline its future research prospects.

In this study, I have explored that the empirical data does not much reinforce the existing concept of *nunchi* and identity in transnational business, however the concept of *nunchi* management through strategic self-presentation does. Therefore, this concept is a construct building on Goffman (1956), Hochschild (1983) and Brannen's (2004) theories of symbols of identity viewing strategic *nunchi* performances of different character groups, all with different kinds of international affiliations and motivations and with links to each other of different approaches.

This concept arguably, offers a more applicable perspective of understanding the significance of *nunchi* in German MNCs in Korea, and the way in which strategic *nunchi* performances in identity affect business activities, than less interpretive theories on identity; it is also more straightforward to the lived experiences of *HanaEins* members, permitting us to bear in mind their connections in the private sphere and the recontextualisation processes of "the Korean Way". The concept additionally, through the discussion of the recontextualisation process and the learning process of *nunchi* rules, offers a way of viewing *nunchi* and identity in MNCs, which does not merely focus on two colliding national identities but on the semiosis of symbols of identity in MNCs. The concept of *nunchi* management through strategic self-presentation, by considering all three character groups as an equal part of *HanaEins* as a unit, provides us with a new way of looking at German MNCs in Korea which allows us to take individual backgrounds and circumstances into consideration.

Consequently, this study's key contribution is the introduction and examination of *nunchi*, as an important organizational phenomenon into the management literature, in offering a way of seeing and understanding *nunchi* as part of the presentation of self, hence performative identity. This study has therefore examined the role of core symbols in "the Korean way" in the recontextualisation process of adopting *nunchi* into strategic self-presentations. Thus the chief concern with the vitalisation and adaptation of *nunchi* is that it becomes an indispensible tool for all actors in Korea in work realted settings and the private sphere.

Out and About: *Nunchi* and strategic self-presentation of *HanaEins* members

The primary contribution of this study is consequently not simply to throw spotlight on the dwelt experiences of German transnational businesspeople in Korea and to produce an inclusive concept of *nunchi* in MNCs, but moreover to suggest a theoretical idea which may allow an improved comprehension of the ways in which *nunchi* is adopted strategically into self-presentation. In the following part I will outline how the concept of *nunchi* management through strategic self-presentation develops upon previous ways of looking at international business management, reinforced by the empirical data in the earlier chapters.

The concept of *nunchi* management through strategic self-presentation, as explored in the past chapters, relies on Hochschild's (1983) emotion management concept, however improves Goffman's (1956) strategic presentation of self theory and Brannen's (2004) model of recontextualising symbols from one identity context into another especially in international business. The subsequent interpretation considers *nunchi* in the strategic self-presentation of transnational businesspeople, regardless of their character group and motivations, as a tool, which necessitates all actors who are participating in business activities across borders, to recontextualise symbols of identity in any given circumstance to deliver the expected *nunchi* performance in order to achieve managerial excellence thus corporate success. The concept of *nunchi* management through strategic self-presentation is formed through the strategic recontextualisation of symbols of national identity of individuals and groups, and also includes the links between different *HanaEins* character groups, and particular Korean entities to the extent that all actors engage in business across borders. The concept of *nunchi* management through strategic self-presentation is therefore a way, which presents a multifaceted, flexible, greatly engaged depiction of *nunchi* and identity in business across borders and identities in German MNCs in Seoul.

As pointed out throughout this study none of the existent definitions regarding *nunchi* and identity with regards to transnational business is quite suitable in the case of *HanaEins* members considered here in the approach the concept of *nunchi* management through strategic self-presentation does. The literature focusing on national identity does highlight the impact of differences in identity within transnational business to some degree, however it tends to take a single perspective, not paying attention to the degree of diversity of strategic self-presentation of different entities within a MNC and with regards to the effect external impacts have upon them. Indisputably, it would have been incorrect to have viewed all *HanaEins* members in Seoul as exclusively, or even largely, as just "German" or "Korean" with respect to their strategic self-presentation and the adoptation of *nunchi*, as my informants engaged in a series of borrowing symbols from two identity contexts rather than having exclusively one or the other. The literature, which stresses the immediate needs of Korean and German managers and employees, enhances the degree of complexity to some extent and points out the specific impacts of symbols of identity, however this approach nevertheless generalises all *HanaEins* members and does not seem very suitable in the event where the informants did not have a fixed formula of *nunchi* management through strategic self-presentation, but numerous altered approaches underlined by dissimilar motivations. Thus, the effect of the three character groups, would have principally been undetected in an approach, which concentrates mainly on national identities. Therefore, theories, which treat national identity as fixed phenomena, consequently do not take into consideration the degree of complexity, which this study identified, in similar terms as a theory paying close attention to the self-presentations and interplay of informants of multiple identity contexts in transnational settings such as Seoul.

Goffman's "strategic self-presentation" theory, while better capable of concentrating on the connections between *nunchi* and identity of German transnational businesspeople is eventually enriched by Hochschild's depiction of "emotion work" and Brannen's theory of "recontextualisation". The combination of the three forms the concept of *nunchi* management through strategic self-presentation, which is more suitable in the case of the German transnational businesspeople in Seoul, because it allows the researcher to take the degree of complexity viewed in the ethnographic data presented in previous chapters into consideration. The conclusion of this book is consequently that, while the three theories might be applied to depict the German transnational businesspeople in loose terms, only in combination do they allow the consideration of, the multifaceted, continuing and performative manners in which they use recontextualised symbols of identity to present themselves according to particular motivations to perform *nunchi*. The concept of *nunchi* management through strategic self-presentation defined previously, though, is able to consider this degree of complexity, as it positions *HanaEins* members in the context of their connections to, and relationships with, other groups possessing different levels of German and Korean identity, cross-border activites and knowledge related to the setting.

In this book, I have considered numerous definitions of *nunchi* at different levels in relation to identity. Once the theoretical background was outlined in the beginning of this study and the combination of the three theories mentioned above suggested, the empirical chapters shed light on the case of the transnational German businesspeople in increasingly more detail, commencing with identity and habitat, concentrating on Germans in the city of Seoul, those working for German MNCs and then, ultimately, considering a particular symbol of their self-presentation, called *nunchi*. Such approach results in myself being able to study the case of *HanaEins* members both in its precise facets, which follows a management studies approach and in the broader societal, historical and identity context, which follows an anthropological approach. In the concluding analysis the definite improvement of the theory is that it permits the researcher to consider *HanaEins* members as a whole and its single character groups at multiple levels and to take both the broader context and the particular situations of individual character groups into consideration. The chosen theory fits the ethnographic data; as it is able to consider the different practises and levels of cross-border activities of *HanaEins* members, and to allow for the links between the three character groups and their subgroups, while at the same time recognizing their different complexions.

In harmonising and strengthening theories in international business management studies with theories originating from sociology and anthropology, researchers may establish a thicker, more inclusive perspective of identity and *nunchi* among *HanaEins* members, permitting scholars to draw out the complexities in researching businesspeople such as *HanaEins* members in transnational settings.

I shall now look at what the combination of the three theories contributes to the study of international business management as an overall discipline.

Thinking Across Borders: Theoretical Contribution

Furthermore, the concept of *nunchi* management through strategic self-presentation not merely relies on and advances previous work in international business management studies, however also contributes to the wider literature on *nunchi* and identity in business and strategic self-presentation. In the following section, I will indicate how this concept amends previous studies on related matters in business, establishes a more detailed way for investigating *nunchi* and identity in business, yields a fresh perspective of viewing *nunchi* across borders and identities in MNCs and renders a different approach on the adoptation and vitalisation process of *nunchi* in identity and strategic self-presentation at work and in the private sphere whilst adding insightful ethnographic data on the everyday activities of most actors in MNCs.

Modifying Earlier Work in business studies

First of all, the concept relies on, and advances, the work of previous academic studies considering similar discourses in organisations such as identity.

Most work in business studies, which addresses *nunchi,* focuses on culture rather than identity (see Morden and Bowels 1998) and tend not to focus on the facets of negotiation within organisations and in most cases marginalise the fact that all actors in German MNCs in Seoul shape and influence each others identity performances, such aspects go missing in a non ethnographic approach taken on by most earlier studies, which predominantly focus exclusively on managers; by taking this study's approach to the world of MNCs, the complexity and multifaceted nature of identity performances can be taken into consideration. Furthermore, identity has become a popular frame through which to examine a wide range of phenomena. Organisational scholars, such as Mats Alvesson, Karen Lee Ashcraft, Stefan Sveningsson and Hugh Willmot are progressively concerned with organizational, managerial, professional and occupational identities and how actors within organisations negotiate subjects surrounding self in workplace settings. Thus, identity may be related to a broad spectrum: from mergers, motivation and sense making, to emotions and managing across borders and in this case *nunchi* (Alvesson, et al. 2008; Alvesson and Willmott, 2001; Alvesson and Sveningsson, 2003; Alvesson, 1994, 2010). The concept of *nunchi* management also avoids forcing symbols of identity performances into either the "national" or "organisational" box as done by many previous studies (e.g. Trompenaars 1994) and thus considers different influences on different presentation of self in MNCs. In opposition to the more impressionistic and elusive approach taken by business anthropologists, however, the concept of *nunch*i management through strategic self-presentation furthermore has concrete applications in that, as was presented, it can be applied as a concept for examining diverse impacts on *nunchi* management during strategic self-presentation in MNCs. The concept of *nunch*i management through strategic self-presentation thus offers a new vista of *nunchi* and identity, in which neither the complexity of identity nor the multi-layered aspects of *nunchi* go missing.

The concept of *nunchi* management through the strategic self-presentation is a combination of the above-mentioned theories and adds a dynamic quality to the combination of these.

In addition, it is worth adding to this that such principles are built up out of negotiations of interactions and with time, furthermore self-presentations are subject to change, in response to internal and external influences and that only considering *nunchi* in terms of national or business specific identity presentations does not allow us to understand the complexity of symbols of identity in MNCs. The concept of *nunchi* management through strategic self-presentation consequently improves the literature to propose an approach of considering *nunchi* and identity in MNCs in the general societal and historical contexts, rather than concentrating on the single self-presentation of a single group in only one setting.

This study thus does not merely transform initial theories of *nunchi* and identity in MNCs in a more applied and inclusive way advocated by the concept of *nunchi* management through strategic self-presentation, however it additionally offers a rare perception on *nunchi* and identity through the choice of the methodology used to carry out this research.

Moreover, beyond the empirical case of *nunchi* this study renders theoretical contributions to the current international business literature in several ways.

Firstly, this study offers its support to theories, stressing the importance of identity in business contexts (Alvesson, 1994, 2010; Alvesson & Sveningsson, 2003, Alvesson & Willmott, 2001; Alvesson, et al. 2008) and symbols of national culture (Brannen, 2004; Moore, 2005). Furthermore, it contributes in highlighting the power and importance of the recontextualisation theory (Brannen, 2004) and its application in business studies. Ultimately, this study supports business management theorists, advocating that using dimension based theories, when studying culture related subjects in business management should be avoided (see Shenkar et al., 2008; Kirkman, Lowe & Gibson, 2006), thus this study contributes to a theoretical paradigm shift from function to meaning (Piekkari & Welch, 2004; Welch et al. 2011; Tenzer et al. 2014) and "distance" to "friction" (Shenkar, 2012, 2001; Shenkar et al. 2008).

I shall now move on to the matter of relating international perspectives to identity specific perspectives through the concept of *nunchi* management through strategic self-presentation.

Developing an international perspective

The concept of *nunchi* management through strategic self-presentation, as well as contributing to earlier discourses, may also provide researchers with an improved perspective of performative identity and the role of *nunchi* in management across borders. I shall now briefly consider what this concept contributes to studies, which consider working and managing across borders.

The concept, initially, raises the subject of the connection between symbols of identity and *nunchi*. The actuality that there are several ways outlining this interplay might propose different perceptions on a specific phenomenon. Nevertheless, following the concept of *nunchi* management through strategic self- presentation, there are a range of distinctive connections and interactions, which in one way or another all, in loose terms, relate to managing across borders. If thus, one regards managing across borders as developing a range of various subsets of the *nunchi* management phenomenon, the different manners of depicting it can be simply integrated as different aspects of the phenomenon. The connection concerning the two is then indicated to be complex and symbolically negotiated, including several ways of acting; in fact when one takes into account the many ways *nunchi* is expressed in identity, it is difficult to speak of one *nunchi* formula, as there appear to be a number of ways of approaching and presenting these performances across borders. Eventually, the concept of *nunchi* management through strategic self-presentation treats the notion of *nunchi* and identity in business as a problem; under the concept of *nunchi* management through strategic self-presentation, a solitary complex phenomenon can be identified, incorporating many definitions of *nunchi* and identity performances, with different relationships emerging between them, which are defined and redefined through the self-presentations of *HanaEins* members in MNCs.

The case of *HanaEins* members in Seoul furthermore proposes that the variety of *nunchi* performances and the different sorts of transnational negotiations of symbols of identity, manifests in the significance of self-presentation relevant to activities related to managing across borders. I have earlier presented how symbols of national identity, Germanness and Koreanness, may be used to express different degrees of cross-border activities, group commitments, and different links with symbolism, in ways which delicately alter as the meaning of symbols used shift from one identity context to another for the actors in the setting. Strategic self-presentation seems to make up the majority of their success, in such context; strategic performances of symbols of identity in MNCs and the private sphere depend on *nunchi*, which implies that it is essentially symbolically constructed. The multifaceted, performative complexion of self-presentation, moreover, makes it an ultimate resource for negotiating between group relationships and positions, meaning that actors make up character groups while strategically presenting themselves, and the act of belonging to a character group impacts their self-presentation. Therefore, this study highlights the fact that symbols of identity and self-presentation are indispensable to managing across borders in international business management.

When merging these two points, this study furthermore establishes that the symbolic complexion of the connection between *nunchi* and managing across borders indicates that *HanaEins* members may make use of performative self-presentation to negotiate between the two identity contexts in German MNCs in Seoul. The *HanaEins* members whom explored in this study recontextualise symbols of identity in both identity contexts, in the case of *HanaEins* members, most notably, Korea and managing across borders. Nevertheless, the act of negotiating between different entities e.g. *HanaEins* members at the office and Koreans, for example, or between international German managers and settled Germans, connects the character groups, making for complex networks of *nunchi* performances between Germanness and Koreanness and managing across borders, and bearing in mind a number of variations of these. Furthermore, this indicates that the way in which *nunchi* is defined becomes more important to international business management than before, because MNCs undergo the process of self-definition on various levels and identity contexts. Strategic *nunchi* performances in transnational business neither belong exclusively to one or the other identity specific context, however they are subject to recontextualisation, had I merely inspected the corporate setting without the private sphere, invaluable social and physical linkages between them would have gone undetected.

The concept of *nunchi* management through strategic self-presentation therefore considers the complexity between identity contexts and character groups, and with regards to the significance of self-presentation, shows how symbols of identity serve to construct and recontextualise meaning when managing across borders. By not solely looking at MNCs as either purely following Korean or German identity, consequently one can establish a different way of viewing managing across borders, which considers the rich range of ways of how identity performances relate to each other. Thus, this is a significant contribution, since the trend in working and managing across borders and identities, tends to transfer a somewhat transnational organizational system, which *nunchi* is not yet part of, but soon perhaps will be.

Formulating New Views of Nunchi in Management

The complexion of the concept of *nunchi* management through strategic self-presentation, in addition with the chosen methodology to develop it throughout this study, furthermore opens up new ways of viewing *nunchi* in transnational business and managing across borders. This subsequently has implications for how managing and working across borders; identity and recontextualisation of symbols of identity in MNCs are perceived.

This study commences with pointing out some of the limitations of earlier studies of *nunchi*, by elucidating the lack of the researchers' backgrounds and missing links to transnational business. Most research on *nunchi* (Yi and Jezewski, 2000; Lee-Peuker, 2004; Chung and Gale, 2008; Kang, 2000; Scherpinski-Lee, 2011, Blackhall, 2001; Stowell, 2003; Meurant, date unknown) tends to have been conducted by Koreans or overseas Koreans or researchers who do not take an ethnographer's approach and predominantly focus on the generalisation of national cultures opposed to symbols of national identity. This study's findings in applying Agar's concept of making the familiar strange, contributes to all previous studies conducted on *nunchi* in making plain the complexity and multi-layered facets *nunchi* entails, as opposed to simply classifying it as "innate" (Kang 2000), "mind reading (Lee-Peuker 2004), "a mysterious 'alpha' hidden in their hearts (Stowell 2003) and non-verbal communication (Yi and Jezewski 2000; Chung and Gale 2008; Kang 2000). Moreover, findings demonstrate that *nunchi* applies to all actors in MNCs and society and not like Stowell claims predominantly to the lower social class to gather the feelings of the higher social class. Additionally, this study proves Suh's (2003) claims that Koreans are more adaptable wrong, in outlining that *nunchi* is a tool used in strategic self-presentation, which is subject to recontextualising symbols of identity in identity specific contexts.

Moreover, the case of *HanaEins'* different character groups emphasises the fact that inward presentations of identity in MNCs may be as important as the outward ones, meaning that sometimes the gap between "Korean" and "German" can be less important than between international German managers and settled Germans. Supposedly, in any multinational corporation, the concept of *nunchi* management through strategic self-presentation infers, the occurance of the diversity of different self-presentations influencing it, which is caused by the company's country of origin, the symbols of national identity used by its members, customers and competitors and many other aspects.

This work also addresses one of the key difficulties with previous research on transnational managers and the concept of emotional intelligence. While a clear trend, stressing that international managers are encouraged to be emotionally intelligent exists (Cooper, 1997; Harrison, 1997; Hesselbein, Goldsmith & Beckhard, 1996; Morris & Feldman, 1996), the same works lack to incorporate non-Western symbols of identity, such as *nunchi,* and fail to address that the recontextualisation of the Western concept of emotional intelligence as defined by Salovey and Mayer (1990) is needed to successfully manage across borders and identities, when vitalising emotional intelligence. Throughout this study *HanaEins* members have been divided up into character groups, all working for German MNCs who might broadly be described as international and managers in one way or another, and in taking a closer look at the strategic performances of symbols of identity at work and the impact of *nunchi* on such self-presentations, this study offers an alternative perspective. Furthermore it demonstrates that recontextualising symbols of identity such as *nunchi*, which includes attributes of emotional intelligence, for instance, self-awareness, emotion management, self-motivation, empathy and relationship management (Goleman, 1995; Salovey & Mayer, 1990) is very useful for transnational businesspeople to produce viable results of managerial success in an identity specific context. This study thus provides an indication of the diverse complexion and forms working across borders can take, and the impact identity specific contexts have on MNCs and emotional intelligence.

Since international business management becomes increasingly identity focused, so the strategic use of self-presentation becomes more significant, and therefore more consideration should be paid to its use in international business, and in organisational studies. This study thus steers in the direction of discovering and examining the part of this development in transnational business.

This book hence contributed to the study of international business management by proposing innovative ways of how emotional intelligence – *nunchi* in relation to transnational businesspeople may be defined and how their strategic self-presentations entailing symbols of identity allows them to relate to their MNCs in an identity context dissimilar to their own. Long term, these contributions may be more useful to scholars researching *nunchi*, German transnational businesspeople and MNCs than theories using a quantitative method; because this study delineates the process of how the recontextualisation of symbols of national identity such as *nunchi* changes in identity specific settings over time in order to be successful instead of serving as a fixed formula of how to to business in Korea.

Creating New Views of Identity

Conclusively, in addition to letting the development of the concept of *nunchi* management through strategic self-presentation form, the methodology supporting this study provides a new understanding of *nunchi* and identity in MNCs in a day and age when a more interdisciplinary approach in perspective may be enriching to researchers.

As stated in the beginning of this study, there have been fairly few ethnographies of managing across borders, and essentially none whatsoever on transnational businesspeople working for German MNCs in South Korea. Moreover, even studies which take a more qualitative approach tend to concentrate on interviews and restricted interaction with the studied population rather than absolute participation; studies of working and managing across borders (e.g. Forster 2000; Harzing 2001a,b; Feely and Harzing 2003; Fredriksson et al. 2006; Tange and Lauring 2009) tend to be grounded on surveys and therefore do not to examine such activites with regards to more general societal and historical meanings. The complexion of the chosen methodology in this study therefore offers a perspective on *HanaEins* members, who are working in German MNCs in Korea, as a population, bound together through shared symbols of identity and part of a broader group, which seperates this volume from many other studies in international business management studies focusing on German and Korean identity.

Furthermore, the fact that *HanaEins* members were being researched at the German MNCs, the pub and their natural environement also provides rare advantages. Not to mention the fact that sociological, case-study-based work on the adoption of *nunchi* in strategic self-presentation in transnational business is relatively rare in general, the position of the ethnographer as a partial outsider to *HanaEins* members infers that this study allows a view of such events which is neither too positivistic, nor strongly influenced by the emotional process of the adoption process of *nunchi* into strategic self-presentation. The conditions of the research supporting this study consequently make it possible to provide a restricted, nevertheless still valuable perspective on a population in our case *HanaEins* members incorporating symbols of identity strategically into their self-presentations.

In essence, nonetheless, this study contributes to international business management as an academic discipline in several different ways. In addition to forming the concept of *nunchi* management through strategic self-presentation, which has implications for the way in which academics and practitioners view *nunchi* in regards to identity, the selected methodology and principles of the study offer a valuable alternative to the strong purely interview based efforts of earlier studies. I shall now move on to consider some of the limitations and troubles of this study.

The Trouble with *Nunchi*: Limitations of the *Nunchi* Management through Strategic Self-Presentation Concept

Like any theory, the concept of *nunchi* management through strategic self-presentation is not exclusive of its limitations. In the following section, I will consider some of the problems brought up by the concept per se, besides by the data and methodology used to underpin it, and recommend ways in which these can be improved.

It might be, for example, said that the concept of *nunchi* management through strategic self-presentation, in criticising more traditional theories of dimensions (Hofstede 1980, 1994, 2001) in MNCs, tends too much in the other direction, being too widespread where former theories were too limiting. Although scholars like Hofstede do not take into consideration the range of identities and the interplay between businesspeople managing across borders, one might likewise argue that the concept of *nunchi* management through strategic self-presentation might be too inclusive. However, taking the diversity of the multi-layered concept of identity into account, allows the concept of *nunchi* management through strategic self-presentation to recontextualise symbols of identity in strategic self-presentation in order to successfully manage across borders and identities. Furthermore, the concept of *nunchi* management through strategic self-presentation provides a theory for discovering the ways in which the three character groups interrelate, and for understanding the function of their different influences and self-presentation in their expressions of business activities in their everyday lives. Moreover, it must also be noted that one of the objectives of this research is to further unpack the pretension of the practise of assuming that symbols of national identity such as *nunchi* are exclusive to particular national groups. The case of *HanaEins* members in this study therefore implies that the concept of *nunchi* management through strategic self-presentation may offer a helpful basis for future research.

Nevertheless, it could likewise be proposed that the concept of *nunchi* management through strategic self-presentation is, in some aspects too limited. Whereas the concept allowed me to feature the different aspects in which informants related to symbols of Korean and German identity, this research does not even make an attempt at covering the diversity of *HanaEins* members. The German members, for example, contained a small percentage of former East Germans who still grew up in the former German Democratic Republic, West Germans, to say nothing of regional German identities e.g. Bavarians, Berliners etc. in total there are 16 official states within Germany, and the Koreans also varied in terms of their regional origin (albeit largely tried to be kept as a secret), class background and religion. Despite the outward mono-identity of the Koreans overall, there still existed two privileged groups among male Koreans, firstly the ones who were chosen to serve in the American army instead of the Korean army and secondly the ones who were allowed to work for a state owned company instead of attending any army service, even though that is a very small percentage. Subsequently, it might therefore be that further research will find measures of approaching and integrating this occurrence of diversity.

The case study of *HanaEins* members working for German MNCs in Seoul also subtly underlines the fact that one has to take into account other effects on transnational businesspeople than merely the influence of symbols of national identity. Also, the empirical chapters and the conclusion, stress the fact that *HanaEins* members do not exist in their own world, however *HanaEins* members frequently voiced the influence of external commercial, governmental and cultural events.

Still, even this level of detail cannot consider the other aspects affecting *HanaEins* members, such as gender, ethnicity and sexuality, besides those reviewed in this study. Factors such as gender, sexuality and ethnic relations could not only affect *HanaEins* members' *nunchi* management through strategic self-presentation, but also the same factors could have different influence on different character groups and their recontextualisation processes. There are thus possibilities for expansion and development of the concept of *nunchi* management through strategic self-presentation in terms of other forms of diversity.

Conclusively, as already mentioned in the methodology section, while ethnographic methodology has provided a number of different understandings into *nunchi* and identity in transnational business, it also has certain weaknesses. The starting point that the ethnographer was a reasonably cheerful, tall Caucasian white, arguably handsome young man, who was willing to drink abundant amounts of *soju* etc., undeniably influenced the responses informants provided and how I was treated; it could thus be useful conducting comparable ethnographies by researchers with unlike demographic starting conditions, or of different ethnicities. Additionally, I was similarly alert that the answers, especially for the recorded interviews which informants gave to me were influenced by my position as a somewhat *HanaEins* member; while I have been able to consider this to a certain degree by informally interviewing at the pub and at the office and by doing follow-up interviews with a fresh role (that of a previous *HanaEins* member who returned back to Germany) the matter that responses which I collected are unavoidably influenced by how I was perceived still exists. After all, correspondingly, all ethnographies are of need personal, descriptive and impressionistic; while this does not weaken their significance as investigation tools, the complexion of the research predictably influences the conclusions made.

In sum, the limitations discussed, while not overthrowing the conclusions inferred, indicate that the concept for *nunchi* management through strategic self-presentation forms a good starting point; more research will be necessary in order to enhance it into something, which carries stronger feasibility. Thus, future development of this research, will allow scholars to gather further insight of *nunchi* and identity in transnational business, which corresponds to their own matters in transnational business management.

Continuing from Here: Areas for Future Expansion

Thus, in advocating new ways of looking at *nunchi* and identity to those formerly employed in business management studies, the recontextualisation of *nunchi* presents options for future research in theoretical, methodological and practical ways. Such suggestion also supports d'Iribarne's (2002) alert to scholars and practitioners to consider general tools and management practices in country specific contexts (p. 225). I will concisely consider some of the routes in which this study could be directed.

Areas for Theoretical Development

First of all, it might be of value taking this study into other fields, to examine to which extent the concept of *nunchi* management through strategic self-presentation operates under other circumstances to those outlined here. One of the potential options would be to modify a single variable within the study, for example, consider Koreans working for German MNCs in Frankfurt or Munich, or consider transnational businesspeople with similar, yet different symbols of national identity, for instance, Swiss, Austrians or Dutch in the City of Seoul.

Having suggested that, it might therefore be useful to consider small multinational businesses, or focusing on international entrepreneurs, with a focus examining whether they come across parallel effects encompassed by *HanaEins* members. Another possibility might also be looking at other transnational German groups in Korea that are not related to business, from the concept of *nunchi* management through self-presentation point of view, to test if the concept is limited to only international business management or whether it can be taken into other areas e.g. Germans working for the Goethe institute, German school, German embassy, adoption agencies and the Konrad Adenauer Foundation. Studies comparing and examining smaller, less influential or groups without a business affiliation in using the same concept therefore might be suitable for proving the concept of *nunchi* management through strategic self-presentation, or for expanding it into other fields of management.

Ultimately, we touch upon the matter of symbolism and symbols of national identity. While the works of Moore (2005) and Brannen (2004) have made pioneering steps in this way, this is a scope, which has received little consideration till lately in international business management studies. This is however tricky when one takes into account that this book stresses the complexity, which recontextualising symbols of identity such as *nunchi* includes, contesting the generalisation of such processes on behave of entire national identities. This process may entail, as witnessed by *HanaEins* members, who all incorporated *nunchi* in one-way or another different motivations and interpretations of semantic fit. Further studies which concentrate on the application and importance of *nunchi* and identity in transnational identity contexts, following a paradigm shift of function to meaning, stressing that meaning matters, are therefor desired to support this study and others, within the body of literature of more complex interpersonal relationships in international business studies (Tenzer, Pudelko and Harzing 2014; Welch et al. 2011; Piekkari and Welch 2004).

Conclusively, this book's outcome raises several prospective areas for future expansion, either in conducting comparative research, or through further investigation on some of the themes of interest emphasised by this study. I shall now take a look at the implications of this research in methodological and practical areas.

Areas for Methodological Development

This study's conclusions additionally throw up methodological implications for the reason to choose ethnography and other qualitative methods in business management studies. Although this subject has been previously noted, it is worth succinctly stressing some of the methodological problems, which this research has created.

Even though it is general business-studies critique of qualitative research that non-statistical, narrative data is a sort of "noise" diverting from the main intention of the exercise (e.g. Hofstede 1980: 314. 339; 1994, 2001), this study proposes that it is much more important than that. Even scholars working more on the mainstream side of theories, admit that there are major limitations and that value-free science is an epitome, which is neither feasible nor anticipated, particularly for social sciences (Tsui, 2016). Alternatively Tsui encourages the transformation of business school research to be both rigorous and useful in practice. As detected in this study, the interplay and connections of the single character groups amongst *HanaEins* members of varying degrees of self-presentation allows them to carry out *nunchi* strategically in German MNCs in Seoul. By employing setting specific knowledge and recontextualising their symbols of identity to strategically incorporate *nunchi* into their self-presentations, they are able to mobilise resources on many levels; when overlooking these processes, and merely concentrating on those facets, which can be quantitatively measured, one looses one of the crucial facets in MNCs. Moreover, it is worth mentioning that regardless of his conveyed interpretations on the matter, Hofstede supports his conclusions considerably with personal and descriptive evidence. Thus there is encouragement for Chapman and others' assertion that ethnographic research produces insights, which non-ethnographic one does not (2002: 254; 1997, 2001; Chapman and Gajewska-De Mattos, 2004). In this study, it is simply by viewing the qualitative data that one is able to identify the connections and interplays, which essentially reveal the investigated phenomena. Former works on identity in anthropology considered it to be a firm, possessable object, but then it was exposed to be more complex and subject to negotiation than appeared at first (Banks 1996). Therefore several researchers are suggesting that changes in research methodology and narrative writing may be needed (Appadurai 1997: 115; Piekkari and Welch 2004, 2006: 395). In this case also, the group that was portrayed as fixed, transnational German businesspeople, in previous studies now appears as dispersion into character groups, increaseingly connected and internally separated. Therefore, it might be useful considering the way transnational businesspeoples' identities are described and considered by researchers, possibly converging on interdisciplinary studies opposed to those of solitary perspectives and methodologies.

Finally, it might be useful running more ethnographic studies in business management, and testing previous quantitative studies with ethnographic fieldwork, in order to gain a richer understanding on *nunchi* and identity in MNCs. This book consequently underlines some of the benefits, which qualitative studies can contribute to international business management studies.

Areas for Practical Development

Lastly, this research's findings have implications for the applied everyday activities of multinational corporations in and outside of Korea. Therefore, it is worth contemplating some of these and how they might have an influence on actors in such settings.

One of the examples is that this study advocates that German interntional managers should adoppt a more qualitative and performative perspective on identity and the way they manage their human recourses. In viewing *HanaEins* members as a group in terms of the incorporation of *nunchi* into their strategic self-presentation described in this study, employing the quantitative approach of Hofstede, decision makers would have overlooked the perspectives on, and concerns connected to, the incorporation of *nunchi* that the different character groups went through. This caused, as presented in the enthnographic chapters, a redundant sum of time spent and energy wasted for the international German managers, who were completely new to the concept of *nunchi*, to realise that the settled Germans could act as sense makers in such process. Whereas Harris' (2001) standpoint that a combination of research methods including ethnographic and others should be employed to give a general overview of management has been acknowledged, and although this suggestion may be suitable for some business studies of national identity, it seems rather problematic to predict what a quantitative approach would have revealed to defining the concerns of *nunchi* and identity of this specific group of transnational businesspeople. Thus practitioners as well as academics would not have gotten to know the key subjects impacting the success of managing across borders and identities.

Conclusion

All in all then, the fundamental finding of this study has been the examination of an importnant organizational phenomenon, *nunchi*, and to advocate that transnational businesspeople, such as the *HanaEins* members in this particular research, strategically present themselves with symbols of national identity, which through identity specific recontextualisation offer them the chance to manage across borders and identities in expressing *nunchi* strategically. Thus *nunchi* should not be considered as a symbol exclusive to merely one identity context, however with support of recontextualisation as a concept helpful to managing across borders and identities all over the world. This conclusion, nonetheless, brings up motivating theoretical and practical matters which possibly influences the approach how self-presentation incorporating symbols of identity is regarded and made use of in international business management, the approach businesspeople of multinational corporations manage across borders and identities, and the approach how *nunchi* in transnational business is perceived.

Ultimately, this study has therefore not only provided a new perspective on *nunchi* and identity in multinational corporations and implied a new theoretical concept for viewing managing across borders and identities, however it has moreover formed innovative areas for research and practical improvement.

Nevertheless, the more detailed implications of the concept of *nunchi* management through strategic self-presentation in international business management might, become clearer with the course of time.

BIBLIOGRAPHY

Adler, N.J. (1997) *International dimensions of organisational behaviour,* (3rd ed.). Cincinnati, OH: South Western.

Adler, P.S. & Kwon, S.W. (2002) Social Capital: Prospects for a New Concept, *The Academy of Management,* 27(1), 17-40.

Agar, M. (1996) *Professional stranger: An informal introduction to ethnography.* 2nd ed. Academic Press.

Ahn, Y. D. (1998) *Traditional Korean management systems as impediments to localisation strategies on United States' subsidiaries.* Claremont, CA: The Claremont Graduate University.

Alston, J.P. (1989) Wa, Guanxi, and Inhwa: Managerial Principles in Japan, China and Korea. *Business Horizons,* 32 (2), 26-31.

Alvesson, M. (1994) Talking in organizations: Managing identity and impressions in an advertising agency, *Organization Studies,* 15 (4), 536-563.

Alvesson, M. (2010) Self-doubters, strugglers, storytellers, surfers and others: Images of self-identities in organization studies, *Human Relations,* 1-25.

Alvesson, M. (2011) *Interpreting interviews.* London: Sage.

Alvesson, M. & Deetz, S. (2000) *Doing critical management research.* London, Sage.

Alvesson, M. & Sköldberg, K. (2009) *Reflexive Methodology, New Vistas for Qualitative Research,* (2nd Ed.), Sage Publications Ltd.

Alvesson, M. & Sveningsson, S. (2003) The good visions, the bad micro-management and the ugly ambiguity: Contradicitions of (non-) leadership in a knowledge-intensive company, *Organization Studies,* 24, 961-988.

Alvesson, M. & Willmott, H. (2001) Identity Regulation as Organizational Control: Producing the Appropriate Individual, *Journal of Management Studies,* 39 (5), 619-644.

Alvesson, M., Lee Ashcraft, K. & Thomas, R. (2008) Identity Matters: Reflections on the Construction of Identity Scholarship in Organization Studies, *Organization,* 15 (1), 5-28.

Anderson, B. (1991). Imagined communities. London. *Verso*

Appadurai, A. (1997) Grassroots Globalization and the Research Imagination, *Public Culture,* 12 (1), 1-19.

Ashforth, B.E. (1998) Becoming: How does the process of identification unfold?

In D.A. Whetten & P.C. Godfrey (Eds.), *Identity in organisations: Building theory through conversations*, 213-222, Thousand Oaks, CA: Sage.

Ashforth, B.E. & Humphrey, R.H. (1993) Emotional Labor in Service Roles: The Influence of Identity, *The Academy of Management Review*, 18 (1), 88-115.

Ashforth, B.E., & Humphrey, R.H. (1995) Emotion in the workplace: reappraisal. *Human Realtions*, 48, 97-125.

Association of Social Anthropologists of the UK and the Commenwealth (1999) "Ethical Guidelines for Good Research Practice," available at http://www.theasa.org/ethics/guidelines.shtml

Atkinson, P., Coffey, A., Delamont, S., Lofland, J. & Lofland, L. (2001) Handbook of Ethnography, *London: Sage*.

Baba, M. L. (1998) Anthropology of work in the Fortune 1000: A critical retrospective. *Anthropology of Work Review*, 18 (4), 17–28.

Babbie, E. (1998) *The practice of social research*. 8th ed. Belmont, CA: Wadsworth.

Bade, K. J. (1992) *Deutsche im Ausland—Fremde in Deutschland: Migration in Geschichte und Gegenwart*. München, Verlag C.H. Beck.

Banks, M. (1996) *Ethnicity: Anthropological constructions*. Routledge.

Barley, S. R. (1996) Technicians in the workplace: Ethnographic evidence for bringing work into organization studies. *Administrative Science Quarterly*, 41 (3), 404–441.

Bartlett, C.A., & Ghoshal, S. (1997). Transnational management: Text, cases and readings in cross-border management *(2nd ed.). Boston: Irwin*.

Bass, B. M. (1985) *Leadership and performance beyond expectations*. New York, Free Press.

Bauder, H. (2008) Media Discourse and the New German Immigration Law, *Journal of Ethnic and Migration Studies*, 34 (1), 95-112.

Baudrilliard, J. (1983). Simulations. New York: Semiotext(e).

Baudrilliard, J. (1988). America. London: *Verso*.

Bauman, Z. (1993) Postmodern Ethics. *Oxford: Blackwell*.

Becker, G. (1998) *Disrupted lives: How people create meaning in a chaotic world*, University of California Press, Berkeley, Los Angeles, London.

Bell, E. (1999) The Negotiation of a Working Role in Organizational Ethnography. *International Journal of Social Methodology*, 2 (1), 17-37.

Bell, E., & Wray-Bliss, E. (2009) Research Ethics: Regulations and Responsibilities.

In D. Buchanan, A & A. Bryman (Eds.), *The Sage Handbook of Organizational Research Methods*, 78-92.

Berger, P. & Luckmann, T. (1966) The Social Construction of Reality: Treatise in the Sociology of Knowledge (Anchor Books ed.) New York: Doubleday & Company, Inc.

Bhappu, A.D. (2000) The Japanese Family: An Institutional Logic For Japanese Corporate Networks And Japanese Management, *Academy of Management Review*, 25 (2), 409-415.

Binney, G. (1993) The British Company and the German Company Compared, In G. Binney (Ed.), *Debunking the Myths About the German Company*, London: Chameleon Press, 15-18.

Birdwhistell, R.L. (2010) *Kinesics and Context: Essays on Body Motion Communication*, University of Pennsylvania Press.

Blackhall, L. J., Frank, G., Murphy, S. & Michel, V. (2001) Bioethics in a different tongue: The case of truth-telling. *Journal of Urban Health: Bulletin of the New York Academy of Medicine*, 78 (1), 59–71.

Blau, P. (1963) [1955] The dynamics of bureaucracy: A study of interpersonal relations in two government agencies. In S. Yebema et al. (Eds.), *Organizational Ethnography Studying the Complexities of Everyday Life*, Sage Publications Ltd.

Boas, M. & Chain, S. (1976) *Big Mac: The unauthorised story of McDonald's*. New York: Dutton.

Boje, D. & Tyler, J. (2009) Story and Narrative Noticing: Workaholism Autoethnographies. *Journal of Business Ethics*, 84 (2), 173-194.

Borneman, J. (1992) *Belonging in the Two Berlins: Kin, State, Nation*, Cambridge: Cambridge University Press.

Boyatzis, R. E. (1982) *The competent manager: A model for effective performance*. New York, John Wiley & Sons.

Brannen, M. Y., & Salk, J.E. (1999). Partnering across borders: Negotiation organizational culture in a German-Japanese joint venture. *Human Relations, 53: 451-487*.

Brannen, M.Y. (2004) When Mickey loses face: Recontextulaisation, semantic fit, and the semiotics of foreignness, *Academy of Management Review*, 29 (4), 593-616.

Bray, D. W., Campbell, R. J. & Grant, D. L. (1974) *Formative years in business: A long term AT&T study of managerial lives.* New York, John Wiley & Sons.

Brewer, J. (2000) *Ethnography.* Buckingham, Philadelphia: Open University Press.

Brewer, J. (2004) Ethnography. In C. Cassel & G. Symon (Eds.), *Essential Guide to Qualitative Methods in Organizational Research:* Sage.

Briner, R.B. (1999) The neglect and importance of emotion at work. *European Journal of Work and Organizational Psychology,* 8, 323-346.

Brubaker, R. & Cooper, F. (2000) Beyond "Identity", *Theory and Society,* 29 (1), 1-47.

Brucks, U. (1998) Arbeitspsychologie personenbezogener Dienstleistungen. *Bern: Huber.*

Bruhn, J. (1994) *Was deutsch ist: zur kritischen Theorie der Nation.* Freiburg, Ca-Ira Verlag.

Brunner, V.W. & Turner, E. M. (1986) The anthropology of experience, Univeristy of Illinois Press.

Bryman, A. & Bell, E. (2011) Business Research Methods (3rd Eds.): *Oxford University Press.*

Buchanan, D. & Bryman, A. (2009) The SAGE Handbook of *Organizational Research Methods:* Sage.

Buchanan, D., Boddy, D. & McCalman, J. (1988) Getting in, getting on, getting out and getting back. In A. Bryman, *Doing Research in Organisations.* London: Routledge.

Burgelman, R. A. (1991). Intraorganizational ecology of strategy making and organisational adaptation: Theory and field research. *Organizational Science, 3: 239-262.*

Burns, J. M. (1978) *Leadership.* New York, Harper & Row.

Burns, T. (1992) *Erving Goffman.* London: Routledge.

Butcher, M. (2009) From 'fish out of water' to 'fitting in': the challenge of re-placing home in a mobile world, *Population Space and Place,* 16, 23-36.

Campbell, J. P., Dunnette, M. D., Lawler, E. E. & Weick, K. E. (1970) *Managerial behaviour, performance, and effectiveness.* New York, McGraw Hill.

Caplan, R.D. (1983) Person-environment fit: Past, present and future. In C.L. Cooper (Ed.), Stress research: Issues for the eighties (pp.35-77). Ann Arbor, MI: Institute for Social Research.

Cavusgil, S. T & Das, A. (1997). Methodology issues in cross-cultural sourcing research-primer. *Marketing Intelligence & Studies of Management & Organization Vol. 15 No. 5 p.213.*

Cha, J.H. (1994a), 'Changes in Value, Belief, and Behaviour of the Koreans over the Past 100 Years', *Korean Journal of Social Psychology,* Vol.8, No.1, pp.40-58.

Cha, J.H. (1994b), 'Aspects of Individualism and Collectivism in Korea' in U. Kim, H.C. Triandis et al. (eds.), *Individualism and Collectivism: Theory, Method and Application.* Thousand Oaks, CA: Sage Publications.

Chaney, L.H., & Martin, J.S. (2011) *Intercultural business communication (5th ed.).* Upper Saddle River, N.J.: Prentice Hall.

Chang, C. S. & Chang, H. J. (1994) *The Korean management system: Cultural, political, economic foundations.* Santa Barbara, CA: Quorum Books.

Chang, C.S. (1983) Comparative analysis of management systems: Korea, Japan and the United States, *Korea Management Review,* 13 (1), 77-98.

Chang, C.S. (1988) 'Chaebol: The South Korean Conglomerates', *Business Horizon,* 51-57.

Chapman, M. (1997) Social anthropology, business studies and cultural issues. *International Studies of Management and Organization,* 26 (4), 3–29.

Chapman, M. (2001) Social anthropology and business studies: some considerations of method. In D. Gellner & E. Hirsch (Eds.), *Inside Organisations Anthropologists at Work.* Oxford: Berg, 19-33.

Chapman, M. & Gajewska-DeMattos, H. (2004) The Ethnographic IB Researcher: Misfit or Trailblazer? In R. Marschan-Piekkari & C. Welch (Eds.), *Handbook of Qualitative Methods for international business,* Cheltenham, UK and Northhampton, MA: Edward Elgar.

Chapman, M., Clegg, L.M. & Gajewska-De Mattos, H. (2002) 'Close Neighbors and Distant Friends: Managerial Perceptions in Cross-border mergers and acquisitions', *European International Business Academy,* 2-26.

Charmaz, K. & Mitchell, R. (1997) The Myth of Silent Authorship. Refelxifity and Voice. R. Hertz. London, Sage.

Chen, G., and Chung, J. (1994), ' The Impact of Confucianism on Organisational

Communication', *Communication Quarterly*, Vol.42,pp.93-105.

Chen, M. (1995) *Asian management systems*. London: Routledge.

Cho, Y.H. (1995), 'Corporate Cultures of Korean Big Businesses' in Y.K. Shin et al., *Management Characteristics of Korean Big Businesses*. Seoul: Seikyungsa, pp.321-77.

Cho, Y.H. and Yoon, J. (2001), The Origin and Function of Dynamic Collectivism: An Analysis of Korean Corporate Culture, *Asia Pacific Business Review*, Vol. 7, No. 4, pp. 70-88.

Choi, H. J., Park, H. S., Oh, J. Y. (2011) Cultural differences in how individuals explain their lying and truth-telling tendencies. *International Journal of Intercultural Relations*, 35, 749–766.

Choi, J. P. & Cowing, T. G. (1999) Firm behavior and group affiliation: The strategic role of corporate grouping for Korean firms. *Journal of Asian Economics*, 10, 195–209.

Choi, S. C. (1997) Psychological characteristics of Koreans. In: Choi, S. C. et al (eds.) *Understanding of modern psychology*. Seoul, Hak-Moon-Sa, pp. 695–766.

Chun, B. G. (2009) Firm's choice of ownership structure: An empirical test with Korean multinationals. *Japan and the World Economy*, 26, 26–38.

Chung, E.Y.J. (1995) The Korean neo-Confucianism of Yi To'oegye and Yi Yulgok. Albany, New York: State University of New York.

Chung, H. & Gale, J. (2008) Family functioning and self-differentiation: A cross-cultural examination. *Springer Science+Business Media, LLC*

Chung, K.H., and Lee, H.C. (1989), 'National Differences in Managerial Practices' in K.H. Chung and H.C. Lee (eds.), *Korean Managerial Dynamics*. New York: Praeger, pp.163-80.

Chung, K.H., Lee, H.C., & Jung, K.H. (1997) *Korean management: Global strategy and cultural transformation*. New York: Walter de Gruyter.

Church, A. & Waclawski, J. (1998) The relationship between individual personality orientation and executive leadership behaviour. *Journal of Occupational and Organisational Psychology*, 71, 99–126.

Cocroft, B. A. K. & Ting-Toomey, S. (1994) Facework in Japan and in the United States. *International Journal of Intercultural Relations*, 18, 469–506.

Cohen, A. P. (1985) *The symbolic construction of community*. London: Tavistock.

Cohen, A. P. (1986) Of symbols and boundaries, or does Ertie's greatcoat hold the key? In: Cohen, A. P. (ed.) *Symbolising boundaries: Identity and diversity in British cultures*. Manchester: Manchester University Press, pp. 1–22.

Cohen, A. P. (1987) *Whalsay: Symbol, segment and boundary in a Shetland Island community*. Manchester: Manchester University Press.

Cohen, A. P. (1994) *Self consciousness: An alternative ethnography of identity*. London: Routledge.

Condon, J.C. (1977), *Interpersonal Communication*. New York: Macmillan.

Conger, J.A. (1998) Qulitative research as the cornerstone methodology for understanding leadership. *The Leadership Quarterly*, 9, 107-121.

Cooper, R. K. (1997) Applying emotional intelligence in the workplace. *Training & Development*, 51, 31–38.

Cooper, R. K. & Sawaf, A. (1997) *Executive EQ: Emotional intelligence in leadership and organisations*. New York, Gosset, Putnam.

Cornwall, G. H. & Stoddard, E. W. (2001) *Global multiculturalism: Comparative perspectives on ethnicity, race and nation*. Lanham, MD, Rowman and Littlefield.

Crang, M. & Cook, I. (2007) *Doing Ethnographies*. London, Thousand Oaks, New Delhi, Sage Publication.

Cunliffe, A.L. (2008) Social Construtionism. In R. Thorpe & R. Holt, The SAGE *Dictionary of Qualitative Management Research*, 200-202.

Czarniawska, B. (1993) The Three-Dimensional Organization: *A Construtionist View*. Lund: Studentlitteratur.

Czarniawska, B. (2007) Shadowing, and Other Techniques for Doing Fieldwork in Modern Societies. *Liber: Copenhagen Business School Press*.

D'Iribane, P. (1991). The usefulness of an ethnographic approach to international comparisons of the functioning of organizations. *International Studies of Management and Organization*, Vol. 26 No. 4 pp. 30-47

D'Iribane, P. (1996). The usefulness of an ethnographic approach to the international comparison of organizations. *International Studies of Management & Organizations Vol. 26 No. 4 p.30.*

d'Iribarne, P. (2002) Motivating Workers in Emerging Countries: Universal Tools and Local Adaptations, *Journal of Organizational Behavior,* 23 (3), 243-256.

Dacin, M. T., Hitt, M. A. & Levitas, E. (1997) Selecting partners for successful international alliances: Examination of U.S. and Korean firms. *Journal of World Business,* 32 (1).

Dalton, M. (1959) Men who manage: Fusions of feeling and theory in administration. In S. Yebema et al. (Eds.), *Organizational Ethnography Studying the Complexities of Everyday Life,* Sage Publications Ltd.

Damasio, A. (1994) *Descartes' error: Emotion, reason and the human brain.* New York, Gosset, Putnam.

Dancey, C.P., & Reidy, J. (1999). Statistics without Maths for Psychology (ed. 5). *Pearson Education limited.*

Darwin, C. (1965) *The expression of emotions in man and animals.* Chicago: University of Chicago Press.

De Rivera, J. (1977) *A structural theory of emotions.* New York: International University Press.

Denzin, N. & Lincoln, Y.S. (2005) Introduction: The Discipline and Practice of Qualitative Research. In N. Denzin & Y. Lincoln (Eds.), *The Sage Handbook of Qualitative Research* 3, 1-32: Sage Publications.

Denzin, N. K. & Lincoln, Y.S. (2003) *Turning points in qualitative research: Tying knots in a handkerchief,* Rowan & Littlefield Publishers, Inc.

Denzin, N.K. (1997) *Interpretive Ethnography,* Thousand Oaks, CA: Sage.

Diener, E. & Crandall, R. (1978) *Ethics in social and behavioral research,* University of Chicago Press.

Dingwall, R. (1997) Accounts, interviews and observations. In: Miller, G. & Dingwall, R. (eds.) *Context & Method in Qualitative Research.* London, Sage.

Dorfman, P.W & Howell, J.P. (1988). Dimensions of National Culture and Effective Leadership Patterns: Hofstede revisited. *Advances in International Comparative Management Vol. 3 pp. 127-150.*

Dowling,P.J., Welch,D.E., & Schuler, R.S. (1999) *International human resource management. Managing people in a multinational context,* (3rd ed.). Cincinnati, OH: South Western.

Duberley, J., Johnson, P. & Cassel, C. (2012) Philosophies Underpinning Qualitative Research. In G. Symon & C. Cassel (Eds.), *Qualitative Organizational Research: Core Methods and Current Challenges.* Sage.

Dumont, L. (1986) Are cultures living beings? German identity in interaction. *Royal Anthropological Institute of Great Britan and Ireland,* 21 (4), 587-604.

Dumont, L. (1994) *German ideology: From France to Germany and back.* Chicago, University of Chicago Press.

Earley, P.C., & Gibson, C.B. (2002) *Multinational work teams: A new perspective.* Mahwah, NJ: Erlbaum.

Early, P.C. & Peterson, R.S. (2004) The Elusive Cultural Chameleon: Cultural Intelligence as a New Approach to Intercultural Training for the Global Manager, *Academy of Management Learning & Education,* 3 (1), 100-115.

Ekman, P. (1973) *Cross-cultural studies of facial expression: A century of research in review.* New York: Academic press, pp. 169-222.

Elias, N. (1996) *The Germans: Power struggles and the development of habitus in the nineteenth and twentieth centuries.* Oxford: Polity Press.

Eliott, S., Scott, M., Jensen, A. & Mc Donough, M. (1982) "Perception of reticence: a cross-cultural investigation." In M. Yi & M.A. Jezewski (Ed.), *Korean nurses' adjustment to hospitals in the United States of America,* Journal of Advanced Nursing, 32 (3), 721-729.

Ellis, C. et al. (1997) *Interactive interviewing,* in R. Hertz (ed.), Reflexivity and Voice. Thousand Oaks, CA:SAGE.

Erramilli, M. K., Srivastava, R. & Kim, S. S. (1999) Internationalization theory and Korean multinationals. *Asia Pacific Journal of Management,* 16, 29–45.

Feely, A.J. & Harzing, A.W. (2003) Language management in multinational companies, *Cross Cultural Management: An International Journal,* 10 (2), 37-52.

Fetterman, D. M. (2009) *Ethnography: Step-by-step*. Applied Social Research Methods Series.

Fetterman, D.M. (1998) *Ethnography: Step-by-Step*. Newbury Park: Sage Publications.

Fine, G., Morril, C. & Surianarain, S. (2009) Ethnography in Organizational Settings. In D. Buchanan, A & A. Bryman (Eds.), *The Sage Handbook of Organizational Research Methods*, 602-619.

Fineman, S. (1993) *Emotion in organizations*. London: Sage.

Flick, U. (2002) An Introduction to Qualitative Research (2nd Eds.), *London: Sage.*

Flucher, G. & Davidson, F. (2007) *Language testing and assessment advanced resource book*. Routledge.

Forster, N. (2000) The Myth of the 'International Manager', *International Journal of Human Resource Management,* 11 (1), 126-142.

Forsythe, D. (1989) German identity and the problem of history. In: Tonkin, E. et al (eds.) *History and Ethnicity*. (vol. 27) London, Routledge, pp. 137–156.

Fredriksson, R., Barner-Rasmussen, W., & Piekkari, R. (2006) The multinational corporation as a multilingual organization, *Corporate Communications: An International Journal,* 11 (4), 406-423.

Gardner, H. (1983) *Frames of mind: Theory of multiple intelligences*. New York Basic.

Gardner, H. (1993) *Multiple Intelligences: The theory in practise*. New York: Basic Books.

Geertz, C. (1973) The Interpretation of Cultures: Selected Essays. *New York: Basic Books, Inc., Publishers.*

Geertz, C. (1988) *Works and lives: The anthropologist as author*. Stanford, CA, Stanford University Press.

Giddens, A. (1984) *The Constitution of Society,* Cambridge, Polity Press.

Gleason, P. (1983) Identifying Identity: A Semantic History, *The Journal of American History,* 69 (4), 910-931.

Glover, L. & Wilkinson, A. (2006) Worlds colliding: The translation of modern management practices within a UK based subsidiary of a Korean-owned MNC. *International Journal of Human Recourse Management.*

Goffman, E. (1956) *The presentation of self in everyday life*. Edinburgh, University of Edinburgh, Social Sciences Research Centre.

Goffman, E. (1959) The presentation of self in everyday life. *London: Pelican.*

Goffman, E. (1961) *Encounters: Two studies in the sociology of interaction*. Indianapolis,

Bobbs-Merril Ltd.

Goffman, E. (1963) *Behaviour in Public places: Notes on the social organization of gatherings.* London, The Free Press of Glencoe.

Goffman, E. (1969) *The presentation of self in everyday life.* London, Allen.

Goffman, E. (1970) *Strategic interaction.* Oxford, Basil Blackwell.

Goffman, E. (1979) *Gender advertisements.* London, Macmillan.

Goleman, D. (1995) *Emotional intelligence.* New York, Bantam.

Goleman, D. (1996) *Emotional intelligence: Why it can matter more than IQ.* London, Bloomsbury.

Goleman, D. (1998) *Working with emotional intelligence.* New York, Bantam.

Gomez- Mejia, L.R. and Palich, L. (1997) Cultural Diversity and the Performance of Multinational Firms. *Journal of International Business Studies,* 309-335.

Gouldner, A.W. (1954) Patterns of industrial bureaucracy: A case study of modern factory administration. In S. Yebema et al. (Eds.), *Organizational Ethnography Studying the Complexities of Everyday Life,* Sage Publications Ltd.

Gray, K. R. & Marshall, K. P. (1998) Kenyan and Korean management orientations on Hofstede's cultural values. *Multinational Business Review,* 6 (2), 79–88.

Grint, K. (2000) The Arts of Leadership. New York: Oxford University Press.

Gudykunst, W.B., Yoon, Y.C. and Nishida, T. (1987), 'The influence of Individualism-Collectivism on Perception of Communication in Ingroup and Outgroup Relationships', *Communication Monographs,* Vol.54 (Sep.), pp.295-306.

Ha, Y. C. (2007) Late industrialization, the state, and social changes: The emergence of neofamilism in South Korea. *Comparative Political Studies,* 40 (4).

Habermas, J. (1994) *The past as future.* Cambridge, Polity Press.

Hackley, C. (2003) *Doing research projects in marketing, management and consumer research.* London, Routledge.

Hall, E.T. (1976), *Beyond Culture.* Garden City, NY: Doubleday Anchor Books.

Hall, E.T. (1989) *Beyond Culture,* New York: Anchor Books.

Hammersley, M. & Atkinson (1994) Ethnography: Principles in practice. London, Routledge.

Hannerz, U. (1983) Tools of identity and imagination. In: Jacobson-Widding, A. (ed.) *Identity: Personal and socio-cultural, a symposium.* Uppsala, Almqvist and Wiksell, pp. 347–360.

Hannerz, U. (1990) Cosmopolitans and Locals in World Culture, *Theory Culture & Society*, Sage, London, Newbury Park and Delhi, 7, 237-251.

Hannerz, U. (1992) *Cultural complexity: Studies in the social organization of meaning.* New York: Columbia University Press.

Hannerz, U. (1996) *Transnational connections: Culture, people, places.* London, Routledge.

Harris, M. (1968) The Rise of Anthropological Theory. London: Routledge & Kegan Paul.

Harrison, R. (1997) Why your firm needs emotional intelligence. *People Management*, 3, 41.

Harzing, A.W. (2001a) An Analysis of the Functions of International Transfer of Managers in MNCs, *Employee Relations*, 23 (6), 581-598.

Harzing, A.W. (2001b) Of Bears, Bumblebees and Spiders: the Role of Expatriates in Controlling Foreign Subsidiaries, *Journal of World Business*, 36 (4), 336-379.

Hatch, M.J. (1999) Exploring the empty spaces of organizing: How improvisational jazz helps redescribe organizational structure. *Organization Studies*, 20 (1), 75-100.

Hays, R.D, Anderson and Revicki, D. (1993). Psychometric considerations in evaluating health-related quality of life measures. *Quality of Life Research Vol.2 No. 6 pp. 441-449.*

Head, D. (1992) *Made in Germany: The corporate identity of a nation.* London, Hodder and Stoughton.

Headland, T.N., Pike, K.L. & Harris, M.E. (1990) *Emics and etics: The insider/outsider debate*, Newbury Park, Sage.

Heckathorn, D. D. (1997) Respondent-driven sampling: A new approach to the study of hidden populations. *Social Problems*, 44 (2).

Henry, G.T. (1990). Practical Sampling. *Newbury Park, Sage.*

Hesselbein, F., Goldsmith, M. & Beckhard, R. (1996) *The leader of the future.* San Francisco: Jossey-Bass.

Hickson, D.J., & Pugh, D.S. (1995). Management worldwide: The impact of societal culture on organizations around the globe. *London: Penguin.*

Higgs, V.D.M. (2000) Emotional Intelligence – A review and evaluation study, *Journal of Managerial Psychology*, 15 (4), 341-372.

Hillman, J. (1961) *Emotion*. Evanston IL: Northwestern University Press.

Ho, D.Y. (1993) Relational orientation in Asian social psychology. In U. Kim & J.W. Berry (Eds.), *Indigenous psychologie:* Research and experience in cross-cultural context (pp.240-259). Newbury Park, CA:Sage.

Hochschild, A. (1979) Emotion work, feeling rules and social structure. *American Journal of Sociology,* 85, 551-575.

Hochschild, A. R. (1983) *The managed heart.* Berkeley: University of California Press.

Hodge, R., & Kress, G. (1988). Social semiotics. Ithaca, NY: Cornell University Press.

Hoecklin, L. M. (1996) *(Re)constructing Hausfrauen: Gender, ideology, 'the family' and social welfare in Southern Germany.* MPhil thesis, ISCA, University of Oxford, Oxford.

Hofstede, G. (1980a) *Culture's consequences: International differences in work-related values.* Beverly Hills, CA: Sage.

Hofstede, G. (1980a). Culture's Consequences: International differences in work-related values. *Beverly Hills, CA: Sage.*

Hofstede, G. (1980b) Motivation, leadership and organization: Do American theories apply abroad? *Organisational Dynamics,* Summer, 42–63.

Hofstede, G. (1980b). Motivation, leadership and organization: Do American theories apply abroad? *Organisational Dynamics,* Summer pp. 42-63.

Hofstede, G. (1984) *Culture's consequences: International differences in work-related values.* Abridged version. London, Sage.

Hofstede, G. (1984). Culture's Consequences: International differences in work-related values, abridged version. *London: Sage.*

Hofstede, G. (1991) *Cultures and organizations: Software of mind.* London, McGraw-Hill.

Hofstede, G. (1991). Cultures and organizations: Software of mind. *London:*

McGraw-Hill.

Hofstede, G. (1994) Management Scientists Are Human, *Management Science,* 40 (1), 4-13.

Hofstede, G. (2001) *Culture's consequences: Comparing values, behaviors, institutions and organizations across nations,* Sage Publications.

Hogan, R., Curphy, G., & Hogan, J. (1994) What we know about leadership effectiveness and personality. *American Psychologist,* 49, 493-504.

Holloway, W. & Jefferson, T. (2000) *Doing qualitative research differently.* London, Sage.

Holstein, J. A. & Gubrium, J. (1997) Active interviewing. In Silverman, D. (ed.) *Qualitative Research.* London, Sage.

Holstein, J. A. & Gubrium, J. (2003) Inside interviewing: New lenses, new concerns. In: Holstein, J. & Gubrium, J. (eds.) *Inside interviewing.* Thousand Oaks, CA: Sage.

Hong, R. (2008) *Shame in the Korean uri culture: An interpretation of self-psychology.* Drew University.

Howard, A., & Bray, D. (1988) *Managerial lives in transition: Advancing age and changing times.* New York: Guilford.

Hsieh, H.-F. & Shannon, S. E. (2005) Three approaches to qualitative content analysis. *Qualitative Health Research,* 15 (9).

Huang, Y. (2002) Transpacific Displacement: Ethnography, Translation, and Intertextual Travel in Twentieth-Century American Literature Berkeley, Los Angeles, London: University of California Press.

Humphreys, M. & Watson, T. (2009) Ethnographic Practices: From 'Writing-up Ethnographic Research' To 'Writing Ethnogrphay'. In S. Yebema, D. Yanow, H. Wels & F. Kamsteeg (Eds.), *Organizational Ethnography: Studying the Complexities of Everyday Organizational Life,* 40-50. Sage: London.

Humphreys, M., Brown, A.D. & Hatch, M.J. (2003) Is Ethnography Jazz? *Organization,* 10 (1), 5-31.

Hur, S.V. and Hur, B.S. (1988), *Culture Shock! Korea.* Singapore: Times Books International.

Hwang, K.K. (1988), *The Chinese Power Game.* Taipei: Giren.

Ibarra, H. & Andrews, S.B. (1993) Power, social influence, and sense making: Effects of network centrality and proximity on employee perceptions, *Administrative*

Science Quarterly, 38 (2), 277-303.

Iser, W. (1989) *From Reader Response to Literary Anthropology*, Johns Hopkins Press.

Jackson, P.T. (2006) "Making sense of making sense: Configurational analysis and the double hermeneutic," In D. Yanow & P. Schwartz-Shea (2nd Eds.), *Interpretations and Method: Empirical Research Methods and the Interpretive Turn*, London: Routledge.

Jaeger, A. M. (1983) The of organizational culture overseas: An approach to control in the multinational corporation. *Journal of International Business Studies*, 14 (2), 91-115.

Janelli, R. L. (1993) *Making capitalism*. Stanford, CA: Stanford University Press.

Jelinek, M., Smircich, L. (1983). Code of many colours. *Administrative Science Quarterly*, Vol. 28 pp.331-338.

Jenkins, R. (1996) *Social identity*. London: Routledge.

Johnson, T.P. (1998). Approaches to equivalence in cross-cultural and cross-national survey research. *Zuma Nachrichten Spezial Vol.3 pp.1-40*.

Judson, P. M. (1993) Inventing Germanness: Class, ethnicity, and colonial fantasy at the margins of the Habsburg monarchy. *Australian Journal, Social Analysis*, 33.

Jullien, F. (2004) A Treatise on Efficacy: Between Western and Chinese Thinking, *University of Hawai'i Press*.

Kamata, S (1983) Japan in the Passing Lane: An Insider's Acount of Life in a Japanese Auto Factory, *George Allen & Unwin*.

Kamsteeg, F.H. & Wels, H. (2004) Anthropology, Organisations and Interviews: new territory or quicksand? *Intervention Research, International Journal on Culture, Organization and Management*, 1(1), 7-25.

Kang, C. I. (2000) Korea teachers of English to speakers of other languages. *Korea TESOL Journal*, 3 (1).

Kasmir, S. (2001) Corporation, self and enterprise at the Saturn automobile plant. *Anthropology of Work Review*, 22 (4), 8–12.

Kaufman, H. (1960) *The Forest Ranger: a study in administrative behavior*, Resources for the Future.

Kay, J. (1993) *Foundations of corporate success: How business strategies add value*. New York, Oxford University Press.

Kearney, R.P. (1991), *The Warrior Worker: The Challenge of "the Korean Way" of Working*. New York: Henry Holt and Company.

Kim, D-Y. & Park, J. (2010) Cultural differences in risk: The group facilitation effect. *Judgment and Decision Making*, 5 (5), 380–390.

Kim, E. J. (2010) *Adopted territory transnational Korean adoptees and politics of belonging.* Duke University Press.

Kim, H. J. (2004) National identity in Korean curriculum. *Canadian Social Studies*, 38 (3).

Kim, H. S. (2003) Exploring Public relations in a Korean multinational organization in the context of Confucian culture. *Asian Journal of Communication*, 13 (2).

Kim, K. (1986) Misunderstanding in nonverbal communication: America and Korea. 1–22.

Kim, N. H., Sohn, D. W. & Wall, J. A. (1999) Korean leaders' (and subordinates') conflict management. *International Journal of Conflict Management*, 10 (2), 130.

Kim, S.H. (1990), *The Military Culture.* Seoul:Ulji.

Kim, Y.R. (1993) "Jeong and Han," In I. Yang (Eds.), *Jeong exchange and collective leadership in Korean organizations,* Asia Pacific J Manage, 283-298.

Kirkman, B., L., Lowe, K.B., and Gibson, C. (2006) A quarter century of *Culture's Consequences:* A review of empirical research incorporating Hofstede's cultural values framework. *Journal of International Business Studies*, 37(3), 285-320.

Kisielewski, S. (1965) *Fragen eines Polen, sind die Deutschen wircklich so?,* Herrenalb/ Schwarzwald: Horst Erdmann Verlag.

Kogut, B. (1991). Country capabilities and the permeability of borders. *Strategic Management Journal, 12: 33-47.*

Kogut, B. and Singh, H. (1988) The Effect of National Culture on the Choice of Entry Mode. *Journal of International Business Studies*, 19(3), 411-432.

Kohls, R. L. (2001) *Learning to think Korean: A guide to living and working in Korea.*

Kostova, T. (1999). Transnational transfer of strategic organizational practices: A contextual perspective. Academy of Management Review, 24: 308-324.

Kotter, J. P. (1982) *The general managers.* New York: Free Press.

Kramer, R.M. (1991), 'Intergroup Relations and Organisational Dilemmas: The Role of Categorization Process', *Research in Organisational Behavior,* Vol.13, pp.191-228.

Kunda, G. & van Maanen, J. (1999) Changing Scripts at Work: Managers and Professionals. *The ANNALS of the American Academy of Political and Social Science*, 56 (1), 64-80.

Law, J. (1994) Organizing Modernity. Oxford, Massachusetts: Blackwell.

Law, J. (2004) After method: Mess in social science research. London, New York: Routledge.

Lawrence, P. (1980) *Managers and Management in West Germany*, London: Croom Helm.

Le Gloannec, A.M. (1994) On German Identity, *The MIT Press*, 123 (1), 129-148.

Lee-Peuker, M.-Y. (2004) *Economic action in South Korea: An heuristic attempt.* Heidelberg University. Discussion Paper Series number 415.

Lee, C.Y. (2001a) *Korean Culture And Its Influence on Business Practice in South Korea*, Kansas, USA: Pittsburg State University.

Lee, D.R. and Suh, D.W. (1998), 'A Longitudinal Study on the Managerial Characteristics of Korean Firms', *Korean Management Review*, Vol.27, No.4.

Lee, H.C. (1998a) Transformation of employment practices in Korean businesses. *International Studies of Management and Organization*, 28 (4), 26-39.

Lee, J., Roehl, T. W. & Choe, S. (2000) What makes management style similar and distinct across borders? Growth, experience and culture in Korean and Japanese firms. *Journal of International Business Studies*, 31 (4), 631–652.

Lee, S. B. (1987) Dissent from abroad. *Third World Quarterly*, 9 (1), 130–147.

Lee, S. H. (1997) A semiotic approach to 'Mom'. In: Kim, C. S. (ed.) *Life and sign.* Seoul, MunhakkwaJisungsa, pp. 42–75.

Lee, S. H. (2000) Argument of Asiatic value and the future of Confucian culture. In: *Korean identity in the new millennium.* The Academy of Korean Studies, pp. 12–27.

Lee, S. M. & Yoo, S. (1987) The D type management: A driving force of Korean prosperity. *Management International Review*, 58, 68–77.

Lee, S.M. & Yoo, S. (1987) Management style and practice of Korean chaebols, *California Management Review*, 29 (4), 95-110.

Lee, T. H. (1998b) *The impact of culture on the practice of Law in Korea.* Seoul, Lee and Ko.

Lee, Y. I. & Trim, P. R. J. (2008) The link between cultural value systems and strategic marketing: Unlocking the mindset of Japanese and South Korean managers. *Cross Cultural Management: An International Journal*, 15 (1), 62–80.

Lee, Y.I. (2001b) Factors to be aware of when dealing with Japanese and South Korean organisations, *International Journal of Management Literature*, 1 (2-4), 263-274.

Levi-Strauss, C. (1963) *Structural anthropology.*

Lim, T.K. (1993) "Communicational base of Korean relationship: Chaemyun, jeong and *nunchi*," In I. Yang (Eds.), *Jeong exchange and collective leadership in Korean organizations,* Asia Pacific J Manage, 283-298.

Lincoln, Y.S. & Guba, E.G. (1985) Naturalistic Inquiry. Beverly Hills, California: Sage Publications.

Lincoln, Y.S., Lynham, S.A. & Guba, E.G. (1998) "Paradigmatic Controversies, Contradictions, And Emerging Confluences, Revisited," In N.K. Denzin & Y.S. Lincoln (4th Eds.), *The SAGE Handbook of Qualitative Research,* Sage Publications, Inc.

Lindlof, T. R. & Taylor, B. C. (2002a) *Qualitative communication research methods.* 2nd ed. Thousand Oaks, CA, Sage.

Lindlof, T.R. & Taylor, B.C. (2002b) *Asking, listening, and telling, Qualitative Communication Research Methods,* Sage Publications.

Lippert, J. (1882) *Die Erziehung auf nationaler Grundlage in Sammlung Gemeinn*ütziger Vorträge, Prague: Verlag des deutschen Vereins zur Verbreitung gemeinnütziger KenntnissePrag.

Locke, K. (1996) A funny thing happened! The management of consumer emotions in service encounters. *Organization Science,* 7, 40-59.

Lofland , J. & Lofland, L.H. (2006) Analyzing Social Setting: A Guide to Qualitative Observation and Analysis (4th Eds.), Belmont, CA: Wadsworth Thomson.

Luthans, F., Hodgetts, R. M. & Rosenkrantz, S. A. (1988) *Real managers.* Cambridge, MA, Ballinger.

Lytle, A.L., Brett, J.M., Barsness, Z.I., Tinsley, C.H. & Janssens, M.A. (1995). Paradigm for confirmatory cross-cultural research in organisational behaviour. *Research in Organisational Behaviour, Vol. 17 pp. 167-214.*

MacIntyre, A. (1971). Is a science of comparative politics possible? In MacIntyre, A. (Ed.), Against the self-images of the age: Essays on ideology and philosophy. *London: Duckworth.*

Malinowski, B. (1979) *The ethnography of Malinowski.* Routledge.

Marcus, G.E. (2007) Ethnography two decades after Writing Culture: From the experimental to the baroque. *Anthropology Quarterly,* 80 (4), 1127-1145.

Martina, Birgit, Susama, Inge, Mijung, Sonja, Beate, Cornelia (2014) *Deutscher Club Seoul.* Available from http://www.deutscherclubseoul.org

Maxwell, A. & Davis, S.E. (2016) Germanness beyond Germany: Collective Identity in German Diaspora Communities, *German Studies Review*, 39 (1), 1-15.

Mayo, E. (1933) *The Human Problems of an Industrial Organization*, Boston: Harvard University Press.

McAuley, J. (2004) Hermeneutic Understanding. In C. Cassell & G. Symon (Eds.), *Essential Guide to Qualitative Methods in Organizational Research*, 192-202. Sage Publications.

McCurdy, D.W., & Spradley, J.P. (1972) *The cultural experience: ethnography in complex society.* Chicago: Science Research Associates.

McSweeney, B. (2002). Hofstede's Model of National Cultural Differences and their Consequences: A Triumph of Faith – A Failure of Analysis. *Human relations Vol.55 No. 89.*

Megerian, L. E. & Sosik, J. J. (1996) An affair of the heart: Emotional intelligence and transformational leadership. *Journal of Leadership Studies*, 3, 31–48.

Mensik, S., Grainger, R. J. & Chatterjee, S. R. (1999) *Trends and transitions in Japanese and Korean management approaches.* Australia: Curtin University of Technology.

Meurant, R. C. (date unknown) *Aspects of face and cultural dimensions, In Kohls' 'Korea: People-oriented and group-centered': A critical review from an Intercultural Communication perspective.* Hyejeon College, Korea.

Miller, J. & Glasser, B. (1997) The inside and the outside: Finding realities in interviews. In: Silverman, D. (ed.) *Qualitative research.* London, Sage.

Moeran, B. (2005) *The business of ethnography: Strategic exchanges, people and organizations.* Berg.

Moore, F. (2005) *Transnational Business Cultures Life and Work in Multinational Corporation*, UK, Ashgate.

Morden, T. & Bowels, D. (1998) Management in South Korea: A review. *Management Decision*, 36 (5), 316–330.

Morgan, G. (1997) Images of organization. Thousand Oaks. CA: Sage.

Morrill, C. & Fine, G.A. (1997) Ethnographic contributions to organizational sociology, *Sociological Methods & Research,* 25, 424-451.

Morris, J. A. & Feldman, D. C. (1996) The dimensions, antecedents, and consequences of emotional labor. *Academy of Management Review*, 21, 986–1010.

Morris, J. A. & Feldman, D. C. (1997) Managing emotions in the workplace. *Journal of Managerial Issues,* 9, 257-274.

Morris, M. W., Leung, K., Ames, D. & Lickel, B. (1999) Views from the inside and outside: Integrating emic and etic insights about culture and justice judgment. *Academy of Management Review,* 24 (4), 781–796.

Nasif, E.G. & Al-Daeaj, H. & Ebrahimi, B. & Thibodeaux, M.S. (1991). Methodological Problems in Cross-Cultural Research: Un Update. *Management International Review Vol. 31 No. 1 p.79.*

Nguyen Huy, Q. (1999) Emotional capability, emotional intelligence, and radical change. *The Academy of Management Review,* 24 (2), 325–345.

Nicolini, D. (2009 Zooming in and zooming out: A package of method and theory to study work practices, In S. Yebema et al. (Eds.), *Organizational Ethnography Studying the Complexities of Everyday Life,* Sage Publications Ltd, 120-137.

O'Reilly, K. (2009) Key Concepts in Ethnography. London: Sage.

Olie, R. (1995). The 'Culture' Factor in Personnel and Organization Policies. International Human Resource Management: An integrated approach. *London Sage Publication pp.124-143.*

Ortloff, D. H. (2009) Social studies teachers' reflections on citizenship education in Bavaria, Germany. *Race/Ethnicity: Multidisciplinary Global Contexts,* 2 (2), 189–214.

Orum, A.M., Feagin, J.R. & Sjoberg, G. (1991) Introduction: the nature of the case study. In A.M. Orum, J.R. Feagin & G. Sjoberg (Eds.), *A Case for the Case Study,* 1-26. Chapel Hill: University of North Carolina Press.

Ottomeyer, H. (2006) Interview with Matthias Matussek and Matthias Schulz. "Vaterland in der Vitrine" , *Der Spiegel,* 22 May 168-72.

Paik, Y. S. & Sohn, J. H. (1998) Confucius in Mexico: Korean MNCs and the Maquiladoras. *Business Horizons,* 41 (6), 25–33.

Paoli, P. (1997) *Second European Survey on the Work Environment 1995.* Dublin: European Foundation for the Improvement of Living and Working Conditions.

Park, J-S. & Chang, P. Y. (2005) Contention in the construction of a global Korean community: The case of the Overseas Korean Act. *The Journal of Korean Studies,* 10 (1).

Park, K.K. and Ahn, H.T. (1998), *Comparison of Personnel Administration Practices in Korea and Germany.* Seoul: Korea Management Association.

Park, W.W., and Lee, B.C. (1996), *Corporate Culture of Korean Companies.* Seoul: The

Chamber of Commerce and Industry.

Parker, M. (2000). Organizational culture and identity. *London: Sage.*

Pekrun, R., & Frese, M. (1992) Emotions in work and achievement. In C.L. Cooper, & I.T. Robertson (Eds.), *International review of industrial and organizational psychology,* 7, pp. 153-198. New York Wiley.

Peters, T.J., & Waterman, R.H. (1982) *In search of excellence.* New York: Harper & Row.

Pettigrew, A.M. (1979) On Studying Organizational Cultures. *Administrative Science Quarterly,* 24 (4), 570-581.

Piekkari, R. & Welch, C. (2004) *Handbook of Qualitative Research Methods for International Business,* Cheltenham: Edward Elgar.

Piekkari, R. & Welch, C. (2006) Introduction to the Focused Issue: Qualitative Research Methods in International Business, *Management International Review,* 46 (4), 391-396.

Pink, S. (2007) Doing Visual Ethnography (2nd Ed.), Sage.

Posen, A. (1993), Less then a Universe of Difference: Evaluating the Reality of German Finance, In A. Bradley Shingleton, et al. (Eds.), *Dimensions of GermanUnification: Economic, Social and Legal Analyses,* Oxford: Westview Press, 43-56.

Potter, J. & Wetherell, M. (1987) *Discourse and social psychology beyond attitudes and behaviour.* London, Sage.

Pratch, L. & Jacobowitz, J. (1998) Integrative capacity and the evaluation of leadership. *Journal of Applied Behavioural Science,* 34, 180–182.

Rabbie, J.M. and Horowitz, M. (1988), 'Category versus Group as Explanatory Concepts in Intergroup Relations', *European Journal of Social Psychology,* Vol.19, pp.171-202.

Redpath, L. (1997). A comparison of native culture, non-native culture and new management ideology. *Revue Canadienne des Sciences de l'Administration Vol. 14 No. 3 p. 327.*

Rice, A.K. (1963) *The enterprise and its environment.* London: Tavistock Publications.

Richardson, L. (2000) Evaluating Ethnography, *Qualitative Inquiry,* 6 (2), 253-255.

Richardson, L. & St. Pierre, E.A. (2005) Writing: A Method of inquiry, In *Handbook of Qualitative Research* (3rd Ed.), ed. N.K. Denzin and Y.S. Lincoln, Thousand Oaks, CA: Sage, 959-978.

Richman, T. (1984) *A tale of two companies.* Inc., pp.38-43.

Risberg, A. (1999). Ambiguities thereafter: An interpretive approach to acquisitions. *Lund University Press.*

Robinson, J. H. (1985) Communication in Korea: Playing things by eye. In: Samovar, L. A. & Porter, R. E. (eds.) *Intercultural communication: A reader.* Wadsworth.

Roethlisberger, F.J. & Dickson, W.J. (1939) *Management and the worker: an account of a research program conducted by the Western Electric Company, Hawthorne Works,* Chicago. Cambridge, MA: Harvard University Press.

Ross, S. & Offermann, L. (1997) Transformational leaders: Measurement of personality attributes and work group performance. *Personality and Social Psychology Bulletin,* 23, 1078–1087.

Rossi, I. (1989). The unconscious in culture. *New York: Dutton.*

Rowan, B. (1999) On the Ajumma: A Political and Economic Perspective on Korean Women, 아세아연구 (Asian Studies), 102 (12), 185-220.

Rowley, C. (1998), *HRM in the Asia Pacific Region: Convergence Questioned.* London: Frank Cass.

Salovey, P. & Mayer, J. D. (1990) Emotional intelligence. *Imagination, Cognition, and Personality,* 9, 185–211.

Salovey, P. & Mayer, J. D. (1993) The intelligence of emotional intelligence. *Intelligence,* 17, 433–442.

Salter, S.B. & Niswander, F. (1994). Cultural influence on the development of accounting systems internationally. *Journal of International Business Studies Vol. 379 No.97*

Sandberg, J. (2005) How Do We Justify Knowledge Produced Within Interpretive Approaches? *Organizational Research Methods,* 8 (1), 41-68.

Sark, K. (2012) Fashioning a New Brand of "Germanness": The 2006 World Cup and Beyond, *A Jouranal of Germanic Studies,* 48 (2), 245- 256.

Schein, E. (1985). Organizational culture and leadership. *Wiley.*

Schensul, S., Schensul, J. J. & LeCompte, M. D. (1999) *Essential ethnographic methods. Observation interviews and questionnaires.* Altamira Press.

Scherpinski-Lee, A. (2011) "Die Bedeutung von Emotionen in der koreanischen

Interaktion," online Zeitschrift für Interkulturelle Studien, pp. 87-107.

Schneider, J. (2001) Talking German: Othering strategies in Public and everyday discourses. *International Communication Gazette*, 63 (351).

Schneider, S. P. & Barsoux, J. L. (1997) *Managing across cultures*. Europe, Prentice Hall.

Schneider, S.P. & Barsoux, J.L. (1997). Managing across cultures. *Europe, Prentice Hall.*

Schwartz, S. H. (1992). Universals in the content and structure of values: Theoretical advances and empirical tests in 20 countries. In Zanna, M. (Ed.) *Advances in experimental social psychology*, Vol. 25 pp. 1-65.

Schwartz, S. H. (1994). Beyond individualism/collectivism: New cultural dimensions of values. In Kim, U., Triandis, H.C., Kagitcibasi, C., Choi, S-C. & Yoon, G. (Eds), Individualism and collectivism: Theory, methods and applications. *London: Sage,* pp. 85-119.

Schwarz, A. (2003) Modes of 'un-Australianness' and 'un-Germanness': Contemporary debates on cultural diversity in Germany and Australia. *Journal of Australian Studies*, 27 (80).

Seliger, H. & Shohamy, E. (1989). Second language research methods. *Oxford, Oxford University Press.*

Selznick, P. (1949) TVA and the grass roots: A study in the sociology of formal organization, In S. Yebema et al. (Eds.), *Organizational Ethnography Studying the Complexities of Everyday Life*, Sage Publications Ltd.

Senge, P. (1990) *The fifth discipline*. New York, Doubleday.

Shenkar, O. (2001) Cultural distance revisited: Towards a more rigorous conceptualisation and measurement of cultural differences. *Journal of International Business Studies*, 32, 519-535.

Shenkar, O. (2012) Beyond cultural distance: Switching to a friction lens in the study of cultural differences. *Journal of International Business Studies*, 43(1), 12-17.

Shenkar, O., Luo, Y., and Yeheskel, O. (2008) From "Distance" to "Friction": Substituting Metaphors and redirecting Intercultural Research. *The Academy of Management Review*, 33(4), 905-923.

Shin, Y.K. (1992), *The Korean Management*. Seoul: Parkyungsan.

Slater, P.L. (1970). The pursuit of loneliness. *Boston, MA: Beacon Press.*

Slote, W.H. (1992) Oedipal ties and the issues of separation-individualism in traditional Confucian societies. *Journal of the American Academy of Psychoanalysis,* 20, 435-453.

Smelser, N.J. (1992). Culture: coherent or incoherent. In Munch, R. & Smelser, N.J. (Eds), *Theory of culture, Berkley: University of California Press pp. 3-28.*

Smircich, L. (1983). Concepts of culture and organizational analysis. *Administrative Science Quarterly,* Vol. 28 pp. 339-358.

Snow, C.C., Snell, S.A., Canney-Davison, S.C., & Hambrick, D.C. (1996) Use transnational teams to globalise your company. *Organizational Dynamics,* 32, 20-32.

Sondergaard, M. (1994). Hofstede's consequences: A study of review, citations and replications. *Organizational Studies Vol. 15. No.3 p. 447 – 456.*

Song, B.N. (1990), *The Rise of the Korean Economy.* Hong Kong: Oxford University Press.

Song, Y.H., & Meek, C.B. (1998) The impact of culture on the management values and believes of Korean firms. *Journal of Comparative International Management,* 1 (1).

Southerton, D.G. (2008) More thoughts on Korean Business and Popular Culture: Volume 2, Bridging Culture Publications Von Gilnow, M.A., Huo,Y.P. and Lowe, K. (1999). "Leadership Across the Pacific Ocean: A Tri-National Comparison", *International Business Review,* 8 (1), 1-15.

Sparrow, P., Schuler, R. & Jackson, S. (1994) Convergence and divergence? Human resource practices and policies for competitive advantage worldwide. *International Journal of Human Resource Management,* 5 (2), 267–299.

Spencer, L. M. & Spencer, S. M. (1993) *Competence at work: Models for superior performance.* New York, John Wiley & Sons.

Spender, J-C. (1998). Pluralist epistemology and the knowledge-based theory of the firm. *Organization, Vol. 5 No. 2 pp. 233-256.*

Sperber, D. (1974) *Rethinking symbolism.* Cambridge: Cambridge University Press.

Spradley, J. P. (1980) *Participant observation.*

Stake, R.E. (1978) The case study method in social inquiry. *Educational Researcher,*

7 (2), 5-8.

Steers, R.M., Shin, Y.K. and Ungson, G.R. (1989), *The Cheabol: Korea's New Industrial Might.* New York: Harper and Row.

Stemler, S. (2001) An overview of context analysis. *Practical Assesment, Research & Evaluation,* 7 (17).

Sternberg, R. (1985) *Beyond IQ: A triarchic theory of human intelligence.* New York: Cambridge University Press.

Sternberg, R. (1997) Managerial intelligence: Why IQ isn't enough. *Journal of Management,* 23, 475-494.

Stowell, J. A. (2003) *The influence of Confucian values on interpersonal communication in South Korea, as compared to China and Japan.* University of Oklahoma, Tulsa.

Strauss, A., Farahaugh, S., Suczek, B., & Wiener, C. (1980) Gefühlsarbeit. Ein Beitrag zur Arbeits- und Berufssoziologie. *Kölner Zeitschrift für Soziologie und Sozialpsychologie,* 32, 629 -651.

Strauss, C. & Quinn, N. (1997) *A Cognitive Theory of Cultural Meaning.* Cambridge: Cambridge University Press.

Strecker, I. (1988) *The social practice of symbolization: Anthropological analysis.* London, Athlone Press.

Suh, E. M. (2002) Culture, identity consistency, and subjective well being, *Journal of Personality and Social Psychology,* 83 (6).

Symon, G. & Cassell, C. (2012) *Qualitative organizational research: Core methods and current challenges.* London, Sage.

Tajfel, H. and Turner, J.C. (1979), 'An Integrative Theory of Intergroup Conflict' , in W.G. Austin and S. Worcherl (eds.), *The Social Psychology of Intergroup Relations.* Monterrey, CA: Books/Cole.

Tang, N.M. (1992) Some psychoanalytic implications of Chinese philosophy and child-rearing practices. *Psychoanalytic Study of the Child,* 47, 371-389.

Tange, H. & Lauring, J. (2009) Language management and social interaction within the multilingual workplace, *Journal of Communication Management,* 13 (3), 218-232.

Tenzer, H., Pudelko, M., &Harzing, A. (2014) The impact of language barriers on trust formation in multinational teams, *Journal of International Business,* 45, 508-535.

Thompson, C.J., Locander, W.B. & Pollio, H.R. (1990) The lived meaning of free choice: An existential-phenomenological description of everyday consumer experiences of contemporary married women. *Journal of consumer research*, 17 (3), 346-361.

Thornton, G.C., & Byham, W.C. (1982) *Assessment Centres and Managerial Performance*, London, Academic Press.

Tinsley, L. R. & Woloshin, D. J. (1974) Approaching German culture: A tentative analysis. *Teaching German*, 7 (1), 125–136.

Triandis, H.C. (1989) The self and social behavior in differing cultural contexts, *Psychological Review*, 96 (3), 506-520.

Triandis, H.C. (1995), *Individualism and Collectivism*. Boulder, CO: Westview Press.

Trompenaars, F. (1994), *Riding the Waves of Culture: Understanding Diversity in Global Business*. Chicago, IL: Irwin.

Tsui, A. (2016) Reflections on the so-called value-free ideal: A call for responsible science in the business schools, *Cross Cultural & Strategic Management*, 23 (1), 4-28.

Tung, R.L. (1994) Strategic management thought in East Asia, *Organizational Dynamics*, 22 (4), 55-65.

Turner, S. (2006) Interview with Ulf Lippitz and Falko Müller. "Berlin fühlt sich freier an als andere Orte", *Zitty*, 29-30.

Tyler, S., & Nathan, J. (1985) *In search of excellence* [Film]. New York: Public Broadcast System.

Ulrich, D. & Lake, D. (1990) *Organisational capability*. New York, John Wiley & Sons.

Ungson, G.R., Steers, R.M. and Park, S.H. (1997), *Korean Enterprise: The Quest for Globalization*. Boston, MA: Harvard Business School Press.

Van Maanen, J. (1979) Reclaiming qualitative methods for organizational research: A preface. *Administrative Science Quarterly*, 24 (4), 520–526.

Van Maanen, J. (2006) Ethnography then and now. *Qualitative Research in Organizations and Management: An International Journal*, 1 (1), 13-21.

Vijver, F. & Leung, K. (1997) *Methods and data analysis for cross-cultural research*. Thousand Oaks, CA, Sage.

Wallerstein, I. (1990). Culture as the ideological battleground of the modern world-system. *Theory, Culture & Society, Vol. 7 pp. 31-55.*

Watson, A. (1995) *The Germans: Who are they now?* London, Methuen.

Watson, T. (2008) Field Research. In R. Thorpe & R. Holt (Eds.), *Dictionary of Qualitative Management Research,* 99-100. London: Sage.

Watson, T. (2011) Ethnography, Reality, and Truth: The Vital Need for Studies of 'How Things Work' in Organizations and Management. *Journal of Management Studies,* 48 (1), 202-217.

Watson, T. (2012) Making Organisational Ethnography. *Journal of Organizational Ethnography,* 1 (1), 15-22.

Waxin, M. F. (2004) Expatriates' interaction adjustment: The direct and moderator effects of culture of origin. *International Journal of Intercultural Relations,* 28 (1), 61–79.

Webb, E. J., Campbell, D. T., Schwartz, R. D., Sechrest, L. & Grove, J. B. (1981) *Nonreactive measures in the social sciences.* Boston, Houghton Mifflin.

Weber, M. (1946) *From Max Weber: Essays in sociology.* Trans. Gerth, H. & Mills, C. New York, Oxford University Press.

Weick, K. (1979) *The social psychology of organizing (2ⁿᵈ ed.)* Reading, MA: Addison-Wesley.

Weidenfeld, W. (1983) Die Identität der Deutschen: Fragen, Positionen, Perspektiven. In Werner Weidenfeld (ed.) *Die Identität der Deutschen.* Bonn, Bundeszentrale für politische Bildung, pp.13–49.

Welch, C., Piekkari, R., Plakoyiannaki, E., & Paavilainen-Mäntymäki, E. (2011) Theorising from case studies: Towards a pluralist future for international business research, *Journal of International Business,* 42, 740-762.

Wetzel, D. (2008) The Heimat Abroad: The Boundaries of Germanness (review), *Journal of Wolrd History,* 19 (1), 119-121.

White, J. (1997) Turks in the New Germany. *American Anthropologist,* 99 (4), 754–769.

Whyte, W.F. (1948) *Human relations in the restaurant industry,* Oxford, England: Mcgraw-Hill.

Wilkinson, B. (1996) Culture, institutions and business in East Asia. *Organization Studies,* 17 (421).

Williams, C.J. (1989) *What is Identity.* Oxford, Clarendon Press.

Willis, P. & Trondman, M. (2002) Manifesto for ethnography, *Cultural Studies –*

Critical Methodologies 2 (3), 394-402. Sage Publications.

Wolcott, H. F. (1999) *Ethnography: A ways of seeing.* Altamira Press.

Yang, I. & Kelly, A. (2009) Assumptions in Korea organizations and their implications in a cross-cultural setting. Emerald Group Publishing Limited, 5, 297–320.

Yang, S. & Chung, M.H. (1995) Discursive contradictions between tradition and modernity in Korean management practices: A case of Samsung's new management, In I. Yang & A. Kelly (Ed.), *Assumptions in Korean organisations and their implications in a cross-cultural setting,* In Advances in Global Leadership, 297-320.

Yanow, D. (2009) Organizational ethnography and methodological angst: myths and challenges in the field, *Qualitative Research in Organizations and Management: An International Journal,* 4 (2), 186-199.

Ybema, S., Yanow, D., Wels, H. & Kamsteeg, F. (2009) *Organizational ethnography: Studying the complexity of everyday life.* Sage.

Yi, M. & Jezewski, M. A. (2000) Korean nurses' adjustment to hospitals in the United States of America. *Journal of Advanced Nursing,* 32 (3), 721–729.

Yim, H. (2002) Cultural identity and cultural policy in South Korea. *The International Journal of Cultural Policy,* 8 (1), 37–48.

Yoo, S., & Lee, S.M. (1987) 'Managemnt Style and Practice in Korean Chaebols', *California Management Review,* 29 (4), 95-110.

Yum, J. O. (1994) The impact of Confucianism on interpersonal relationships and communication patterns in East Asia. In: Samovar, L. A. & Porter, R. E. (Eds.), *Intercultural communication: A reader.* Belmont: International Thomson Publishing, pp. 75–86.

Yum, J.O. (1987) Korean Philosphy and Communication, In D.L. Kincaid (Eds.), *Communication Theory: Eastern and Western Perspectives,* New York: Academic Press.

Yum, J.O. (1988), 'The Impact of Confucianism on Interpersonal Relationships and Communication Patterns in East Asia', *Communication Monographs,* No.55, pp.374-88.

Zapf, D. (2002) Emotion work and psychological well-being A review of the literature and some conceptual considerations. *Human Resource Management Review,* 12, 237-268.

INDEX

t refers to table

A
Agar, M., 107, 242
Alvesson, Mats, 101, 103, 109, 120, 238–39

B
Brannen, Mary Yoko
  communicating and managing effectively across borders, 17
  core competences and semiotic framework, 210, 210t4 –211t4
  "the Korean Way's" core competencies, 209
  model of recontextualising symbols from one identity context into another, 235
  people create meanings through systems of signification, 24
  process model, 220
  semiotic theory building, 209
  symbols carry various meanings, depending on the social context, 24, 36
  symbols in international management, recontextualising, 24
  symbols of identity, theories of, 233–34
  symbols of national culture, 239
  symbols of national identity, 249
  theory of recontextualisation, 11–12, 24–25, 209, 236, 239

C
case studies
  Andrea, 160–61
  EJ, 162
  ethnographic, 13
  Peony, 205–6
  Rainer, 159
chameleons (German speaking Koreans)
  character group three, 161–62, 163t3
  educational props, 168–69
  German speaking Koreans, 15, 160–62
  Korean blood discourses of identity, 193
  Korean identity presentations, frustrated with and judgmental of, 191–92
  "the Korean Way's," core competencies of, 212
  "the Korean Way's" symbols of self-presentations and recontextualisation, 219
  nunchi and, 161–62, 165–68, 192–93
  nunchi and strategic self-presentations of German and Korean symbols of
    identity, 194, 212

set of attributes such as self-awareness, emotional management, self-motivation, empathy, and relationship management, 14–15

social intelligence: ability to supervise one's own and others' emotions, 13–14

study of symbols in the anthropology and, 24

transformational leadership and, 14

verbal and non-verbal appraisal and expression of emotion, 14

Western concept of, 16–17, 243

ethnographic
  case study, 13
  data collection, 47
  methodology, 247
  process, 17

ethnographic study (studies)
  of attitudes and experiences of truth telling, 54–55
  in business management, 107, 250
  on HanaEins, 118
  of nunchi, 11
  on paediatricians, 33
  of strategic self-presentation of transnational businesspeople, 11
  of theories of strategic self-presentation, 11
  of transnational German businesspeople, 99

G

German Club Seoul, 109, 112t2, 114t2, 117, 124, 145

German embassy, 248

German international managers. See also German multinational corporations (MNCs) in Seoul
  Chameleons and Korean colleagues not invited to social events, 218
  character group one, 157–59, 163t3
  cross-border expression of symbols of identity and management of identities within HanaEins, 15
  educational props, 168–69
  German MNCs, 157–58, 193
  "the Korean Way's" recontextualisation as strategic front stage performances, 219–20
  Koreans are inflexible, 192
  Koreans criticised for being inflexible, 192

German multinational corporations (MNCs). See also Korean MNCs
  actors working for German MNCs, 20
  business management style, South Korean, 16
  chaebols, favourable attitudes of, 200
  chameleons and frustration with Korean counterpart's identity presentations, 191–92
  chameleons and nunchi, 161–62, 165–68, 192–93

Korean(s)
    aggression in men is seen as masculine and a positive behaviour, 231
    behaviour and benefits gained from investing in a relationship, 186
    blood discourses of identity, 193
    Himnae (cheer up, chin up), 213
    identity inflexibility and the lack of worldly attitudes, 193
    identity seen as being a "one way street," 193
    inflexible, German international managers and settled Germans criticised Koreans
        for being, 192
    international managers deliberately lied to or not taken seriously because of age
        and marital status, 190
    Jemi-obda (no fun, not interesting), 213
    language facility, Korean vs. German responses to, 190–91
    performative lying and Korean identity, 212
    self-presentations, differences in Korean and German, 190
    symbols of identity, Korean vs. German, 191
    taboos, especially about sexual discourse, 187
Korean households, 208
Korean language barrier, 123
Korean management, 97
    authoritarian management style and close supervision, 88, 95
    chaebols, symbol of identity, 86–91, 95
    changes in, 89
    Confucian thought in, 91–95
    influenced by inwah (harmony) and nunchi (emotional intelligence), 90
    nunchi, harmony by application of, 62
    nunchi as symbol of Koreanness in business, 95–96
    nunchi is linchpin in performances of, 31, 63
    nunchi performed to avoid losing social face, 31, 62
    organizational control in, 31, 63
    practices, informal, 19
    practices and nunchi, 21–23
    'relation-based behaviour,' 96
    scientific management of jobs, 88
    shouting in an authoritarian style, 226
    style and business practices of chaebols, 97
Korean MNCs. See also German multinational corporations (MNCs)
    Buddhism in, 92–93
    Confucianism in, 92–94
    country selection for FDI, 93
    expansions abroad and human resource management, 22
    group affiliations in, 46

human recourses as crucial factor in, 88

low-trust/low-investment approach, 88

management practices in, 87–88

management styles in, 88

preferences in ownership structure, 90–91

three elements investigated, 46

Korean positioning process to gain orientation, 186

Korean team leader, 151

"Korean wannabe cosmopolitan," 208

"the Korean Way," 209–10. See also managerial change by adoption of Nunchi

about, 195–96

"is absolutely not logical," 217

authoritarianism, 199–200

in business practices, 202

case study: Peony, 205–6

collectivism and national identity simulacra, meanings of, 216

conclusion, 203, 220–22

Confucian policy, 196–98

core competencies of, 21, 209–10, 210t4–211t4, 212, 220

different kinds of strategic self-presentations and nunchi management required in different settings, 228–29

enables Korea to maintain pretense of an "imaginary" theme of living in a collective and harmonious society, 215–16

essential features of, 200–201

form of ideological hegemony or "pre-punched model of life," 217

HanaEins, analytic model applied to, 209–11t4

HanaEins' group assets, recontextualisation of strategic self-presentations in "the Korean Way" as, 210–11t4

human resource management (HRM), 202–3

ideologies, 214–20

imposed on everyone, 208

inflexibility, 219

military and family, 201–2

military mind-set, 198–99

narrative trope used in Korea to control and shape citizens as products of an imagined society, 215

origin of, 196–203

performative strategic lying engrained in, 213

"pre-punched model of life" narrative of, 215–16

recontextualisation and symbols of identity, 221

recontextualisation and symbols of self-presentations, 219

recontextualisation changes identity specific settings over time, 221

Hweshik ritual, 174–79

initial contact: identity and nunchi, 184–87

nunchi, background to integration of, 172–74

spiral of silence, 183–84

mind reading, 47, 242

MNCs. See German multinational corporations

"mysterious 'alpha' hidden in their hearts," 242

N

national identity. See also symbols of identity

business studies of, 251

core competencies, 12

HanaEins members, 154–55

nunchi and strategic self-presentations symbolic of, 11

symbols of, 13, 17–18, 249

symbols of, recontextualisation of, 11–12, 19, 35, 39, 100, 244

non-verbal communication, 49, 55–56, 59–61, 99, 242

nunchi (emotional intelligence). See also emotional intelligence; kibun (feeling of balance); managerial change by adoption of nunchi; symbols

ability to empathize, 47

complex and multi-faceted concept, 195

conclusion, 35–36

emotion work concept in the literature, 32–35

German and Koreans strategically perform lies for the sake of nunchi, 180

identity, concept of, 25–26

identity, Goffman's 'back-stage' performance of, 29–32

identity, Goffman's 'front-stage' performance of, 28–29

identity by studying differences, 27

identity performance and Goffman's theory, 27

involves deep acting, imagining emotional memory and the use of personal props, 232

kibun, provides guidance to understand another person's, 47

knowledge, innovation and advances in, 19–21

Korean management practices and nunchi, perceptions of, 21–23

"the Korean Way," nunchi is vulnerable to recontextualisation of, 221

non-verbal communication, 59–61

nunchi, conceptual framework, 23

nunchi, illustration of, 19f1

recontextualisation, concept of, 24–25

research, known gaps in the, 13–16

research questions, 16–17

research study, significance and contribution of, 17–18

study focused on culture vs, identity, 238

www.ingramcontent.com/pod-product-compliance
Lightning Source LLC
Chambersburg PA
CBHW080556030426
42336CB00019B/3207